Praise for *Leadership Presence*

"An entertaining twist on the typical interpersonal skills book."
—*Publishers Weekly*

"Read *Leadership Presence* and give the gift of presence to all those you touch. Halpern and Lubar take a fresh approach to leadership by providing the tools to authentically express yourself as you genuinely create value with others."
—Kevin Cashman, CEO, LeaderSource; author of *Leadership from the Inside Out and Awakening the Leader Within*

"As a leader, you are always in the spotlight. *Leadership Presence* teaches how to be masterful under that bright light . . . connecting more profoundly to those you lead and to yourself. A thought-provoking and highly practical guide to realizing your leadership potential."
—Jay Conger, professor, London Business School; author of *Building Leaders*

"The foundation of success in business (and in life) is the ability to authentically engage and connect with others. Using the profession of acting as the perfect metaphor, this book is a masterful guide for achieving true leadership success. I loved the mix of personal stories from clients and well-known actors and found *Leadership Presence* to be a powerful teaching tool. This book isn't just for business leaders, it's for anyone who wants to bring more passion, empathy, and presence to all their relationships. I highly recommend it!"
—Cheryl Richardson, author of *Take Time for Your Life* and *Stand Up for Your Life*

"Finally there is a book where the insights of theatre, transformation, and organizational learning have been brought together. Leaders of organizations have much to learn from those who have spent their lives understanding the nature of performance, keeping the beat going, and the power of truly showing up. In the end, productive and humane institutions depend on the integration of art and commerce. This book is a great beginning."

—Peter Block, author of *The Answer to How Is Yes, Stewardship, Flawless Consulting,* and *Empowered Manager*

"It is relatively easy to describe what makes a leader, it's teaching people how to communicate the qualities of leadership that is difficult. *Leadership Presence* does just that. It doesn't just tell you what to do, it tells you how to do it."

—Mark C. Mazzarella, coauthor of *Reading People* and *Put Your Best Foot Forward*

Leadership Presence

Dramatic Techniques
to Reach Out,
Motivate, and Inspire

Belle Linda Halpern *and* Kathy Lubar
Cofounders of The Ariel Group

GOTHAM BOOKS

AUTHORS' NOTE

To protect the privacy of our clients, most of the client stories herein have been disguised by changing names and industries. Some are several cases merged into one to illustrate a particular insight. They are all based on actual Ariel engagements. Occasionally we have used real names with permission from our clients and colleagues.

GOTHAM BOOKS
Published by Penguin Group (USA) Inc. 375 Hudson Street,
New York, New York 10014, U.S.A.
Penguin Books Ltd, Registered Offices: 80 Strand, London WC2R 0RL, England
Penguin Books Australia Ltd, 250 Camberwell Road, Camberwell, Victoria 3124, Australia
Penguin Books Canada Ltd, 10 Alcorn Avenue, Toronto, Ontario, Canada M4V 3B2
Penguin Books (NZ) Ltd, Cnr Rosedale and Airborne Roads,
Albany, Auckland 1310, New Zealand

Published by Gotham Books, a division of Penguin Group (USA) Inc.
Previously published as a Gotham Books hardcover edition.

First Gotham Books trade paperback printing, October 2004
30   29   28   27   26   25   24   23   22   21

Gotham Books and the skyscraper logo are trademarks of Penguin Group (USA) Inc.

The Library of Congress has cataloged the Gotham Books hardcover edition as follows:
LIBRARY OF CONGRESS CATALOGING-IN-PUBLICATION DATA
Halpern, Belle Linda.
Leadership presence : dramatic techniques to reach out, motivate, and inspire /
by Belle Linda Halpern and Kathy Lubar.
p.   cm.
ISBN 1-592-40017-5 (hardcover : alk. paper)   1-592-40086-8 (pbk.)
1. Leadership. 2. Interpersonal relations. I. Lubar, Kathy. II. Title.
HD57.7.H34 2003
658.4 ' 092—dc21   2003010586

Printed in the United States of America
Set in Stone Serif with Eras Medium display
Designed by Sabrina Bowers

To our parents, Merril Halpern, Phyllis Miriam,
and Gary and Lorraine Lubar

and

To The Ariel Group Ensemble

2003

Abigail Van Alyn

Mel Auston

Chris von Baeyer

Liz Callahan

Greta Cowan

Pat Dougan

Priscilla Douglas

Trisha Fennessey

Joel Gluck

Amy Goldfarb

Ron Goldman

Harvey Greenberg

Steven Holt

Christine Johnson

Lucy Kaplan

Sean Kavanagh

Jeffrey Korn

Pete Kovner

Patricia Mulholland

Maryann O'Connor

Kenny Raskin

Arthur Roberts

Reba Rose

Robert Salafia

Sarah Stevenson

Anja Struchholz

Johannes Theron

Bob Walsh

Chris Webb

Nat Warren-White

Marjorie Zohn

Contents

Acknowledgments

There are three people without whom this book would not have come into being.

First and foremost we thank Kent Lineback, with whom we wrote this book. His dedication, infinite patience, and talent shaped ten years of our work and ideas into a coherent whole. We feel so lucky to have found someone with his elegant style, intelligence, and openness. He was always a joy to work with and he bears responsibility for only the best parts of this book.

The second person without whom this book would never have existed is our CEO, Sean Kavanagh. From encouraging us to write a book (and not letting up), to writing sections himself while running the company, Sean kept the project moving. His unflagging spirit and sense of humor made the process fun, and his perspective and wisdom helped us craft a more accessible and relevant book.

And finally, we would like to thank our agent, Paul Fedorko, for his initial idea to write this book and his enthusiasm throughout. His commitment and support of this project went above and beyond the call of duty.

We would like to thank Mark Rittenberg and Penny Kreitzer, pioneers in theater-based corporate training through their firm, Corporate Scenes. It's because of them that we met and through training with them that we became business partners. We thank them for mentoring and inspiring us, and for their profound thinking about the application of theater in a business context.

We would like to thank Jean Claude van Itallie for his mentoring, his innovative work on storytelling, and his orientation to theater as a healing art. The wonderful teachers of Roy Hart Theatre in France inspired us with their approach to using the voice as an instrument of transformation. Exercises have been inspired by the work of Augusto Boal, Kristin Linklater, Ira Progoff, and Viola Spolin. Other teachers who have been important to our growth as performers and people are: Warren Bennis, Bill Castellino, Pema Chodron, Steve Cummings, Kermit Dunkelberg, Alvin Epstein, Daena Giardella, Ildri Ginn, Edwin Gray, George Kinder, Mariel Kinsey, Josephine Lane, Larry Lane, Alan Langdon, Kim Mancuso, Toni Packer, Shelley Prencipe, Chogyam Trungpa Rimpoche, Ron Roy, Martha Schlamme, Duncan Scribner, Maureen Stuart, Judy Swanson, Leah Taylor, and Christopher Titmuss.

We would like to thank our wonderful, talented team at Gotham Books. Our editor, Brendan Cahill, was both patient and encouraging as he coaxed us toward the ever-looming deadlines. We thank Bill Shinker for recognizing the potential in our work, and Erin Moore and Lauren Marino for their insight and guidance. The cover design is based on The Ariel Group company logo, which was designed by Scott Williams.

We would like to thank the following people for their interviews, which added so much richness to our book: Jane Alexander, Donna Berg, Barbara Berke, Jory Berson, Mark Blaxill, Steve Chambers, John Clarkeson, Marjorie M. Connelly, Pat Dougan, Bob Garland, Joel Gluck, Kenneth Jay, Kris Holland, Madeleine Homan, Dennis Liberson, Glenn Mangurian, Gaby Meyer, Susan Miele, Nigel Morris, Laura Olle, John Perkins, Kenny Raskin, Judy Rosen, Ken Rosenberg, Nat Warren-White, Catherine West, and Rabbi Sean Zevitt.

We would like to thank our readers throughout the process for their invaluable feedback: Tom Ascheim, Chris von Baeyer, Greta Cowan, Pat Dougan, Michael Even, Tony Gallo, Norm Gaut, Amy Goldfarb, Tim Hall, Merril Halpern, Steven Holt, Kate Kavanagh, Peter Kovner, Stuart Krantz, Aaron Lieberman, Lorraine Lubar, James Mauch, Phyllis Miriam, Patricia Mulholland, Anne Murphy, Joanna Nikka, Brock Reeve, Anne and Loren Rosenberg, Ken Rosenberg, Rob Salafia, Alice Stone, Carolyn Schwartz, Tracey Sloan, Bruce Tanenbaum, Christopher Webb, and Marjorie Williams.

We would like to thank the following people for their research and writing: Chris von Baeyer, Liz Callahan, Andy Wolfendon,

Margie Zohn, and especially Joel Gluck for his tremendous contribution to Practices and Exercises.

We would like to thank Schon Beechler, Gabrielle Davis, Mike Fenlon, Carol Franco, Rob Galford, B. Z. Goldberg, Charlie Green, Madeleine Homan, Lucy Kaplan, Barbara Lubar, Willie Pietersen, Cheryl Richardson, Pat Scheuer, Bob Steinbach, and Elizabeth Weed for their support and guidance.

We feel so blessed to have had such incredible clients who have challenged us and helped us to evolve in so many ways over the years. We also want to thank The Ariel Group facilitators and consultants for inspiring us over the past decade with their talent, depth, and dedication.

We could never have successfully completed this book without the support of our amazing staff—as devoted a team as anyone could wish for. A special thank you to Sarah Stevenson for her hard work, enthusiasm, and flexibility during this process.

We also both feel much gratitude to the circle of friends who have encouraged and supported us on our journeys, especially our dear friend and colleague Pat Dougan, vice president of The Ariel Group, whose outstanding work with key clients is reflected throughout the book.

We are deeply grateful to our parents and our families for their love, inspiration, and belief in us. And finally, we thank our husbands, George Kinder and Mitch Rosenberg, who have offered unconditional support and greatly appreciated counsel, read and critiqued numerous drafts with nuance and insight, and kept us sane during the whole messy process of writing. They are our greatest teachers, best friends, and loving partners.

We're sure there is someone we've overlooked. Thank you all, the missing and the mentioned, for the many gifts you have given us.

Foreword

Georges Braque famously said, "The only thing that matters in art is the part that cannot be explained." You could also say that about leadership. There *is* something missing in leadership studies: those parts that resist explanation. *Leadership Presence* does identify one of those important things that *do* matter, the natural and obvious—but eerily overlooked—connection between leading and acting. They are unavoidably yoked together, these two, by a common social purpose: *the creation of mutuality, of transforming feeling into shared meaning.*

Like great actors, great leaders create and sell us on an alternative vision of the world—a better world of which we are an essential part. They suspend us, to paraphrase Max Weber, in webs of significance. Churchill idealized his countrymen with such intensity that in the end they approached his ideal. Gandhi, it has been said, made India proud of herself. Washington and the other founding fathers also had that great leader's gift of making people believe they could be part—that they *were* part—of a great nation. Martin Luther King Jr., a rhetorician of rare power, had that same genius. When you consider such towering and theatrical leaders, you come to realize that leadership is not just a performing art, it may be the greatest performing art of all—the only one that creates institutions of lasting value, institutions that can endure long after the stars who envisioned them have left the theater.

Over the years I've been pondering this convergence of leadership and performance, occasioned by everything from movies and plays I've seen, conversations with insightful friends—including my actor daughter, Kate—and other entertainment industry professionals. In this book, the cofounders of The Ariel Group, Belle Linda Halpern and Kathy Lubar illustrate, reify, explain, and show what this convergence is all about. If there is such a thing as "principled envy"—and I hope there is—that's how I felt when I finished this engaging book.

The authors tell us in a variety of ways that leadership is a role, a part that a person plays. And so I'm not surprised that the writer who seems to have known the most about leadership, as indeed he knew the most about everything, was also a man of the theater. William Shakespeare was acutely aware of the leader as actor. He understood that there was nothing like a play about power—its achievement, its use and misuse, its loss, and the way it changes the person who has it—to hypnotize his audience, be they groundlings or nobility. One way or another, all of Shakespeare's tragedies, all his history plays, and even a number of his comedies are about the rise and fall of leaders. Indeed, the link between leadership and drama was recognized long before the highly theatrical Age of Elizabeth. Aeschylus, Sophocles, and other ancient playwrights knew intuitively that audiences would be riveted by plays about legitimacy, succession, and other leadership matters—perhaps because the playwrights understood that the power leaders have over the rest of us means that their lives are inextricably bound up with our own. Some men may, in fact, be islands, but no leader ever is.

Palpable in Ancient Greece and Elizabethan England, the link between leadership and performance is even more obvious today in a nation where at least one president—Ronald Reagan—was previously both a member and a leader of the Screen Actors Guild. This reminds me of an anecdote about an encounter between Orson Welles and Franklin Delano Roosevelt. The first time FDR met Welles, the president graciously said to the fabled young actor, "You know, Mr. Welles, you are the greatest actor in America." "Oh, no, Mr. President," Welles replied, "you are."

The star power that FDR and Welles had is an example of what is sometimes called "charismatic leadership," a fuzzy but apparently irresistible term. Halpern and Lubar incisively hone in on this and rescue the term from its meaningless charm by teaching us how leaders cause us to care deeply about them, how they induce in us a response that normally requires the presence of powerful pheromones. W. H. Auden expressed it well: "A great actor can break your heart at fifty feet." It goes back to the second word in this book's title, *presence*.

Shakespeare, of course, has something to say on this point. In *Henry IV,* Part I, we encounter the Welsh seer, Glendower, boasting to Hotspur. "I can call the spirits from the vasty deep." And Hotspur, in a hilarious outbreak of candor replies, "Why, so can I, or so can any man, but will they come when you do call for them?" Genuine leadership, as this book shows, requires more than putting on the trappings of power. It requires the ability to find that magnetic core that will draw together a fragmented audience— not just to call the spirits, but to make them come when they are called. Former President Clinton did this brilliantly in his speech accepting his party's first nomination when he spoke so movingly of there being "no 'them,' only 'us.'" In essence, the leader is able to create community.

Halpern and Lubar know this; they understand community. Listen to their definitive words on the subject: "A world where people authentically engage with one another and unlock their most generous selves." That's their wish for the readers of this volume. I think you'll find it hard to resist that invitation.

—Warren Bennis
Santa Monica, California

Prologue

Executive presence is so important to our success as consultants. I believed if our consultants could speak with clarity and confidence—if they could find their voice—then they would show up as credible advisors, capable of assisting our clients with their most challenging problems. Your impact went much deeper than that. With your guidance, we worked on our connections to each other, on making vulnerability safe, and most of all, on being authentic in whatever roles we played—as consultants and leaders. We moved from playing our roles to being those roles.

Judi Rosen, then Managing Director, CSC Index Eastern Region
1993

WE FOUNDED THE ARIEL GROUP IN 1993, AND IF YOU'D ASKED US then what we were doing, we'd have said we were teaching leaders to be better communicators. We thought the skills and techniques we'd learned as professional actors and performers would be helpful.

They were, and The Ariel Group prospered. But as we worked with more companies and more leaders, we began to realize that something beyond better communication was going on. The use of dramatic skills and techniques was leading to something richer in the lives of people we worked with.

Two women attending one of our corporate programs for a giant financial services firm had been struggling for months to complete a budget. They couldn't resolve the issues that kept them apart. In our program they did a listening exercise together over lunch. That evening, fueled by their newfound understanding of each other, they put the budget together in less than two hours and sent it off to their boss in London, who happily approved it without change.

Better listening skills? Certainly. But their newfound ability to collaborate went beyond listening.

We worked with the executive team of a software company. They were preparing to present an important new strategy in a town meeting for all employees, and they wanted to do it in a way that broke the mold of previous presentations. Rather than the old PowerPoint slide show, they wanted to model a collaborative and cohesive spirit among the executive team, to communicate how the strategy needed to be implemented throughout the company. Not only was the presentation more powerful and creative but, as a result of our work, they told us afterward they had "never before been this cohesive, except during two crises—9/11 when we had a large contingent of people in New York and during a major workforce reduction." Better presentation skills? Of course. But their teamwork inspired the organization too.

We deliver our work as volunteers in a Boston-area program for prison inmates called Houses of Healing. One of the inmates in the program was a man whose street name was Nitro. When he was asked in an exercise to illustrate his life story, he drew a chain of railroad cars climbing a steep mountain. Each car was another event from his life. As he began to describe each car, he dissolved into tears. By the end of the program he'd changed his street name from Nitro to Patience, as he understood, for the first time, that he had the power to create a life for himself beyond drugs and violence.

Greater self-confidence? Yes. But personal transformation too.

As we saw these moments of change, and countless others like them, we began to understand the power of the concepts we were bringing from the theater.

It wasn't just communication. It was about authentic connections between people. The two women making a budget found a way to connect with each other. The executive team making the strategy presentation found ways to connect with company employees in a new way. Nitro found a way to connect with himself and in the process became Patience.

We've found these kinds of transformation everywhere as we've worked with a diversity of private and public organizations. From

U.S. Customs officers to senior partners at a major accounting firm, from school teachers to management consultants, from Wall Street financiers to prison inmates. Over thirty thousand senior executives in fourteen countries. We've worked with companies like GE, Mobil, Capital One, Boston Consulting Group, Merrill Lynch, City Year, Jumpstart, and many others.

Our work over the years convinced us that the ability to connect authentically—which we call *Leadership Presence*—is crucial if leaders want to motivate and truly inspire their colleagues, their managers, and their clients.

Our understanding of presence comes from our experience on the stage. Both of us have been performers most of our lives. Kathy majored in theater at Stanford and worked as a professional actress for fifteen years. In 1985 she cofounded the New Repertory Theatre in Boston, where for eight years she was a leading actress. Belle, born to a musical family, decided at age fourteen she wanted to be a cabaret singer. After graduating from Harvard-Radcliffe, she trained in voice and theater and performed her one-woman shows all over the world.

When we met in 1992 we had already discovered how useful our stage skills and experience could be to people outside the performing arts. Kathy had taught acting to nonactors at the New Repertory Theatre. Businesspeople, doctors, lawyers, teachers, and many other professionals filled her popular classes. Week after week they returned with stories of applying—with powerful results— what they had learned in class to their interaction with coworkers, students, even spouses. Belle had taught successful singing workshops in the United States and Europe for individuals convinced they could not sing. She discovered that conquering the fear of singing liberated her students to conquer fear and doubt in other parts of their lives.

Within a year of meeting we combined our resources and began offering workshops together. A senior manager from Computer Sciences Corporation attended one of our early programs. He came in a skeptic, but at the end he said: "Before taking the workshop, I thought expressing myself fully was an act of self-indulgence. After taking the workshop, I think expressing myself fully is an act of generosity." His comment moved us profoundly then and still inspires us today.

We wrote this book because we feel strongly that by developing the skills of Leadership Presence, by making profound, authentic connections with one another, employees will be more fulfilled, teams will be more motivated, and organizations will be more inspired. The need for Leadership Presence is greater today than ever before, whether it's to lead an organization through difficult economic times, restore trust in an environment of corporate malfeasance, or build consensus among countries. The world won't survive if people can't connect in deep and genuine ways.

We hope you find inspiration in this book that allows you to go beyond standard ways of communicating and helps you connect more generously and authentically with those you lead, your coworkers, your friends, and your family.

Belle Linda Halpern and Kathy Lubar
April 2003

Leadership Presence

CHAPTER 1

Presence: What Actors Have That Leaders Need

All the world's a stage,
And all the men and women merely players.
They have their exits and their entrances;
And one man in his time plays many parts. . . .
William Shakespeare, *As You Like It*

GREAT ACTORS HAVE IT. GREAT POLITICAL LEADERS HAVE IT TOO, AS do great business executives. Laurence Olivier. Meryl Streep. Marlon Brando. Katharine Hepburn. Martin Luther King, Jr. Eleanor Roosevelt. John F. Kennedy. Gandhi. Winston Churchill. Alfred P. Sloan. Oprah Winfrey.

But it's not limited to people in mighty positions. Your local pizza guy may have it. Your doctor may have it. Your daughter's piano teacher may have it too.

All these people—well known or not—are compelling individuals who attract your attention almost effortlessly. They have something, a magnetism that pulls others to them.

When they enter the room, the energy level rises. You perk up, stop what you're doing, and focus on them. You expect something interesting to happen. It's as though a spotlight shines on them.

What is it they have?

They have *presence*.

In the eyes of most people, it's the ability to command the attention of others. Peter Brook, the eminent English stage director, expressed it this way:

One actor can stand motionless on the stage and rivet our attention while another does not interest us at all. What's the difference?

What other words, besides *presence*, come to mind when you think of these people? Here are the words we hear most often when we ask that question in our workshops: *Inspiring. Motivating. Commanding. Energized. Credible. Focused. Confident. Compelling.* Kathy tells this story about working with an aspiring actor:

In the mid-1980s I played Hypatia in a production of George Bernard Shaw's Misalliance *at the New Repertory Theatre. A young actor, playing a relatively minor role, had caught my attention in rehearsals but I was completely unprepared for what happened on opening night.*

He stepped out on stage and simply seized *the room. He was playing the part of the gunner who popped up out of a Turkish bath where he had been hiding. Without saying a word, he was absolutely hilarious. It felt like a full minute before he even opened his mouth and the audience was absolutely riveted by him and when he finally delivered his line there was another twenty-second round of laughter.*

I remember the director, Larry Lane, commenting, "This guy really has what it takes to be a big success." It turns out Larry was right. The actor's name was Oliver Platt and he went on to make a name in films like Working Girl, Bulworth, *and* Indecent Proposal, *as well as on television, including an Emmy-nominated role on* The West Wing.

Presence doesn't have to be a billion-watt nuclear reactor. While some people, like Oliver Platt, can "fill" an entire room or auditorium, the presence of others may not be so large. But it's no less genuine, for these people may be great conversationalists, or they may lead great meetings. Even some actors who have great presence in an intimate medium like movies or television don't have that ability to fill an auditorium. And some great stage actors have trouble "pulling it back" for television or a movie.

Still, whether their presence is large or more intimate, they have it, and when you look at them, it may be with a pang of envy.

Does everyone want to be a billion-watt reactor? Most of us don't seek to be center of attention all the time. But when we join a group or enter a room, we want our arrival acknowledged. When we speak, we want others to listen. When we offer an opinion, we want it treated with respect. We want to be taken seriously. We want our existence to have weight and substance for others.

It's the same thing, just not writ quite so large. We all want presence because no one wants to be ignored.

What is presence?

A moment ago we said most people think of presence as the ability to command the attention of others. But "commanding attention" is only one outcome of presence, not its essence or even its most valuable outcome.

We prefer to think of presence in a different—and deeper—way. For us, presence is *the ability to connect authentically with the thoughts and feelings of others.* Most people think you are born with presence, or without it, or that circumstances lead you, if you're lucky, to develop it at an early age. And if the right circumstances never quite align? Well, too bad.

Fortunately, that's not the case. Presence is the result of certain ongoing choices you make, actions you take or fail to take. In fact, presence is a set of skills, both internal and external, that virtually anyone can develop and improve.

However, when we say anyone can improve his or her presence, we don't mean it's an easy task. It requires you to give up habitual patterns of behavior that you maintain because they make you feel safe. Developing presence will require you to go places and do things that feel uncomfortable, at least initially. Given that hurdle, we're absolutely convinced anyone can develop his or her presence.

The premise of this book is that presence can be developed and you will be a more effective leader when you invest some time and energy toward that goal. Our purpose in writing it is to describe how anyone, including you, can increase your presence.

We know people can develop presence because we have been helping leaders do it for over a decade. Thousands of managers and leaders have gone through our workshops, or worked with us in one-on-one coaching, and improved their ability to connect with others.

More than just skin deep

Let's confront an assumption you may be making.

This is not a book about simply making a better impression. It's not the behavioral counterpart of *Dress for Success*.

Presence includes these things, and anyone working to develop more presence will pay attention to them, because others pay attention to them, but true presence goes far beyond such superficialities.

Just because you've won the lead in a play or a leadership title at work doesn't mean you automatically hold any more sway over your audience or your people. It is your "performance," in both the theatrical and the organizational sense, that will grant you the authority the title or role implies. The presence you bring to your role—how you show up, how you connect, how you speak, listen, act—every move you make on the corporate or real stage, combine to create the impact you have.

Presence comes from *within*. It begins with an inner state, which leads to a series of external behaviors. Sure, you can put on the behaviors, but by themselves they'll lack something essential. They'll be hollow noise and nothing else. We've all heard politicians say, "I feel your pain," when we know they're simply saying what they think we want to hear. Compare that to Martin Luther King, Jr.'s "I have a dream" speech, which obviously sprang from his deeply held beliefs and motivated a generation to overturn four hundred years of assumptions and behaviors.

Presence varies with each individual. In our workshops we

never use a cookie-cutter approach; rather, we help each person discover his or her own unique presence in all its richness and variety.

Learning from theater

The second reason we know presence can be developed is that there exists a whole group of people who work diligently and successfully to develop it. That group of people is actors, and their success, even their livelihood, depends on presence. They must excite us when they step onstage, or they will fail. For the actor and performer, presence is not a happy accident of genetics or upbringing; it's the result of training and practice. *We will draw heavily on the acting profession for concrete principles, practices, and stories about the development of presence.*

At this point you may be thinking what can "serious" business leaders or teachers or politicians or government managers hope to learn from actors? Sure, they can learn how to speak better, to project their voices, to stand up straight. But actors play for a living. They pretend to be other people. What could they know about the "real" world that a lawyer or a Fortune 500 CEO doesn't?

Think about the last time you were really moved by an actor in a live theatrical performance, a movie, or even a television program. We mean really moved to feel something deeply, to understand something more completely, to think about something from a new perspective or even, perhaps, to change your mind about something. Now think about the last time you were truly moved in the same way by a presentation made by a leader in your organization. We're not saying moved to tears but moved to understand a different point of view, be excited about a new possibility, or be motivated to adapt and grow with changing times.

Of course the goal of the actor or the leader in these instances is the same—to connect with you in some fundamental way. Unfortunately most people will say that this experience is much more rare at the office than it is at the movies.

Which is exactly our point. The skills that actors use to move, convince, inspire, or entertain have direct and powerful applications in the worlds of business, politics, education, and organizations in general. They are not only useful for leadership, they are essential. Great leaders, like great actors, must be confident, energetic, empathetic, inspirational, credible, and authentic.

That leaders and actors share some skills and characteristics should come as no surprise. Actors and leaders face a common challenge. They must form connections, communicate effectively, and work with others as a team. They must be prepared to play different roles, as the situation requires. They must be prepared to influence and move people every day.

Just for the record, though, we need to say the analogy isn't perfect. If you list the qualities and skills needed by great leaders, there would be many items on the list that actors don't need, such as the ability to create a great vision of the future, skill in negotiating, the ability to plan and coordinate, and the courage to make decisions that will change peoples' lives.

All we're saying is that leaders can learn many things from actors. We're certainly not suggesting that leaders be actors.

Authenticity

When people hear us define presence as connecting *authentically* with others, they say something like: "I can understand how leaders might learn some things from actors. But how can we learn to be more authentic from people who *lie* professionally? After all, isn't that what acting is really about at the end of the day? An actor steps onto a painted set and pretends to be someone else by performing rehearsed actions and reciting words written by others. What could possibly be more *in*authentic?"

There are two answers to that question. Just as actors play a variety of roles, we all play roles, as people and as leaders. How many roles do you play each day of your life? Manager, parent, spouse, engineer (or some other profession), Scout leader, churchgoer, citizen. Do you behave differently in each role? Are you therefore faking it? No, beneath all those roles is the same person: you. The same can be said of actors.

That leads us to the second answer, which has to do with how actors do what they do. A century ago, it was typical for actors to demonstrate emotion through exaggerated, stylized sets of gestures, vocal intonations, and facial expressions. Look at some early silent movies, and note the back of the wrist held to the forehead to indicate distress, or the furrowed brow and clenched fists to portray anger.

Then a pioneering Russian teacher of acting, Konstantin Stanislavsky, taught that a more accurate and engaging approach would be for actors onstage to actually experience the emotions they were portraying. Thus, to portray a character's anger, for example, an actor should find real anger within himself and express that in his performance. In short, he claimed that the emotion needed to be authentic.

Actors worry about the authenticity, the "truth," of a portrayal almost more than anything else. F. Murray Abraham, a well-known stage actor, acting teacher, and winner of an Oscar for his portrayal of Salieri in *Amadeus*, speaks of the actor's search for truth:

> *What you have to do is find the truth, because that's the essential element that is the middle of all art. It's the middle of acting, whether it's for the camera or on the stage. . . . It's the center of our lives. . . . Once you capture the truth in your own terms, nothing can happen that will bother you.*

It's a paradox of the theater that, in order to pretend, the actor must be real. That need requires the actor to delve inside himself, because the only way an emotion can be authentic is if it comes from within the actor. Actors, consequently, are probably more aware of authenticity than anyone else, because they've studied it, and themselves, so carefully. Over the course of this book, we'll examine how actors approach this demanding part of their craft and what leaders can learn from them. It's a crucial part of presence.

Presence and Leadership Presence

Because it's about connections between people, presence is useful for anyone who engages with others. That's virtually every one of us. Connecting authentically with the thoughts and feelings of others can only improve and deepen our relationships. You don't have to be a leader to enjoy the benefits of presence.

But leaders, in particular, need presence, because at its core leadership is about the interaction, the connection, the relationship between a leader and the people she leads. When we talk about leadership, you may think first of those in organizations who have positions of formal authority—the CEO, the director of marketing, the supervisor of customer service, and so on. The people in these positions are leaders by definition. Maybe you're one of them.

What we say about presence for leaders obviously applies to them. But when we talk about leaders, we include anyone who tries to foster achievement and positive change in any group of people. It can be a family, a PTA, a social club, a volunteer organization, a huge government agency, or giant corporation. A leader is anyone who tries to move a group toward obtaining a particular result. You don't need a title to lead.

But with or without a title you do need presence.

Leadership is about results and outcomes, and so leaders want the hearts and minds of others directed toward some purpose, some result desirable for the group or organization. Presence is the fundamental way a leader can engage the full energies and dedication of others to a common end.

This use of presence we call *Leadership Presence: the ability to connect authentically with the thoughts and feelings of others, in order to motivate and inspire them toward a desired outcome.*

The elements of Leadership Presence

Combining our years of theatrical and performance experience with what we've learned from teaching presence to leaders of all kinds, we've developed a model of Leadership Presence. In that model we break Leadership Presence down into four elements, each of which represents both a state of mind and a way of behaving.

Here are the four elements of Leadership Presence: We call this the PRES model.

The PRES Model of Leadership Presence

P stands for *Being Present*, the ability to be completely in the moment, and flexible enough to handle the unexpected.

R stands for *Reaching Out*, the ability to build relationships with others through empathy, listening, and authentic connection.

E stands for *Expressiveness*, the ability to express feelings and emotions appropriately by using all available means—words, voice, body, face—to deliver one congruent message.

S stands for *Self-knowing*, the ability to accept yourself, to be authentic, and to reflect your values in your decisions and actions.

Leadership Presence is more than the sum of these elements. When we're around someone with Leadership Presence, we feel it and know it as one thing, not the accumulation of four related but disparate skills.

Each element possesses both an interior and an exterior aspect. The interior aspect has to do with the state of mind and heart from which each element springs, while the exterior aspect has to do with the behavior that reflects and reveals the interior aspect. Focusing on the exterior and ignoring the interior is like being courteous without caring. It may work for a short while, but its hollowness soon becomes obvious.

The four elements are a convenient way to teach and learn Leadership Presence because each builds on, and gains power from, the preceding element. They're cumulative. *Being Present* is the first step. *Reaching Out* and *Expressiveness* cannot work in practice unless you are fully present—in the moment, focused, completely there. Being Present allows you to effectively reach out to others, to really listen and to see things from their perspective. Expressiveness is certainly possible all by itself. But unless it builds on a foundation of being present and Reaching Out, it will only lead people to think of you as loud or flamboyant. To be *Self-knowing*, to know where you came from and what you stand for, to be authentic, enables you to integrate all the previous elements of the PRES model in your interactions with others.

Prior to attending a coaching session or workshop, we ask our clients to reflect on their own Leadership Presence. We encourage you to consider your own abilities in this area, and to help you we have created a simple, online self-assessment tool. To obtain a preliminary measure of your personal Leadership Presence please log on to *www.leadershippresence.net* and complete the questionnaire. You will receive a confidential, baseline report that will help guide you as you read this book and work to enhance your skills.

The benefits of Leadership Presence

The applications and benefits of Leadership Presence are widespread. Throughout large and small organizations leaders need to move, influence, inspire, and motivate people to achieve goals. Leadership Presence is a powerful tool for mobilizing and energizing people, sometimes toward great achievement.

We have worked at the senior levels of Fortune 500 companies, in government, in nonprofits, in education, and even in the prison system. The list of ways to apply the skill of Leadership Presence grows with every client. Consider the following list.

- Developing deeper and more trusting relationships with your clients

- Inspiring your teammates to sprint to the finish on an important project

- Persuading a reluctant recruit she has what it takes to charge up that hill

- Convincing your investors to fund your next great idea

- Inspiring a classroom of students to become lifelong learners

- Encouraging your employees to hang in through tough times

- Creating enthusiasm in your organization for a difficult change

- Negotiating a complex contract that benefits all sides

- Nurturing a corporate culture that engenders loyalty and retention

Do any of these tasks look familiar? Are they similar to the challenges that you face? Would your ability to connect authentically with your audience help accomplish these things? In other words, would Leadership Presence help? We think so.

It's not hard to imagine all the relationships and situations where these abilities will be useful in building consensus around common goals, making a work group into a real team, creating long-term relationships with customers, improving collaboration with colleagues, anywhere relationships are critical to accomplishment.

Leadership Presence—More than just charisma

As we write this book, the notion of charisma has fallen into disfavor. Too many companies in recent years have come to wrack and ruin, led by so-called charismatic leaders who have led their organizations over the edge of the cliff, while making barrels of money for themselves in the process.

Charisma itself is not necessarily the villain, but narcissistic charisma is. That's the kind of charisma that allows an individual to sway the masses and stir up followers while maintaining emotional distance or even disdain for those followers. Charisma as an element of true Leadership Presence can be a tool for good, as long as the other elements are also in place.

Leadership Presence combines power with humility. It's about where you *and those you lead* want to go and what *all of you* want to accomplish and how all of you can benefit from your work together. It's about relationships and connections between people. To use our PRES model again, Leadership Presence is about:

- Being Present—not pretentious.

- Reaching Out—not looking down.

- Being Expressive—not impressive.

- Being Self-knowing—not self-absorbed.

We said a moment ago that self-knowing is what integrates the four elements of the PRES model into one thing—Leadership Presence. Self-knowing is what separates Leadership Presence from self-centered charisma. For Self-knowing involves knowing your values and living according to those values. A leader can possess charisma and still have Leadership Presence. But for the narcissistic charismatic leader, the chief value is "me," and the problem is that followers inevitably discover that value, causing the luster to wear off.

Achieving Leadership Presence is a four-act drama

Because our experience has shown us that Leadership Presence is most easily learned around the four elements, we have organized the rest of this book around them, in four acts. Each act contains two chapters that cover the interior and exterior aspects of the element. The second chapter in each act provides rules and practical advice to help you apply what you learned in the first chapter.

Act I: Being Present

Chapter 2 discusses the value of living *in the moment*, which is the state of mind that compels or energizes Being Present. Chapter 3 then uses improvisational theater to explore *flexibility*, the key feature of how you act when you're fully present.

Act II: Reaching Out

Chapter 4 delves into *empathy*, the state of mind that drives Reaching Out, followed by Chapter 5 on *making connections*, which covers all the actions we can take to create a relationship with another person.

Act III: Expressiveness

Chapter 6 talks about expressing emotion and focuses on a concept every actor and leader will recognize—*passionate purpose*—which influences all the ways we express ourselves. Chapter 7 then describes the way we communicate our passionate purpose by *congruently* using all means of communication at our disposal.

Act IV: Self-knowing

Chapter 8 explores the heart of Self-knowing for a leader, which is the development of explicit beliefs and values through self-reflection. Chapter 9 discusses *authenticity*, which is based on accepting yourself and living your values.

Practices and exercises

At the end of each chapter we include easy-to-use practices and exercises based on our actual work training and coaching executives. These are the reference sections of the book, designed so readers can learn and apply the principles we discuss in each chapter. Some of you may jump into these right after each chapter, others may choose to return to them after digesting the entire book. We encourage you to pick and choose from these sections depending on your personal preferences and needs.

The practices are actions and behaviors that you can apply, on a daily basis, to your everyday life. The exercises are to be done outside of work at a time you have set aside, in the same way you might do physical exercises to stay fit. These activities, which come predominantly from our acting training, are designed to maintain and strengthen your skills of Leadership Presence.

BEING PRESENT

The ability to be completely in the
moment and flexible enough to
handle the unexpected

Introduction to Act I

Eighty percent of success in life is showing up.
Woody Allen

ON SEPTEMBER 11, 2001, AS ALL OF US WATCHED THE UNFOLDING tragedy on television, a crucial aspect of leadership became crystal clear.

It was comforting to see Mayor Rudy Giuliani of New York on the scene. His simple presence and concern reassured the country. In contrast, everyone wondered about the president. Was he all right? Where was he?

His absence left a void.

Through no fault of his own, President Bush was missing for most of that terrible day. Believing with good reason that the president was in danger, the secret service put him on *Air Force One* to take him out of harm's way. Unfortunately, the effect was to remove him from public view when the country desperately needed his visible presence.

Leaders need to "be present," and being literally, physically present is the fundamental meaning of that term. We're always surprised at how many leaders we encounter who spend most of their time in their offices or on "executive row." They seldom show themselves to those they lead. It was over twenty years ago that the groundbreaking book *In Search of Excellence* pointed out the virtues of "management by walking around." Mayor Giuliani certainly demonstrated the wisdom of that practice.

More than showing up

But being present means more than just physical presence, important as that is. It means being present *in the moment*—focused totally and completely on what is happening right here and right now. It means, when you're with people, giving them your full attention, so that they will feel recognized and motivated. When you're not present to the people you lead, it weakens their willingness to commit.

And being present also means being *flexible*, able to deal spontaneously with rapid change. Think of being present as a focused but flexible dance with the world in which the leader can instantly change step or tempo as the music changes.

In the days following September 11, President Bush tended to the country's wounds, and we sensed, particularly as he spoke to the rescuers at Ground Zero, with his arm around a fireman, that he was present to them (and all of us) in that moment, in spite of all the other national concerns on his mind. Someone handed him a bullhorn and he began to speak. "Can't hear you!" the crowd called. He tried again. "I can't hear you!" the crowd called again. "I can hear you," he answered. "I can hear you. The rest of the world hears you." It was a moment, as a journalist later wrote, that "summed up, with simple eloquence, the nation's gratitude to these men and women."

A few years ago we worked with Margaret, the head of a biotech company. On several occasions we attended Margaret's meetings with her staff, all of them senior managers themselves. Her entry never failed to produce the same response—it was as if a surge of electricity had walked in. That spark perked everyone up. Eyes and attention focused on her, waiting eagerly for what was next.

In contrast, when Howard, who worked for Margaret, entered a meeting of his people, a somber fog would settle over the group. Any life and energy in the room would dissipate like the last bubbles from a glass of warm beer.

Margaret always came into meetings focused on the people there and the work to be done. She began with a series of un-

planned questions, sometimes personal, sometimes business related, and people had to be on their toes. There was humor and
wit; people laughed a lot. Howard, on the other hand, always
seemed distracted. He would start by shuffling his papers, barely
noticing the people around the table. He might even begin the
first agenda item without looking up and making eye contact. In
Howard's meetings no one ever laughed.

Here was the difference: Margaret was present. Howard was
not. Margaret's meetings woke you up. Howard's put you to sleep.

Being present comes first

Being present is fundamental to the work of an actor. The worst
insult you can give an actor is that he "phoned in" his performance, that he wasn't present, that he simply reeled off his lines
and hit his marks. Being fully present is the first requirement of
acting—be there, in the moment, alive, energized. From that quality
springs all else in the theater. So it should come as no surprise that
actors spend a large amount of time training to be completely focused and concentrated in the moment.

We're sometimes asked why actors need to be present. The
words they speak are provided in the script. How they move, what
they physically do, is worked out in rehearsal or specified in stage
directions. Everything is prescribed. So why do they have to be
"present?"

Imagine you're an actor in a romantic drama. In the middle of
the play, you split up with your beloved. You believe the relationship is over forever. It's the darkest day you can imagine. You'll
never be happy again. At least that's what your character thinks.
You, the actor, know better, of course, because you've read the
script. You know at the end you'll be back together and live happily ever after. Knowing that, how can you authentically portray
the end-of-the-world, I'll-never-be-happy-again grief your character feels? Only by being so fully submerged in your character, in
the moment, that you literally don't "know" until the end how
the story comes out.

So, Being Present is the starting point of our PRES model for leadership Presence. At the same time, the simple act of being present can be transformative, can lead to great joy, and to the appreciation of each moment as it arises. The discipline of Being Present allows us to find calm in the most difficult situations and to appreciate being alive in the midst of great chaos.

There is a Zen story that captures the notion of Being Present:

A man runs through the jungle chased by a hungry tiger. He comes to a cliff and grabs a vine hanging over the edge. He looks down and sees another tiger waiting below. Two mice begin to gnaw through his vine. He has only moments to live. He sees a berry growing from the cliff before him. He plucks it and drops it in his mouth. It is the sweetest, juiciest berry he's ever eaten.

CHAPTER 2

Being Present in the Moment

Do you have the patience to wait
till your mud settles and the water is clear?
Can you remain unmoving
till the right action arises by itself?
The Master doesn't seek fulfillment.
Not seeking, not expecting,
she is present, and can welcome all things.

Lao-Tzu

WE JOINED MICHAEL IN HIS OFFICE ONE MORNING AS HE PREPARED for an important meeting.

He was a forty-year-old vice president of strategic development for a large publicly traded healthcare company that The Ariel Group had been working with for several years. Trained as a doctor, Michael had joined the company in the 1980s when it was a small HMO. He'd worked on the medical side for years, but as the company grew he'd become increasingly interested in organizational issues around delivery of medical care. Finally, he'd moved out of practicing medicine itself and held a number of positions in the HMO before taking his current post. We were working with him because a reorganization had expanded his role to make him, with the CEO and the CFO, one of the executives who dealt with outside financial analysts.

It was part of his job to communicate his company's new vision for the future. No one understood that vision better than he, its chief architect. But in this expanded role, he was a fish out of water. Never comfortable making presentations to a group of any size, he found analysts especially intimidating. Born disbelievers, their written opinions, analyses, and recommendations could make a real difference in the company's stock price.

Later that morning, he would face ten to fifteen analysts specializing in the healthcare industry. In the next few months, he and his colleagues would go on a "road show," presenting their plans to more groups around the country.

Michael emerged from his office. It wasn't yet 10 A.M., but we were his fourth meeting of the day and it showed in his tired eyes. He wore a rumpled suit and gave us a warm, slightly distracted smile. People told us he was probably the smartest guy in the company, and a key contributor to its current success. But this morning his mind seemed to be somewhere else. As we talked, he took two quick phone calls and looked at something his assistant shoved under his nose.

He said he welcomed the chance to work with us and he recognized his own problems. Plus, his new son-in-law was an actor and he was eager to learn how a theatrical approach might work.

We spent half an hour with him and then walked to the twelfth-floor conference room where the analysts were waiting. Just before eleven o'clock, Michael, the CEO, and the CFO all trooped in and sat at the head of the large U-shaped conference table.

The CEO said a few words and then introduced Michael who then stepped to the podium, cleared his throat, and began reading his remarks.

His forehead glistened. The pointer shook slightly in his hand when he poked it at the slides on the wall screen behind him. His voice quivered a little. He cleared his throat again and again. His obvious discomfort made us nervous.

In a few minutes he finished reading and slowly looked up. This was the moment he dreaded. We knew what he was thinking, because he'd told us:

> When I'm presenting to a group, especially analysts, my mind will suddenly go blank. First there's nothing there. Then I panic. My heart goes crazy, sweat's rolling down my back and all I can hear is this little voice saying, "Failure! They'll never write anything good about the company!"

We asked how often this happened to him. "Maybe twice in a typical meeting," he said. "Problem is, I'm filled with panic *the whole time* it'll happen any second. I wait for it to happen. It's all I can think about."

When we asked how we could help, he said:

I want to be like Larry Bird at the free-throw line. Larry could stand there, fans screaming, two seconds left on the clock, totally focused, like he was the only guy on the court, and he'd drain that free throw.

As nerves go, Michael's were probably worse than average. But they were hardly the worst we've seen. We've worked with people whose anxiety before any kind of public presentation was so bad they had to take tranquilizers or heart medicine. Some could barely speak. Some threw up.

Maybe you know how Michael felt. As you move into positions of leadership these pressure-filled situations seem to occur more and more often. And you have less time to think, less time to prepare, and less time to recover between meetings.

Michael's blanking out might seem extreme, but we deal with many executives who find it hard to stay totally focused in high-stakes meetings, particularly when there seems to be ten meetings like that every day. Actors can teach us something about handling this kind of stress. They put themselves in similar, high-pressure situations night after night.

Great actors handle pressure before every performance

Laurence Olivier, whom many consider the greatest actor of the twentieth century, once described the moment just before the curtain rose as he played Richard in Shakespeare's *Richard III* in this way:

I was in the slips and ready. The noise of the audience was still removed, but audible, which meant that the house lights were still up. I glanced round the stage. This was to be my world for the next three hours. . . . I looked into the corner and saw (the stage manager) press the final bell for the bars. Far off I could hear it ringing.

Last questions: Was I prepared? Of course I was. The spider in the stomach again. God, I should have gone to the lavatory. Deep breath . . . perfect. Control . . . control . . . everything geared to a fine edge, sharp as a razor. . . . Come on, get that curtain up, I've been here an hour.

. . . the chatter in the front of house slowly ceased. The lights had dimmed and the warmers were on the curtain. Yet another switch and a green light winked.

"Now," I thought. "Now." Up went the curtain and there we were: the audience and Richard, face to face for the first time.

The warmth from a full house is amazing. As the curtain rises, it rushes across the footlights like a great giant's breath. It fills your nostrils.

"Now is the winter . . ." I was inside the skull, looking out through Shakespeare's eyes.

The contrast between Michael and Olivier could hardly be more stark.

Look again at Olivier's description of that time and place. He was totally focused on what was happening around him—the lights, the stage manager, the audience, sounds, the "giant's breath" of air.

He was in the moment, there, his senses fully alive to the world around him and in him, concentrated but calm, eager to begin, mind clear and empty, not lost in thoughts. He was present. Reviewers of his performances always found him electric, mesmerizing, absorbing.

How about Michael? He was distracted, nervous, withdrawn, panicky, expecting failure. He was physically in the room but not present.

And he paid a stiff price for that. He made us nervous but he made the analysts skeptical. We could tell by the looks on their faces and their body language. Michael needed to inspire confidence, not only for his plan, but most of all for his and his colleagues' ability to lead the company. But without Being Present, he couldn't even begin to connect with the analysts. It was like trying to start a car with a dead battery.

Being Present in your world

You've probably been fully present many times in your life—experiences when you were totally in the moment, undistracted by anything past or future, sharp as a razor, alive to everything around you.

It happens, if you play sports, in the throes of a close game. A jazz musician improvising a riff is present. Some mothers have described giving birth as their most intensely present moment. Soldiers describe combat as the time they feel most alive and awake. Many of us experience it when we fall in love.

We remember seeing an ad for skydiving years ago. It said something like, "When you step out of the plane into thin air, whatever was on your mind, whatever was worrying you, will disappear, replaced by the wind, the thrill of falling free, the ground rushing up like a freight train." These moments of being fully present are often thrust upon us by intense circumstances. But you can create them yourself any time you want. You can avoid the embarrassing situations that even the most qualified executive like Michael encounters.

The advantages of Being Present are obvious. You're at your best when you're fully in the moment, totally focused. Seems like a pretty simple concept doesn't it? But why is it so difficult?

It's hard to be present in today's fast-paced world

Being Present is difficult for many reasons, but most of all because the "moment" keeps changing. Every second the world swirls around you and tests your ability to remain present.

Think of the world as a movie. It's going by as a series of still pictures moving so fast our brains blur them into a sense of continuous motion. The temptation sometimes is to reach out and seize one of those still pictures and say, "That's the world! That's it!" when, of course, a split second later, it's not the world anymore. Something has changed. Every moment we must change simply to remain present to the world as it reveals itself.

The way people work in business and organizations presents special challenges. Today's flatter, leaner organizations with stronger technology tools mean more work and responsibility for each individual. Everyone is trying to do several things at once—look through mail or read the paper while talking on the phone, carry on a conversation while doing e-mail, take cell phone calls in meetings or at meals. Yet, when we do many things at once, no one activity or person receives our complete attention. Everyone laments the cost but feels compelled to do it anyway.

All that frantic activity only exacerbates the underlying problem—how we react to our own feelings of fear.

The underlying culprit:
Fear—and how you handle it

In one form or another, fear is what keeps us from Being Present. Fear of failure. Fear of what others think. Fear of being hurt emotionally. Fear of not being good enough. It was fear that caused an executive as accomplished as Michael to blank out during meetings. But here's the critical distinction: When you feel fear, it's not the feeling itself that keeps you from Being Present. It's the *thoughts* you attach to the fear that create the problem. We can be present with fear. Fear is just a physical sensation. Remember Olivier's "spider in the belly?" To see how this works, we need to look at the two basic ways we all react to fear—the "fight or flight" response and the "inner critic."

Fight or flight

One of the biggest obstacles to being present is the adrenaline rush that comes when humans face a threat. It's called the fight-or-flight response. All animals have it. It's extremely useful in the face of danger. The body goes into hyperdrive, as adrenalin prepares it to fight an attacker or run away at top speed. If a mugger is chasing you, the fight-or-flight response can make you run faster.

When the physical threat is real, the fight-or-flight response can save our lives. But in the modern world many of our pressure-packed, high-stakes, day-to-day experiences, like key meetings or major presentations, can provoke that adrenaline rush needlessly. How useful is that when you need to be present? Not very. It was certainly working overtime against Michael.

In our day-to-day lives, instead of being useful, the fight-or-flight response sabotages us. The thoughts and feelings it generates take us out of the present moment.

The inner critic

Most people describe the inner critic as a voice inside their heads that constantly evaluates their behavior. For some it's a single voice. For others it may be a chorus of voices. But, the message is always the same: *This is really bad. You're not good enough. If you don't pass this test, get by this hurdle, you're a failure. You'll fail at every effort to measure up.*

It was the voice Michael heard screaming in his head after his mind would go blank.

To the extent it spurs you to greater effort and higher achievement, the inner critic is useful. Unfortunately, it usually goes far beyond that beneficial role. For many people, the inner critic is so powerful that they fail because it keeps them from ever trying.

Some people have learned to handle it better than others, but we've never met anyone without an inner critic, at least to some degree. Even the most confident among us have this Achilles' heel.

We know it well ourselves because, as performers, we've given it many opportunities to shout in our ears, and, as coaches, we've worked with hundreds of people trying to get rid of it.

Three guidelines for getting present

When actors struggle with fight or flight and the inner critic, they call it stage fright. It may surprise you that stage fright can strike even the most accomplished actors.

Olivier struggled with it, at least for a period in his life. As he wrote in his book, *On Acting*:

> *Let me give you a brief insight into stage fright. It is an animal, a monster which hides in its foul corner without revealing itself, but you know that it is there and that it may come forward at any moment. . . . He is always waiting outside the door, any door, waiting to get you. You either battle or walk away.*

Of course, opening night jitters are worst of all, but that moment of throwing yourself, vulnerable, in front of an audience, can elicit fear no matter how often you do it. So actors work their whole lives on Being Present. It's a constant effort, for it's possible to have an electric sense of Being Present one night, only to lose it the next.

Actors have developed excellent techniques for dealing with the fearful or anxious thoughts and feelings that plague us all. Some of the techniques involve the body, things you can do physically; some involve the mind, the way you think; and some involve the heart, the way you feel.

From acting and our own experience working with leaders like Michael, we've distilled three guidelines for getting present:

1. Focus on the physical.

2. Change your perspective.

3. Let thoughts go, let feelings be.

Being Present guideline #1:
Focus on the physical

We talked to Michael after his meeting with the analysts. We told him that actors apply two basic physical techniques to get themselves present in the midst of fear—"being in the body" and breathing. Both techniques, simple but very powerful, would help him contend with what actors call "being in the head"—consciously thinking and worrying too much.

It's common for a director during rehearsal to ask an actor who doesn't seem fully present, "Where are you now? What's going on with your breath? Are you in your body?"

Be in the body

We told Michael about our colleague Madeleine Homan, an actor who played the lead in a national tour of *Evita* and who is now a vice president of a prominent corporate training and coaching company. She was asked to speak on a news show about the "coaching movement" in corporate life. She went on not knowing that the show had also invited another commentator, a vitriolic career counselor who considered all corporate coaches incompetents and frauds. Madeleine found herself under attack from the first few seconds. She said:

> *I literally broke into a sweat. I could feel the sweat dripping down my back. My ears were ringing—internally, it sounded like I was standing next to a fire engine. I'm unable to think—like a deer in the headlights—when I get that scared, which I think is a normal reaction. When I realized what was going on, I had the conscious thought:* Feel your feet. *I knew Laurence Olivier, when suffering from unpredictable bouts of stage fright, would feel his feet— he would literally, consciously, feel the nerve endings, the soles of his feet, on the ground, and that helped him stay in his body. It keeps you from floating off in your head and getting thrown by the alarm bells. It really helped me. When I looked at the video*

afterward, I actually looked calm and sounded articulate! Only I knew the turmoil under the surface. They say that the adrenaline an actor's body produces on an opening night would kill a horse, and I believe it. One of the things that acting training does is prepare you to manage the extraordinarily intense physical response of terror. I know my acting background helped me stay grounded in the face of incredible discomfort and fear.

Michael agreed to give our exercises a try. We asked him to sit upright in his chair. Pay attention to your body, we told him. Feel yourself grounded on the chair and your feet firmly planted on the floor as if you had roots going down into the earth. Starting with your feet, focus on each part of your body, working up your legs, body, and finally, your head. Observe how each part feels. Note any sensations, like pressure, warmth, anything. If any part seems tense, note that, tense it even more, and then relax it.

By inhabiting the body in this way you can get present. Focusing on that sense of your physical self will reduce the effects of fight or flight and the inner critic.

Breathe

Next, we taught Michael diaphragmatic breathing. We asked him to relax into his chair and notice his breathing. We had him place his hand on his belly to see what was happening there as he inhaled and exhaled. We showed him how to breathe so that he was inhaling with his belly—that is, when he breathed in his belly expanded, and when he exhaled his belly contracted.

We suggested that he pay attention to his breathing before and during meetings. We recommended that he consciously move his breath to his belly whenever he felt his mind going blank. He was politely skeptical that such a simple thing could make any difference, but he agreed to try it.

Breathing is something we cover very early in working with clients. It's such a fundamental and powerful tool for overcoming the obstacles to being present. When afraid, stressed, or excited, people often move the breath into the chest. That's entirely normal. It's part of the fight-or-flight response. Animals do it—you can see them start to pant when they're threatened. But many people move their breath there so often—when they overreact to minor threats, for example—that it stays there virtually all the time.

By breathing purposefully in the belly, we can inhibit the fight-or-flight response, actually telling the brain to stop sending in adrenaline. That's why the simple practice of moving the breath back into the belly holds enormous power. In all our years of teaching, it's been the one practice that has had the most impact on the most people in the shortest period of time. You can't avoid being in the present, if you concentrate on your breath.

Try it now, as you read. Consciously take four or five deep breaths in the belly. Notice the sense of calm it gives you. When you feel stressed or anxious, like Michael, you can consciously move your breathing into the belly.

We gave Michael some homework. We asked him to practice breathing in his belly while lying down, right before he went to sleep at night and just after he woke up in the morning. If you practice when you are most relaxed, the diaphragmatic breathing will become automatic.

When we returned a month later, Michael said he'd been pleasantly surprised. Being in the body and belly breathing had turned out to be effective antidotes for losing his train of thought. Some deep breaths would cause his panic to subside and his mind to clear. Once he'd used it successfully a few times, he lost his constant sense of terror, because he knew what to do if he felt it happening. Simple as this may sound, it was a major step for him.

Being Present guideline #2:
Change your perspective

In addition to physical techniques, there are things you can do mentally to ward off the fearful thoughts that prevent you from being totally present. When your inner critic raises its negative voice, the first level of response is conceptual. That is, you can learn to think of it differently.

Recognize the inner critic as a distinct voice that's *not* you, and that's not necessarily even correct. Think of it as a person separate from you, someone other than you, perhaps an amalgam of voices from your past.

Once you've identified it this way, you can recognize it, and you can literally respond to it, "Oh, that's my inner critic. That's her (his) opinion."

Michael admitted to some continuing anxiety about meetings, so we asked him a series of questions: What goes through your mind as you approach one of those meetings? What are you telling yourself?

"The analysts won't like me," he said. "They'll see how nervous I am. They won't have confidence in me." As he spoke, it became clear to him that he was making negative predictions about the outcomes of the meetings. We asked him to write all the negative predictions on the whiteboard in his office.

Once he could see his thoughts reduced to actual words, we asked if they represented reality or if they were just his thoughts. He had to admit in almost every case he was guessing, imagining, making assumptions. The company was doing well. What analysts had written so far had been mostly positive.

This exercise, which took an hour or so to talk through, represented another turning point for Michael. He'd never made his assumptions explicit, either by saying them aloud or writing them down. And he'd never examined them critically or logically. Once they were expressed clearly and he could think about them, he realized how his inner critic was sabotaging him.

After that, when those thoughts began to prey on him, he would remind himself they were just thoughts and not reality.

Reframe your perspective. . . . come from a bigger place

Many performers handle the inner critic by viewing it through the lens of something obviously more important, something that makes their fears about themselves seem petty or trivial. That's what we mean by "a bigger place."

Belle herself discovered the power of changing perspective when she sang one night at New York's Town Hall, where Judy Garland had recorded her famous album, *Judy Garland at Town Hall*. It was a high-stakes performance, a cabaret festival, with a full house and reviewers from major papers.

In my career, I had had a long struggle with my own inner critic. The voice in me that wanted me to be good was so strong it had been sabotaging my ability to connect with people. It was saying, "The audience is there to judge you, and if they don't think you're good, then you're nothing." So I had put up armor to protect me from the judgment of the audience. What every performer wants is to connect with the hearts of the audience. You want your story to touch the stories in their hearts, but if you have armor on, you can't do it.

It so happened that on the day of her performance an earthquake hit Santa Cruz, California, where her brother attended college. As soon as she and her family heard of the quake, at about two o'clock in the afternoon, they all tried to call him. But the phone lines were down and they couldn't reach him or get any word. All they knew was that television newscasters kept saying how serious it was and how much damage had been done.

I started on my whole preperformance ritual. I got in the shower, I washed my hair. It was four o'clock. I ate something light. By six o'clock I was at the theater and I was starting to warm up, putting my makeup on, all that stuff. I kept checking in with my mother, checking radio and TV. Nothing. We heard how devastating it was but were not able to get much detail. It was six-thirty, seven, seven-thirty, still nothing. I had to go on at eight o'clock. I was doing my routine, warming up my voice, thinking through the words to my songs, talking to my pianist about beginnings and endings.

Usually as I'm warming up, I'm trying to open up, trying to get the armor down. But on the day of this concert, the armor wasn't there at all. Whether the audience liked me or not seemed so unimportant, compared with my concern and love for my brother. The armor simply disappeared.

Undisturbed by the inner critic, I was free to choose what I wanted to do in the concert, and what I wanted was to be generous and give something to the audience that would touch them in their lives. I went on with that attitude and it totally shifted the performance. Without the armor, I was able to come from a bigger place of generosity. I simply offered my music as a gift, rather than an effort to be judged.

It made a difference. Until that concert, people would tell Belle, "Wow, you have a beautiful voice," or, "Wow, that song was funny." After the Town Hall concert, people said things like, "I was so moved by your performance."

At two o'clock that morning, twelve hours after hearing about the earthquake, Belle and her family finally heard from her brother. Though shaken, scared, and without power for many hours, he was fine.

The inner critic is a contracting, diminishing voice. As it grows louder, you become smaller, weaker, less open, less generous. You're stuck in your head, not actually in your feelings. So almost any way of remaining expansive and coming from a bigger place will help keep the inner critic at bay.

We tell those we coach to think of whatever gives them confidence—moments in their lives when they felt proud, when they accomplished something difficult or were recognized—like graduation, winning a game, giving birth. Or, we suggest they remember a person who always gave them wholehearted support and love—a parent, grandparent, friend, anyone. Keep that person in mind, we advise, and recall the way she or he treated you.

Humor can help too. Laugh at yourself. Exaggerate the inner critic's claims ("The world will end, if they don't like me!").

Focusing on your goal, what actors call their "intention," can also silence the inner critic. You want to excite or warn or change people, whatever it is. Get this clear in your mind and focus on it and the inner critic will recede.

Focusing on others, instead of yourself, can help too. William Hurt, the Broadway actor and Oscar-winning star of *Broadcast News* and *Children of a Lesser God*, uses this approach:

> When I come out on the stage I'm generally frightened, momentarily, before I can figure out what to concentrate on. I need something real to get outside of myself—and for me that's always the other actor. I drench myself in the other actor instead of thinking about myself.

Being Present guideline #3:
Let thoughts go, let feelings be

Meredith Monk is a performance artist who combines movement, song, music, and images. Recognized for her "unique style of music-theater enchantment," she won a MacArthur Foundation "genius" grant. In the summer of 2000 the Lincoln Center in New York gave a retrospective of her work.

> I turned fifty, feeling great, thinking, "Boy, this is an easy transition." And then suddenly I was getting onstage and experiencing this incredible existential fright. It was like, "Here I am, and there are two thousand people out there!" And I would just start shaking. Some of it had to do with my (voice): I couldn't get my high E's anymore. . . . I wondered, would anyone really want to watch a woman who's over fifty, you know? There were some performances where people could see that I was frozen in fear.

Then she read a story about Milarepa, a Buddhist saint who lived in a cave. Demons came and demanded to be let in. He denied them, argued with them, pleaded with them, commanded them, fought with them. Nothing worked. Whatever he tried, their demands became more insistent. Finally, feeling frustrated

and at his wits' end, he invited them to come in and have tea—
and to his complete surprise, they vanished.

> *I was doing a performance in San Francisco, and I remember get-*
> *ting onstage and feeling fairly relaxed, and then this incredible*
> *fear started up again. But this time, instead of pretending that*
> *it wasn't there, I let it come. It was like, "Come in." I wasn't*
> *thinking this, of course, because you're not really thinking when*
> *you're performing, but it was happening—it just came, like the*
> *ocean, and then it went and then it would come back, and then it*
> *would go.*
>
> *That was the beginning of working my way through. I don't*
> *feel that way these days. I've found a deep relaxation as a per-*
> *former. I don't even expect anything vocally anymore. My voice is*
> *feeling great, relaxed, very flexible—and I feel that what is going*
> *on, is going on!*[5]

What allowed Meredith Monk to move through her fear was
the most profound response possible—acceptance. She let go of the
thoughts she'd wrapped around the fear—too old, voice failing—
and just experienced the fear. "What is going on, is going on."

By separating thoughts from fear and letting them go, we can
free ourselves. George Kinder, author of *The Seven Stages of Money
Maturity*, calls this practice: "Let thoughts go. Let feelings be."
These are skills an actor uses all the time.

How leaders can "let thoughts go, let feelings be"

Steve Chambers trained as an actor and worked regularly on TV,
before getting an MBA to begin a career in marketing and sales. He
is now executive vice president of marketing and sales at a cutting-
edge communications firm. He said:

> *One technique I used to use from acting training that helped me a*
> *lot in business, I call* experience the experience. *If I was feeling*
> *nervous, I would say to myself, just experience the experience—*
> *your heart's beating faster, your palms are a little cold. I would*

label things that were happening in the moment. Once I could process what was happening the nervousness would dissipate. It really worked.

As we worked with Michael to help him distinguish the voice of his inner critic and understand that these were thoughts of his own creation and not reality—a major insight for him—he was learning to let the thoughts go. Just release them, we told him.

The remaining step for him was simply to feel his feelings. We asked him to notice, when fear or anxiety arose, where it was in his body. He said he noticed a tightness and shallow breathing in the chest and a fluttering feeling in his stomach. We encouraged him to do nothing but bring his attention fully to these sensations, while continuing to release the thoughts he'd hooked to those sensations.

"I'm afraid they'll grow stronger if I focus on them," he told us.

We encouraged him to stay with the sensations and continue to breathe. He did, and to his delight discovered—as Meredith Monk did—that the fear lessened and eventually dissipated, along with the other sensations.

By practicing and applying all these techniques, Michael made great progress in being present in important meetings, in spite of his fear and anxiety. That allowed him to communicate the company's vision to the analysts in a more compelling and convincing way. He was able to instill the belief that he and his colleagues were capable of carrying off the challenges in front of them. His hands stopped shaking, the fear of blanking out went away, the moments of silence as he struggled to get his mind back on track became shorter and shorter. He began to feel a new sense of calm and confidence.

Later he told us, "Now when I feel anxiety or fear, I embrace it in the way you taught me and actually feel energized by it!"

Being Present can transform you in many ways

After working with Michael for a few months, he came in one day and told us this story. One evening in January, he came home from a day of back-to-back meetings and asked Patty, his daughter, how she was doing with her college applications. It was a touchy subject between them because Patty was determined to attend art school and Michael wanted her to attend a liberal arts college.

It was a running battle, fought almost daily for a year and now coming to climax. The college applications, each of which required lengthy and time-consuming essays, were due in a few days. This evening Patty, defiant with her purple hair, informed her father she was absolutely not applying to liberal arts schools. Only art schools.

"What's the point?" she said. "I'm not going there. Why should I write all that junk for the applications?"

As they sat at the kitchen table Michael repeated all his arguments: "You don't know what you want to do. If you go to art school, you won't be prepared for anything else. You can study art at a liberal arts school. Then, if you're still interested, take an advanced degree in art. You'll be glad later. I know what's best."

Patty repeated all her answers. "Why should I do what I know I don't want to do? I want art, to study art, to *do* art. Liberal arts schools don't provide the same experience."

Once again, the discussion became an argument and reached the impasse it always did. Finally, Michael and Patty could only glare at each other.

In this moment of total frustration, Michael realized he was in a state he had never wanted to be in—on the edge of his chair, voice raised, arms crossed, shooting out angry arguments at his only child, who was shooting arguments back at him.

For a moment Michael mentally stepped back and consciously reminded himself to become truly present, something he was now doing regularly at work.

He physically settled into his chair, uncrossed his arms, got his feet grounded, and focused on what was going on in his body, using his breath to center himself.

For the moment, he completely dropped his goal of convincing Patty. He dropped any thought of what was going to happen in the future. He dropped the story he was telling himself that Patty would ruin her life if she went to art school.

He let all his thoughts go and just focused on how his body felt. His chest felt tight, he realized, his heart beating fast. A lump filled his throat. Suddenly he realized the lump was not anger but fear and sadness. He looked at Patty and could see fear in her as well.

Realizing her father had gone silent, Patty said defensively, "What?"

But instead of more arguments, Michael said quietly, "I'm starting to realize how scared this makes me." Then he added, "You must be feeling the same way."

Patty began to cry.

In a split second, everything changed. They gave up the arguments they'd been throwing at each other for months. They became free to understand what was going on. Michael's wife, Patty's mother, had died several years earlier. Her last wish to Michael was that he watch over their little girl as she grew up. Somehow, Michael had taken that to mean Patty had to get a good general education. His greatest fear was breaking the promise he'd made.

Michael's becoming present didn't settle the differences between them, but it allowed them to listen to each other for the first time. It created the possibility of resolution.

The simple act of Being Present can transform your life, as it transformed that moment and the relationship between Michael and his daughter.

Have you ever come home from work exhausted, stressed, and preoccupied, until your child runs up and commands your full attention? Your mood shifts from anxiety to joy in a flash.

Children can be the greatest examples and teachers of being in the present moment. Kathy experienced this recently.

I was riding in the backseat with my niece, Jennifer, to the Savannah airport. My mind raced with all the things I had to do on returning to Boston.

Suddenly Jennifer put her face right up to mine and said, "Where are you?"

I was shocked right into the moment. I was sure she was a Zen teacher reincarnated into a six-year-old body. The rest of the time with her I was completely present.

Children live in the present moment more than most adults. You can see it in babies, in the way they're wide awake to everything around them. Only as we grow older do we learn to live in our minds rather than the present moment.

Without Being Present, you cannot go on to the remaining elements needed for real Leadership Presence. As we said, it's like trying to start a car with a dead battery.

Lao-Tzu says, "If you're present, you are alert, fluid, clear, and able to welcome all things."

That last benefit—"able to welcome all things"—is the subject of Chapter 3.

Being Present in the Moment

Being Present guideline #1

Focus on the physical

Give Attention and Focus in

Purpose: To handle multitasking and information overload

Practice: In today's organizations we are all trying to do several things at once—talking with colleagues, clients, and customers while e-mailing, surfing the Web, reviewing documents, etc. The cost is that no one activity or person receives our complete attention—and in small and large ways, our relationships with others can suffer. Here are some key practices for breaking the habit of multitasking:

- Give Full Attention. When someone comes into your office unexpectedly, try doing the following:
  - Stop what you are doing. Turn your body to face the person and make eye contact.
  - Instead of seeing him or her as an interruption, see what happens if you can smile and breathe.
  - Decide if you're able to talk with the person right then or schedule a meeting later.
  - No matter what you decide to do, try to leave the interaction with a genuine feeling of having made personal, human contact, even if it was momentary.

- Focus In. The next time you have an important task, see what happens if you . . .
  - make a commitment for a set period of time (e.g., one hour) to focus on this one task.
  - arrange your office environment to eliminate all

distractions: turn off the radio, close all unneeded applications and documents on your computer's desktop (especially e-mail), turn off your cell phone, and disconnect or shut off the ringer of your desk phone.

- Take a moment to clear your *inner* environment: relax your body by stretching; take a deep breath or two into your belly, exhaling on a relaxed sigh; and close your eyes for a moment and notice how you feel. You may wish to get up from the computer and repeat this relaxation process every twenty to thirty minutes.

Be in the Body

Purpose: To deal with nerves and tension

Exercise: ■ Sit comfortably, with your back straight, your head erect, your eyes closed, and your feet flat on the floor.
■ Starting from the top of your head, move your awareness slowly down through your body, noticing and releasing any tension. For example, as you scan through your face, let your jaw relax, and allow your mouth to drop open slightly. As you scan through your torso, relax your shoulders, and consciously let go of any tightness in your abdominal muscles.
■ Bring your attention to the body as a whole, just noticing for a moment how you feel. Enjoy the feeling that you are sensing your body fully, nerve endings are awake, and all parts of your body feel alive.

Breathe

Purpose: To deal with fear and anxiety

Exercise: If you are having trouble finding your belly breath, the best way to practice this is to lie down on your back, preferably on the floor:

- Lay one hand on your belly and one hand on your chest, so you can notice where your breath is. When we sit or stand, our habit is to breathe up in the chest. But lying down, you may notice it's immediately easier to feel the belly rising with each inhalation and falling with each exhalation.

■ If you have trouble feeling the breath in the belly, imagine you're breathing through a straw. Or, imagine the hand on your belly is resting on a balloon that's inflating as you breathe in and deflating as you breathe out. Also try inhaling through your nose. With all of these, let your mouth and jaw relax as you breathe out.

■ You can also experiment with filling your entire lung capacity, breathing into both the belly and the chest. Imagine your inhalation is like filling a glass with water, beginning from the bottom—the lowest part of the belly—and filling to the top—the top of the chest. Once you have taken this very big breath in, try letting it out on a big sigh of relief with sound: "aaaahhhhh!"

■ Finally, return to your regular breathing, just noticing the rise and fall of the belly with your breath.

Practice: The goal of these practices is to train the body to breathe with the belly automatically:

■ *Training Regimen.* The best way to become a natural belly-breather is to undertake a two- to three-week daily practice. Since it's easiest to locate belly breathing when lying down, take two minutes before you go to sleep at night—and when you wake up in the morning—with your hands placed on your belly and on your chest, doing the exercise above. After a couple of weeks, you will notice yourself more naturally breathing this way as you go about your day. This was the homework that made a big difference for Michael.

■ *At Your Desk.* One of the best times to practice is when you're at your computer or doing some solo activity, and you notice that you are stressed. Stop what you are doing and take two or three belly breaths, each followed by a sigh of relief. As you do so, let your body relax, particularly your jaw and shoulders. Notice how your mood changes when you do this.

- *Before a High-Stakes Meeting.* The most important time to practice, and the real test of the belly breath, is when you find yourself leading a group or giving a presentation— any time you find yourself "on the spot." The most subtle breath is taken in and out through the nose—filling the belly, while still allowing the exhalation to be free and easy. After a few belly breaths, your heart rate will slow down. See what happens if you let your mouth form a gentle smile as you do this. Your audience may never notice, but you will immediately feel the difference: more grounded and relaxed, less tense.

Being Present guideline #2:

Change your perspective

Transform Your Inner Critic

Purpose: To deal with self-judgment that inhibits productiveness

Exercise: Your inner critic consists of the voices inside your head that constantly evaluate your behavior. It can be enormously useful to confront your inner critic and get these voices out in the open:

- Write a letter from your inner critic to yourself that includes all of the nasty, judgmental things it wants to say to you. Explore why and in what situations your inner critic thinks that you're not good enough or that you're a failure. Try to accurately capture the authentic tone as well as the content of your inner critic's voice.

- Then write a response letter, appreciating the inner critic for its usefulness in your life, but also distinguishing which of its messages you choose to listen to, and which are no longer useful. End by finding a way to make peace with your inner critic, acknowledging your continuing, maturing relationship. (If you find this hard, recall Meredith Monk's story about the Buddhist saint Milarepa: What would it take to invite your own inner demons in for tea?)

Practice:
- Review the "Seven Ways to Disengage from the Inner Critic," to follow. Choose three you feel would make the biggest difference for you and that feel doable.

- Make these three steps your practice.

- If you find it helpful, make a sign for your workspace that lists the three practices. You might also include a reminder to breathe and be in the body, two of the best ways to inhibit the inner critic.

- Mark the events in your calendar where your inner critic will most likely show up, and use your practices to prepare for those events.

Seven Ways to Disengage from the Inner Critic So You Can Be Present

1. Humor. Make jokes. Lightheartedness helps. Exaggerate. Make the inner critic's claims so outlandish they're funny. "Right! If I make a mistake, the world will stop spinning. Everyone will die instantly!"

2. Acceptance. Accept that you may not be perfect. If your inner critic says you may screw up or fail, say "You know, I might." This kind of acceptance disempowers the inner critic.

3. Pleasure. Do something pleasurable, because the inner critic hates pleasure. Many performers incorporate pleasurable things—hot baths or showers, eating something delicious, for example—in their preperformance rituals. Anything that feels good will take you away from the cold, ugly place where the inner critic lives.

4. Intention. Focus on your goal, the reason you're doing what you're doing, rather than on the reaction of the audience. In theater, actors focus on their intention in each scene—to get the other character to go out on a date or to cheat on an exam, for example—and not on what the audience is thinking. This works just as well in any setting. If you can get your intention clear and strong enough, focus on it.

5. *Focusing on Others.* This is a corollary of focusing on your intention. Focus on the other people in your meeting, on what they need, and on making them feel comfortable. Concentrate on being generous and open and giving. Imagine that you're giving a party in your home and you're going to give each person a million dollars, or some other gift of enormous value.

6. *Inner Support.* Think of things that give you confidence. Moments in your life when you felt proud of yourself, when you accomplished something difficult, or when you were recognized—graduation, winning a game, giving birth. Pick such a moment and imagine yourself in it again. Or think of a person who has always given you wholehearted support and love—a parent, grandparent, a friend, anyone. Recall that person and the way she or he treated you.

7. *Using Imagery.* Many people find it useful to visualize the inner critic in some way. It may be some skinny red-faced guy in a tuxedo who's always yammering at you through pursed lips. Or, your image might be of a swarm of attacking bees. Perhaps you don't visualize the critic itself, but the image of its effect on you—for example, you're up on a pedestal where everyone is watching and evaluating you. Whatever the image, get it clear in your mind's eye and then imagine that image changing to something different, something that feels more comforting. Morph that skinny guy into someone friendlier. Imagine those bees becoming butterflies that caress you with fluttering wings.

Being Present guideline #3: Let thoughts go, let feelings be

Let Thoughts Go, Let Feelings Be

Purpose: To deal with fear and anxiety around the unexpected

Exercise:

- Sit comfortably, with your back straight, your head erect, and your eyes closed. Scan through your body (as you did in the "Being in Your Body" exercise) until you can fully sense your body in the chair.

- Send your awareness to your breathing, noticing the rise and fall of the belly.

- As thoughts arise—which they inevitably will—simply notice that you are thinking and bring your attention back to the breath. (Some find it helpful when they notice a thought to say "Thinking" inside their mind, and then return to the breath.) When you notice a thought, neither judge nor congratulate yourself. Just accept what you are noticing and return to the breath. The breath serves as an anchor to bring us back to the present moment.

- If you notice a feeling arise of any kind—irritation, sadness, joy, anger, impatience, peacefulness, anxiety— let go of any thought attached to the feeling and just feel the feeling itself. Notice the location of the feeling in your body. Notice the quality of the feeling. For example, you might experience anxiety as a tightness in your chest or joy as a lightness in your head.

- Move your attention to whatever feelings arise. If there is no feeling present, just keep letting the thoughts go and return to concentrating on breathing. Try this at first for five to ten minutes.

Practice: One more meeting and you find yourself getting bored and irritated by the agenda items, which have nothing to do with you. You find yourself getting more and more anxious and annoyed. It's coming out in your body language.

- While in the meeting, get into some kind of grounded position, make sure your spine is straight, make sure your breathing is in your belly, and take several belly breaths.

- If you're filled with irritation or some other emotion, notice the feeling. If it's irritation, say to yourself, "Irritation." Feel it in your body, letting the thoughts go. Stay with it for as long as you can. Accept the feeling without fighting it.

- Now focus on your breathing for a few seconds. Collect yourself.

  Now just listen to the meeting. When another feeling arises, notice what it is, how it feels, and where it's located in the body. Then return your full attention to the meeting.

CHAPTER 3

Being Present in Action—Flexibility

Every time an actor goes up on stage, they have to slay the dragon. I walk on stage every night with no idea of how to slay the dragon, or perhaps I have a good idea but I cannot be certain it will work, I do not know what the other actors or the audience are going to be like and there's the burrito I ate for dinner that's doing funny things to my stomach. There are just too many variables, so if you have the bravery to throw out all preconceptions and improvise from moment to moment on stage, you will feel like you are on the hero's journey.

William H. Macy, nominated for an Oscar for the movie
Fargo and well known for his role as Dr. David
Morgenstern on the television series *ER*

ONE LOVELY FALL DAY NOT LONG AGO WE FOUND OURSELVES WINDing along a country road through Appalachian forest, on our way to a client's annual strategy meeting. As we rounded the last curve, we saw rustic buildings up ahead, nestled on the side of the mountain. A clump of cars in the gravel parking lot was the only sign of life. The tennis courts were empty, the golf course bare of players.

Inside was no different. The lobby was deserted, save for a solitary receptionist who checked us in and gave us a message to meet in the Davy Crockett Room for a brief meeting before cocktails and dinner. We were just in time.

We found twelve or so executives—the management team of Genlex Corporation, usually a boisterous group—waiting somberly for Margaret, the CEO, to begin the meeting. This was the same Margaret we mentioned in the Introduction whose entrance always brought a surge of electricity.

Not this time. She walked in and her husky voice said her news was not good. She'd just gotten off the phone with the Food and Drug Administration. Trixinol, Genlex's revolutionary drug for high blood pressure, introduced three years earlier and the engine of the company's phenomenal growth rate since then, was off the market for good because of serious side effects discovered only after long-term use. Public announcement of the withdrawal would be made in four days.

The implications of the withdrawal couldn't be more serious. The company's stock price would drop precipitously, probably putting most employees' options underwater. Genlex's growth rate, over 63 percent a year for the past three years, was projected to drop to under 20 percent for at least the next two years.

Margaret outlined a simple agenda. She had almost postponed the long-planned meeting but decided at the last minute to go ahead. It would be useful to get together and begin confronting the coming problems. Now, she said, there were two key items the group needed to begin addressing right away. First, the budget. A drastic decline in revenue required drastic cuts in expenses. Some of those cuts would have to be people. How do you downsize while keeping the best people and attracting first-rate candidates?

The second issue was growth. Where would growth come from? Trixinol's demise couldn't have come at a worse time. Genlex had promising drugs moving through the research and approval pipeline, but they were nowhere near release. Could they be speeded up? Should the company abandon its policy of organic growth and look for acquisitions? Could the company survive a period of slow growth, in the eyes of investors and employees, current and prospective?

In fact, there was another agenda item that only Margaret and we knew about, though it was intuitively clear to all there.

Margaret's goal in the meeting, and the real reason she proceeded with it in spite of Trixinol's withdrawal, was to begin selecting key members of her management team for a company turnaround. All her key executives had joined a company growing by leaps and bounds. Virtually all of them had created the domains they managed. They all had participated in making the company what it was.

But which of them could help her take the company through the next two years? Who could tolerate turbulent times, uncertain roles, a shifting organization? Who could develop and pursue a new strategy, then change on a dime to a better approach based on new market information or clinical data? Who was willing to change jobs every two or three months, sometimes even accepting an assignment that seemed less glorious than the last? Who could develop the new and different skills the company needed now?

We weren't at the meeting because we were expert in pharmaceuticals and the drug business. We'd coached Margaret and several members of her executive team, and run programs for other groups of managers, but we certainly weren't strategy gurus.

We were there because we knew something about the quality she now needed most in her leadership group: flexibility. We were there to help develop this skill in her senior executives.

As we sat in that first session while Margaret talked, every person seemed fully present. No one left to take a cell phone call. No one leafed through reports, listening with half an ear. No one whispered to a neighbor. She had their undivided attention and we suspected she would have it for the full two days. The stakes almost guaranteed it. Budgets would be cut, programs slashed, strategies added or abandoned. If you blinked, you might find your key people in somebody else's division, or your pet project postponed. More than that, jobs—your job—might change or even disappear.

If Chapter 2 was about how you get present, then this chapter is about *how you act once you are present*. How do you respond to the world around you, once being present allows you to do more than simply react? What does the behavior of one who is present look like?

The key characteristic of that behavior, we think, is flexibility. It's the willingness and ability to move and adapt freely as circumstances prescribe *right now*.

Flexibility is what you need to take full advantage of the freedom created by being present. Without flexibility you'll be unable to handle the world as it changes constantly around you. You'll always be operating either in the past, on old assumptions, or in the future, on worries about what might happen.

How flexible are you? How can you become more flexible? Later in this chapter, we'll offer three rules for fostering flexibility that you can use in your journey as a leader.

Flexibility—handling the unexpected

What we know about flexibility comes from our backgrounds in theater. Theatrical lore is filled with stories of actors who coped with the unexpected and even turned potential problems into something positive. Actors train their entire careers, in fact, to develop this ability.

During a production of Tom Stoppard's *The Real Thing* at the New Repertory Theatre, which Kathy cofounded near Boston, a sudden thunderstorm dropped sheets of rain on the roof of the building. Just as the second act began, water began dripping from the ceiling right onto the middle of the stage. The actors forged ahead gamely, ignoring the drip, but the more the actors ignored it, the more the audience was transfixed by it. Then, finally, one actor, while delivering a long and energetic monologue, paused to catch his breath, reached out to catch a few drops, licked the water from his palm, and then continued his monologue. That simple act put the audience immediately at ease, for it incorporated the drip into the play itself. The audience was again able to enter the reality of the story because this actor had the flexibility to respond to what was happening in the moment.

Kenny Raskin, a senior consultant with The Ariel Group who enjoyed a long run on Broadway in *Beauty and the Beast* and was a lead clown with *Cirque du Soleil*, once played an eighty-year-old man in *I'm Not Rappaport*. A scene set in a park opened—the stage lights came up—with his character sitting on a bench by a bridge. One night, a new lighting person turned up the lights before Kenny had positioned himself on the bench. In fact, Kenny wasn't even onstage yet. He was in a small entrance tunnel built to look like the open space under the bridge. He couldn't just wander onto the set from that entrance—the audience would wonder, what was he doing under the bridge? So, as he stepped onstage, he zipped up his fly, as though he'd been under the bridge relieving himself. It was completely in character and the audience laughed, none the wiser.

Laurence Olivier was preparing for a performance of *Hamlet*. However,

> *Pouring, drenching rain meant that we could not open outside as we had intended to, and consequently, after a hurried discussion, it was decided that we would perform in the ballroom, which meant a rapid restaging. . . . All the movements had to be changed.*

For *Hamlet*, with its court scenes, plays within a play, graveyard visits with a ghost flitting about, not to mention the final swordfight, this was no small thing.

> *There is nothing better [Olivier said] than a group of actors being presented with a problem of this kind and having to improvise. . . . It is at such times that you can ask for the impossible, and get it. "I'm afraid the only way you can play this scene is by hanging from the chandelier, dear boy." Without a moment's hesitation, the reply would come back, "Of course—no problem."*

Margaret was looking for people who would hang from the chandelier and say, "Of course—no problem." In Bill Macy's more serious words, she needed people who had the "bravery to throw out all preconceptions and improvise on a hero's journey."

When circumstances change—Improvise!

If acting by its nature requires flexibility, then the crucible of flexibility is improvisational theater, where improvisation is not just the way to solve some unexpected problem, but the very heart of the performance.

What better place to look, then, for ways to foster flexibility?

Imagine this: a bare stage bathed in light. An audience of perhaps a hundred people. Onto the stage walks a group of three women and two men. They line up shoulder-to-shoulder facing the audience. A woman follows them onto the stage and stations herself downstage between the actors and the audience. Facing the audience, she smiles and says, *"An object, please."*

"Arsenic!" calls out a voice from the dark at the back of the audience.

The woman onstage turns to face the row of actors, waits a moment. Suddenly she points to one of the men. The man immediately begins talking.

"I was late to work this morning and I no sooner walked into my office than . . ."

He stops talking instantly because the woman in front, who's conducting this performance—it's a kind of improvisational acting called a conducted story—suddenly points to another of the men, who immediately picks up the first man's sentence.

". . . my office assistant told me she hadn't finished the folders for my meeting in five minutes. I wanted to kill her. Then the phone rang and it was . . ."

The conductor points to one of the women, who immediately begins speaking, in the same nervous, angry, slightly whiny voice the first two actors used.

". . . my boss. He yelled at me that there was a problem with the report I stayed up 'til three o'clock in the morning to finish. The problem was something he made me do at the last minute, but he talked like it was my fault. He said we had to meet right away. I said . . ."

The conductor points to one of the women.

". . . I was tied up all morning, but lunch was open. 'Could you meet for . . . lunch?' He said. . . ."

The conducted story continues, each actor called by the conductor to invent the next step, until the actors bring the story to a conclusion involving arsenic in some way.

Imagine you're one of the actors in the conducted story we just heard.

You listen to what your fellow actors say, ready at any moment to spin out the next piece of the story. If you're suddenly called on, you can take the story anywhere you want, *except you must build on what's already been said.*

You must listen carefully and remember everything. But you cannot spin out the story in your mind in anticipation of being called. For if you're *not* called, another actor will spin out the story in a different way, and you'll be left behind. So you cannot plan ahead at all, not even a few seconds. You must be totally absorbed in the moment, totally present, anticipating nothing, acutely aware of the story as it unfolds second by second, but not preoccupied with it. If your mind wanders for any reason, even for a split second, and you're called, you and everyone else will know immediately that you've lost touch with the moment and you'll be embarrassed.

In fact, improvisational acting can take many forms—the conducted story is only one—but in general it includes any kind of performance without planning or preparation.

It usually begins, as did the conducted story, when someone, often an audience member, throws out an object, a single word, a setting. Triggered by that opening idea, an actor offers an extemporaneous line of dialogue (called the "initiation"). Another actor responds. And thus, in a few words, unfolds a story with characters, relationships, a setting, situations, and problems, all done in the moment in front of the audience.

You can imagine, if you've never seen improv theater, how electric the atmosphere is. No one knows what will happen next.

John Belushi, an original cast member of *Saturday Night Live*, was an expert improviser. According to Bill Murray, another *Saturday Night Live* alumnus, Belushi would "make a decision to do something, and as soon as he did it, it was such a strong move that the entire scene just shifted to that direction. . . . It never looked like he was thinking furiously. It was almost like a martial art. To have a guy who could do that was like having one guy who could swim. He's your best friend."

How does improv relate to business?

Have you ever had a meeting in which everything came together magically to produce a key insight or inspiration? Most people in business do, sooner or later. Afterward, everyone says, "Wow! How did that happen?" Improv actors have learned to create those moments regularly.

Fine, you may say, you understand the need for flexibility, but business is about planning and control, with leaders and managers and rules and constraints. Improv is free form. It can go anywhere it wants, do anything it wants.

We accept that difference, to a point. There is much planning and control in business, but we think it's more accurate to say that business is about *trying* to plan and control in the face of a constantly shifting world. Anyone with experience knows that implementation usually requires some significant changes when a plan meets reality. The military philosopher Karl von Clausewitz talked about the "fog of war," meaning battle plans go out the window with the firing of the first shot. Business isn't much different.

The conducted story and the way it works reminds us of a small session we watched at Genlex's planning meeting at the Appalachian conference center.

Robert, a Ph.D. chemist with an MBA and, at thirty-five, probably the most junior manager at the meeting, had joined Genlex three years earlier as a project manager. Within two years he had talked management into making an exception to its no-acquisition growth strategy.

Tall, gaunt, looking exactly like a fevered scientist, Robert was expert in an esoteric field of biochemistry that held great promise. He had convinced Margaret and the board of directors it made more sense for Genlex to track the many small startups in the field and then buy one or two as leaders emerged.

So Robert had been named head of the only group in the company committed to an acquisitions strategy. For the previous eight months he and his small group, operating out of cheap space in a strip mall, had been surveying the field, getting to know the startups and beginning to make seed investments in several as a window into their technology. He was at least six to eight months, possibly more, from making a significant acquisition.

At the end of the first day of the planning meeting, Margaret asked Robert to meet with her, the CFO, and the COO at breakfast the next morning.

When Robert arrived, he found he was the guest of honor and the purpose of the meeting was to reexamine his division and its approach. For an hour and a half he answered a barrage of questions about his work, the field he was pursuing, and why acquisitions were the right strategy.

At first he thought Margaret and the others were thinking about dropping the idea of acquiring startups. With the coming drop in Genlex's stock price, acquisitions could be expensive. He was convinced it remained the right approach and so he wheeled out all his old arguments for acquisition versus internal growth. The harder he dug in his heels, the harder the others pushed. Before long, as his waffles cooled in front of him, Robert realized he would lose this argument if he stubbornly hung on to his own agenda.

He decided to treat the discussion as an exploration of all alternatives. Instead of resisting all ideas the others brought up, he embraced them and took the lead in exploring them as fully as possible. They reviewed all the reasons for acquiring startups in light of the last eight months' experience. They reviewed again the possibility of Genlex's entering the field itself. Perhaps that made more sense now. They looked at dropping the field entirely. They looked at combining acquisition and internal growth. They looked at rolling Robert's little group into another, larger division. In the end, Margaret and her colleagues decided the company needed to question its policy of organic growth. Acquisitions might make more sense now.

It was a discussion not far different from the conducted story improv of a moment ago. Each line of thought took on a life of its own, with each person building on what had just been said. Margaret, as CEO, guided the discussion from person to person. The skills needed for improv—inventiveness, flexibility, quickness, the ability

to incorporate new ideas as they appeared moment to moment—
were precisely the same skills Robert and the others needed in their
discussion.

Let's return, then, to improv theater and try to understand
how it works, because what makes improv work can make virtually any business discussion more productive.

Getting to "Yes, and . . ."

Improv actors improvise, within a shifting framework and not
in a vacuum, just as businesspeople like Robert must improvise
within a set of constraints.

Oddly enough, to understand the source of flexibility in improv acting, we have to address the *rules* of improvisation.

The first rule, never broken, is *accept the offer*. All statements by
improv actors are called "offers." Whatever an improv actor
says—"Hey, it's great to be back in the Amazon jungle!"—the
other actors must accept it as reality. They can't say, "No, we're in
an ice-cream store." This is the rule that makes improv theater
possible.

What makes it work—what allows a group of improv actors to
create a satisfying, coherent story in real time—is the second rule,
an extension of the first—the *Yes, and . . .* rule.

This is the core rule of improvisational theater because it incor-
porates the rule of accept the offer (*Yes!*) while requiring that an
actor build on and extend what's been offered (Yes, *and . . .*).

First Man: *Hey, it's great to be back in the Amazon jungle!*

Second Man: (Yes, and . . .) *Look out for that twenty-foot snake!*

The importance of this rule cannot be overemphasized. Improv
simply goes nowhere without it, for without it, no coherent story
will ever emerge and the cast of players will never become a true
team.

Margaret adapted this approach at the Genlex planning meeting. The first morning she opened a traditional discussion of how
to cut the budget. By the end of this unhappy, contentious ses-

sion, all her key managers had described how others should cut and why they could not. Angry, Margaret ate lunch alone, while she thought through a different approach. From working with us, she was familiar with improv techniques, and so when she opened the afternoon session, she laid out different ground rules: "Each of you," she said, "one by one, will suggest one or two strategic ways we can reduce our costs, and the rest of you will then volunteer ways you and your units can actively support and build upon that approach." The key words, she said, were "build upon."

Margaret had to enforce her ground rules more than once. Initially she had to drag ideas and opinions from some managers. But by the end of the afternoon, virtually everyone there had truly entered the spirit of the exercise. Not only did the company create a list of promising budget strategies, but everyone present felt the meeting had been a turning point for the group in facing problems openly and with mutual respect and support.

Another company we worked with instituted a practice they called, "Big Bad Idea," any time someone had a brainstorm in a meeting, they could announce "Big Bad Idea!" and state the idea. Then their colleagues were obligated for the next three minutes to support and develop the idea. The company claimed that 20 percent of all Big Bad Ideas turned out to be worth pursuing.

In both cases, colleagues were required not only to support an idea but to build and expand on it, rather than pursue the more typical "yes, but . . ." we all see in business. The value of good Big Bad Ideas often came not from the original idea but from the idea as it evolved in the three-minute development discussion.

While you cannot always apply the rules of improv directly and consistently to business, we do suggest three rules that foster flexibility for leaders.

1. Be open to unexpected outcomes—"Yes, and . . ."

2. Adapt your role to the reality.

3. Be generous toward others.

Flexibility rule #1:
Be open to unexpected outcomes—"Yes, and . . ."

Improv roles and story direction can suddenly change. Your role
may be central to a scene when suddenly the story shifts and your
character is instantly minor. You may think your relationship in a
skit is turning romantic, when suddenly the other character is revealed to be your parent. Improv players cannot take these shifts
in stride if they become attached to a direction or outcome.

Business revolves around goals, expected outcomes, and you
may feel bound by them. But changing circumstances can open
them to renegotiation. Even if an objective is immutable for the
moment, the subgoals and action steps around it usually remain
flexible.

The first danger is not so much that we *are* trapped by the constraints of work but that we *feel* more constrained than we really
are. We trap ourselves.

In our experience, less is set in concrete than people think. Be
clear about what is truly fixed and what is open to change.

We love the business lore around the invention of the Post-It
note at 3M Corporation. As the story goes, a researcher there
failed in his search for a better glue and produced in the process a
"useless" compound that made paper stick together, sort of. Then
in church, as he stuck slips of paper in his hymnal to mark the
songs to be sung—of course, the slips of paper kept falling out—
he realized there was a use for a "sort of" glue. He made up a
batch of the sticky little notes and gave them to secretaries around
the office. When they asked for more, he knew he'd found something. If he hadn't been open to an outcome other than "glue,"
the world wouldn't have those little pieces of paper we stick all
over the place.

The second danger is that you, as leader, have the power to set
constraints for others. You can demand outcomes that are un-
necessarily rigid. And you can force outcomes, from a meeting, for
example, that prevent something better or more truthful from
emerging.

A colleague recalls a strategic planning retreat he attended when he was a senior manager. In one session the executives split into pairs and went off to generate a list of creative alternatives for dealing with employee turnover. On returning, each pair would present its ideas and the group would select the best. Our colleague happened to be matched up with the chairman, the gray-haired founder of the business. The two of them sought out a beautiful spot overlooking the ocean, ideal for generating ideas. But instead of being willing to brainstorm, the chairman pulled from the pocket of his windbreaker a typewritten list of alternatives, which he obviously meant to be accepted as-is. End of discussion. The chairman then presented his ideas to the group as a whole, which felt compelled to accept them. As a consequence, the retreat produced the same employee retention strategies that came out of every planning session and had never worked.

Improv teaches the value of absorbing and accepting information without preconception or bias, and being open to new possibilities.

Business goals and actors' intentions

There's an interesting parallel in the world of acting that may help illuminate this tension between flexibility and goals. For every scene, an actor will have an "intention." It might be to obtain a confession from another character. It might be to look smart. It might be to convince another character that she's misguided. What we see all the time in young, inexperienced actors is too much intensity and energy focused on that goal, whatever it is, to the exclusion of everything else going on in the scene. They portray a monomaniac, someone obsessed with only one thing. In the process, the reality, the authenticity, of their character is lost.

An adept actor prepares thoroughly beforehand. If you could see the script of an experienced actor learning a part you would find it completely covered with notes, with many of the notes focused on what the character wants at every step—to excite, to seduce, to hoodwink, etc.

The actor sorts through all that in advance, experimenting in rehearsal with various ways to communicate each intention. But when the actor goes onstage, she doesn't think about that any more. By performance time, she's internalized it, so she can simply "be" and "do" in the moment, informed by those intentions and guided by them unconsciously.

Christine Lahti, nominated for an Oscar in *Swing Shift* and an Emmy-winning star of the television series *Chicago Hope*, described how she does this. "I try to think about objectives. . . . I think about what this character really wants in her life, scene by scene, I do all this background stuff, break down every scene, and personalize everything, and then I try to forget everything I've done, and go on the set, or into rehearsal, and go from my gut." As Mark Twain reportedly said, "It takes three weeks of rehearsal to be spontaneous."

In our work we've had the opportunity to observe many companies and the men and women who lead them. The most successful leaders we've seen are those who embrace change, both large and small, who are willing to give up past expectations and adapt to new and different circumstances or needs. Measurable goals that everyone rallies around are crucial to business. If they become an obsession, however, they will keep you from the moment and thus, ironically, weaken your ability to lead others.

Be open to outcomes, but "open" means neither "obsessed with" nor "indifferent to." Experience and awareness will help you find the balance that allows you to be present and flexible with others while leading the organization to a desired objective.

Flexibility rule #2:
Adapt your role to the reality

Imagine how dull it would be if improv players invented the same characters with the same characteristics in every scene. That's exactly what beginning improv players often find themselves doing. They discover a comfortable character and keep inserting her into every new sketch.

We all have habits, predispositions, and favorite ways of handling problems. When we find something that feels right and seems to work, we do it over and over.

The way we lead is no exception.

Much of leadership is about finding a balance between two often-conflicting activities: asserting authority and responding to others' needs. Your actions as a leader can fall anywhere on a scale between those two poles, from completely authoritative ("Do it now!") to completely responsive ("How would you like to do it?"). No one position on the scale is always appropriate, and the fully effective leader must be able to move back and forth on the scale as required by people and circumstances.

LEADERSHIP SCALE

Asserting Authority	Responsive to Others
("Do it my way.")	*("How would you like to do it?)*

Of course there are several stages between these two poles. As a handy way to think about the alternatives, we've identified the most common positions on the scale and given them names:

Asserting Authority			Responsive to Others
Captain	**Conceiver**	**Coach**	**Collaborator**
"Do it this way."	*"Here's the future. Follow me."*	*"You can do it!"*	*"I'll help you do it."*

The *captain* primarily uses authority. ("Do it this way.") This approach works best in a crisis or emergency. Its negative side is that it can be dictatorial ("Do it *my* way") and, used regularly or inappropriately, can breed resentment and reduce the accountability of followers.

The *conceiver* leads based on the authority of a vision. ("I have seen the future. Follow me.") This works best when a group needs to rally around a distant goal, but it can be detached from day-to-day concerns and problems.

The *coach* guides and educates, combining some authority (usually in the form of wisdom and experience) with doses of responsiveness. Learning to play this role is often difficult for those just promoted into leadership roles. It requires a shift in mindset from "I do it best" to "I'm going to develop someone else to do it best." It usually takes time before you see any results.

The *collaborator* works side-by-side with someone, highly responsive to their needs and only occasionally asserting authority. This role is best when bringing together new members of a team around a common purpose and when it's critical to brainstorm and elicit input from a variety of perspectives. On the negative side, it can hinder quick decision-making, and make it difficult to give negative feedback.

The leadership scale is simply a handy way to think about the alternatives you have as a leader to respond flexibly to the people and circumstances around you.

Everyone prefers one of these roles. It's the role you tend to use over and over. You may even think your preferred way is superior to all others.

In fact, all roles have their place. There are times when each is the most appropriate. If you're guiding people from a burning building, it's not time to be a collaborator. In a crisis, the captain role generally works best. Yet there are many times the captain role is entirely inappropriate.

It's possible to take on different roles. While our fundamental preferences may not change, we can learn to behave differently. Captains can learn to be more sensitive to the needs of others. Coaches and collaborators can learn to recognize situations calling for strong direction and to provide it. Though these changes are uncomfortable, especially in the beginning, we've seen many instances where strong, natural captains and confirmed collaborators have effectively expanded their behavior. In fact, it's not unusual, as you learn new behaviors, to become fully comfortable with different roles.

Brian, a middle manager we coached at Genlex, had moved into a leadership role because of his superior technical skills. But he was indecisive and wanted to be everyone's friend. He strongly preferred to be a collaborator. Stories he told in one of our workshops made clear he feared that being directive would destroy relationships and leave him alone. Whatever the reason, being a captain, even when he knew it to be the appropriate role, filled him with anxiety. Consequently people were confused about where they stood with him. He couldn't make decisions that might upset someone. He couldn't decide who was on the leadership team, because he didn't want to exclude or hurt anyone. Because of his anxiety he talked too fast, often failed to finish sentences, and usually failed to reach clear and definite conclusions.

We worked with him on the way he talked, getting him to ground himself physically, breathe properly, slow down, use lower tones in his voice. He also learned to handle his difficult feelings. We had him role-play in order to practice saying difficult things and learn how to handle the anxiety and fear that arose in him when he said such things. He learned that he could go through difficult situations and still survive personally. He learned to be tougher when it was necessary.

Based on our experience with hundreds of leaders seeking to expand their leadership skills, we've found that successful change requires three things:

1. Your mindset must change. You must believe genuinely that various roles are truly appropriate at different times.

2. You must practice being in the moment with people. That's the only way you can properly assess which role is appropriate to play.

3. You must possess the skills to play different roles authentically. (Acts II and III, on reaching out and expressiveness, will discuss these skills in some detail.)

Look at the roles and identify the one you prefer, your default role. As a check, ask those who work for you which role they see you use most often. Don't be surprised if your self-perceived role is somewhat different from your role as perceived by others.

Just as there are preferred roles, everyone has a leadership role he or she avoids, the way Brian feared being a captain. In our workshops, when we ask people to identify the role they feel least comfortable with, the majority pick captain. Which role is the one you least prefer? Is it one you never use? Or can you use it when necessary? Are there times when you know you should use it, but you don't because you dislike it so much?

The effective leader must have the ability—the flexibility—to vary his or her role, even moment by moment.

Flexibility rule #3: Be generous toward others

Recall our earlier description of how improv works and its basic rule: *Yes, and.* . . . Each actor must accept whatever is offered by another actor.

But agreement and acceptance—the Yes!—cannot be merely intellectual or temporary. As a player, you cannot go along with another actor's offer while thinking to yourself, "This is dumb. I'll go with it until I can get it back where I want to go." No. You must accept *completely*, heart and soul, what your partner has offered. You must bring your full energy and commitment to it and build on it. Then, of course, your partners must accept and build on what you offer. This is not merely feel-good advice. Improv simply won't work otherwise.

In fact, you must accept and build on your partner's offer, *even if it's a mistake*. What's a mistake? Usually, it's a break in the momentum or the shape of a story that's beginning to emerge.

"It's great to be back in the Amazon jungle!"

"Look out for that twenty-foot snake!"

"Oh, I dropped my ice-cream cone on my pajamas!"

Of course, it's never a mistake in the sense of being objectively "wrong" or incorrect. Instead, a mistake will feel like a diversion rather than an extension of the developing story line.

When that happens, you must agree with the offer and incorporate it into the emerging story. And your partners must do it for you when you make a mistake. Sometimes, of course, "mistakes" open new avenues of possibility.

"Bobbie, get back in the Winnebago!"

On many occasions in improv, for example, when someone makes a mistake, actors are tempted to make a joke or a witty remark. If they do, they may get the laughter they sought, but they will have killed the momentum and energy in the emerging story.

Woman: *I want a divorce.*

Man: *Oh, no! How will I live without you? What about the kids?*

Woman: *We don't have any children.*

The audience laughs, but the man looks foolish and the story dies. The actor playing the woman got a laugh by rejecting the "offer" of children as part of their world.

Outright jokes and wit usually resound to the glory of one player, at the expense of the others. For an improv actor, there's nothing more frightening than working with someone who will sacrifice them and the scene for a quick laugh. Once an improv actor gains a reputation for making jokes, and trying to be funny himself, he'll find that no one wants to go onstage with him.

This third rule of flexibility—be generous toward others—is in fact what animates all improv acting and creates those magical moments both actor and audience long for. The deep spirit of generosity among the actors is based on the belief, as they all go onstage and put themselves at risk, that no one of them succeeds unless they all succeed, that the best way to look good is to make everyone look good.

Have you ever worked with someone, or for someone, who diminishes others to build herself up? This is the kind of person who thinks nothing of sacrificing a colleague to look good. She tears down other people's ideas, or takes them as her own.

As a leader you serve as a model. If you make an effort to share credit, to acknowledge the contributions of others, others will do the same. As Margaret did in her afternoon budget meeting, you can make it clear that destructive behavior is unacceptable. Make ground rules. Take people aside to counsel them that you expect "Yes, and . . ." behavior, rather than the more common "Yes, but . . ." responses and attitude.

A client we worked with launched a new software product that turned out to be badly flawed, and the company's customer service group couldn't keep up with the complaints. Team meetings turned into blame sessions. "How did this happen? Why did you do that? You're not doing your share." More and more energy went into covering up and avoiding responsibility. Problems mounted. In desperation, the team finally admitted the product was failing and something had to change. It took a number of steps but, most importantly, the group decided to react to mistakes and problems in a new way. Whenever a new problem appeared, team members would say, with genuine enthusiasm, "Yay, breakdown!" and then fix the problem without blame. This was far more than a simple change in procedure. Without condoning mistakes and errors, team members decided to trust that everyone on the team wanted to do good work and would learn from their mistakes. It took a little while for the new approach to take hold, but team members began voluntarily admitting problems and asking for help. The product survived and went on to great success.

The full benefits of being present come only to the person who approaches every moment with a deep sense of openness and generosity toward others.

Steve Chambers, the former television actor we mentioned earlier who's now an executive vice president of marketing and sales, headed an executive team running a program with a key customer. One day he told this team, "Guys, this project we're doing, I have never felt more naked and alone. I'm asking you for help and all I'm getting back are questions about why not this, why not that. I need you to show up and step up. I don't want to be a hamburger without a bun. Be my bun."

He got a positive response, so positive it surprised him a little. It didn't surprise us. We knew from watching him that people trusted him because he was generous. In fact, that was a word people used to describe him. He was generous about their gifts and what they brought to the table and he gave them room. He didn't take credit for their ideas.

With this kind of spirit, a leader, and his or her group, are capable together of creating something impossible for anyone of them to do alone. What better definition of leadership than to foster that kind of extraordinary accomplishment?

As you read the rest of this book, you'll find that this rule—indeed, all the rules of flexibility—are the foundation of all that follows.

Being Present in Action— Flexibility

Flexibility rule #1:	Be open to unexpected outcomes

"Yes, and . . ."

Purpose:	To overcome a lack of creativity and problems collaborating
Practice:	The fundamental skill of successful improvisation is being able to accept another's offer, and then to build on it. This requires listening, flexibility, and creativity. Try practicing "Yes, and . . ." behavior in your work:

- First, notice any existing tendency you have to being attached to your own ideas, to automatically critique others, or to give a simple thumbs up or down on what your colleague, team member, or customer is saying.

- Then, see what happens if you try using "Yes, and . . ." behavior. Consciously listen to their idea. Let your first thought be: *"What can I agree with here?"*

- In your response, accept and acknowledge your colleague's idea, and then build on and extend it. Notice his reaction.

- Try doing this in a variety of different conversations and notice what results you achieve.

Big Bad Idea

Purpose:	To encourage cooperative, supportive behavior
Practice:	Be like the client of ours that has instituted the Big Bad Idea brainstorm at their company. Allow anyone to call

out, *"Big Bad Idea!"* at a meeting and for two minutes people must only add to or say positive things about that idea. After that, they can say what they want. This rule encourages people to take risks, builds an ethic of positive thinking and support, and allows the intelligence of the group to develop the idea. If 20 percent of the Big Bad Ideas turn out to be *great* ideas, as was the case for our client, that's a fairly good percentage. Try it with your work team and notice the effect.

When you are leading a "brainstorming" meeting:

- Make sure to specify ground rules like "no judging ideas at first, no thumbs down," etc.

- Suggest an amount of time for throwing out ideas without judgment.

- Write down all ideas.

- Choose a clear process for funneling the best ideas and building on them. (Some vote by show of hands; some give everybody sticky tabs to rate the ideas.)

Flexibility rule #2:	Adapt your role to the reality

Leadership Styles

Purpose:	To broaden your choice of leadership styles
Exercise:	Leadership styles are a useful way to think about the alternatives you have as a leader to respond flexibly to the people and circumstances around you. Take a look once again at the description of the four leadership styles—captain, conceiver, coach, and collaborator—on page 63. Then take some time to answer the following questions in your journal:

- *Most Familiar/Comfortable Style.* Everyone prefers one of these roles. It's the role you tend to use over and over, your core competency, or the one you default to in times of stress. You may even think it is superior to all others.

Pick the style you find most familiar or comfortable and answer these questions:

- Jot down a personal story or anecdote that represents your experience with this style.

- Brainstorm the skills and behaviors you'd associate with this style.

- Identify the "shadow side" of the style. In which situations does the style *not* work so well?

■ Least Familiar/Stretch Style. In fact, all roles have their place—there are times when each is the most appropriate. While our fundamental preferences may not change, we can learn to behave differently. Pick the style you'd say is furthest from your normal behavior, and write about these points:

- Why did you select this style as the most challenging? Give an example of how it has not worked for you and an example of where you think you could use it.

- Brainstorm the skills and behaviors you'd associate with this style.

- What is blocking you from employing this style?

■ Incorporating All Four Styles. Complete this exercise by exploring the following:

- How might you go about using each of the four styles in a given day or week?

- What would change about your current situation or challenges if you applied a greater variety of styles?

- Name five leaders, four of whom each embody a different one of the four styles, and one who manages to balance all four styles. Which qualities of each leader would you like to emulate?

Practice: Take a look at the "Skills, Behaviors, and Workplace Actions" chart to follow. Locate your stretch style and pick three new behaviors or actions to try on in the coming week. Ask team members to give you feedback on how well you are incorporating this new style.

Leadership Styles—
Skills, Behaviors, and Workplace Actions

Captain

Skills and Behaviors	Workplace Actions
■ Confidence—self-trust ■ Energy—positive "can do" attitude ■ Discipline—rigor—logic ■ Presence—powerful use of voice and body ■ Risk taking—willing to be wrong ■ Quick decision-making—thinking on feet ■ Articulately and powerfully stating views	■ Making decisions—taking initiative ■ Deciding on resource allocation ■ Having heavy input into work plans ■ Having high share of voice in meetings ■ Taking a position/stand ■ Prioritizing options ■ Taking responsibility ■ Leveraging position and hierarchy

Conceiver

Skills and Behaviors	Workplace Actions
■ Confidence—self-trust ■ Being inspiring ■ Positive outlook—passion ■ Imagination—creativity—inventiveness ■ Presence—inspiring use of voice and body ■ Risk taking—willing to be wrong ■ Storytelling	■ Sharing vision ■ Reasoning, building the case ■ Developing a strategy ■ Seeing the big picture ■ Imparting knowledge, context ■ Using credibility to drive action ■ Influencing decisions ■ Motivating behavior

Coach

Skills and Behaviors	Workplace Actions
■ Listening and empathy ■ Acknowledging others' strengths ■ Sharing examples/analogies ■ Asking questions ■ Challenging respectfully ■ Sense of humor ■ Showing you care ■ Sharing personal stories	■ Standing back—empowering others' leadership ■ Letting people make mistakes ■ Offering options ■ Delegating ■ Unsolicited reaching out ■ Being specific in feedback ■ Supporting others' ideas

Collaborator

Skills and Behaviors	Workplace Actions
■ Listening and empathy ■ Acknowledging others' strengths ■ Social skills ■ Sharing vulnerability ■ Sense of humor ■ Asking open-ended questions ■ Patience and flexibility ■ Facilitating decision-making	■ Taking time for and getting things done through relationship building ■ Carefully building trust/consensus ■ Being generous with information ■ Communicating outcome as group product ■ Looking for minority opinions—valuing all voices ■ Encouraging brainstorming

Flexibility
rule #3: Be generous toward others

Be Generous

Purpose: To defuse a competitive, cutthroat work environment

Practice: To be truly flexible is to have a spirit of generosity toward others, based on the belief that as we all put ourselves at risk—onstage as in life—we all must take care of one another. It is the conviction that no one succeeds unless all succeed, that the best way to look good is to make everyone look good. As a leader you serve as a model. If you practice generosity, it will spread to your team, and eventually to the entire organization:

- Share credit, acknowledge the contributions of others. It's particularly powerful to do this in public settings, such as meetings.

- Make clear the kind of destructive behavior that's unacceptable. Set ground rules that encourage team members to support one another and give credit where it's really due.

- Take people aside to counsel them that you expect "Yes, and . . ." kind of behavior, rather than the more common "Yes, but . . ." responses and attitude.

- Before you go to sleep at night, make a practice of wishing others well—even people with whom you are having difficulty.

ACT II

REACHING OUT
The ability to build relationships
with others through empathy, listening,
and authentic connection

Introduction to Act II

We can telegraph and telephone and wire pictures cross the ocean; we can fly over it. But the way to the human being next to us is still as far away as the stars. The actor takes us on this way.

Max Reinhardt, renowned German theater director

IN THE 2002 ELECTION CAMPAIGN, RUDY GIULIANI, EX-MAYOR OF New York City, came to Boston to help Mitt Romney, the Republican candidate for governor of Massachusetts, drum up votes. Giuliani and Romney were trolling through Boston's North End, the city's historic Italian district, and dropped into Mike's Pastry shop. According to the *Boston Globe*, a "rumpled local with a ten o'clock shadow" called out, "Let me buy you guys a cannoli."

To which Romney replied, "No thanks, got to run," and headed to the door, probably worried about the next stop in their schedule for the day.

Instead of heading out with Romney, Giuliani walked over to the local guy, put his arm around him and said, "Let me buy *you* the cannoli."

Is there a lesson here? (Besides "Never turn down a good cannoli"?)

We think so. It's a simple one: Leaders reach out and connect with people, and they fail to do so at their peril.

To be fair to Mitt Romney, he did win the election. In the intensity of a campaign for public office it is hard to be "on" every moment. Perhaps some of Rudy's street smarts rubbed off on him. Which proves our point that the ability to reach out, while more natural to some than others, can be learned. It is clear that on that day Giuliani may have salvaged some support for Mitt. His reaching out to the fellow Romney rejected apparently "tickled pink" the people in the shop.

The columnist who reported that small incident went on to talk about what politicians call "the gift," the ability to connect instantly with anyone. Clearly he felt Giuliani had been blessed with it and Romney hadn't.

We take exception to the notion of a "gift" in this case. We believe the experiences of actors, and of the many leaders we've worked with, demonstrate something different: The ability to connect with others is a crucial *skill*, and it can be developed.

In a nutshell, that's the message of this act.

It's up to you

There's another lesson to be drawn from the affair of Mike's Pastry shop.

What was particularly unfortunate about Romney's behavior was his failure to reach out when someone else said to him, "Here I am!"

Poor is the leader who merely waits for such opportunities. We believe it's the leader, instead, who must reach out. And to reject someone who has reached out to you is even worse.

Creating connections with other people is the leader's responsibility—your responsibility. As we work with hundreds and thousands of people in workshops, we sometimes come across an attitude. Not usually expressed outright, but just under the surface, it's the belief that when you have "presence," or when you're the designated leader, you don't need to reach out and make those people connections. It's as though the spotlight will shine on you and all eyes will move to you automatically.

We take a different view.

We think presence has to do, not with the spotlight shining on you, but with reaching out and shining the spotlight on others.

If there are to be connections, you must make them.

A colleague, Frank, once found himself working closely on an engineering project with someone widely known for being cantankerous, brusque, and even downright rude. This other fellow, Daniel, always found fault, trusted no one, and complained constantly.

Frank did his best at first to avoid Daniel as much as possible, but work made that impossible. He hoped, over time, Daniel would soften a little.

Finally, he realized their relationship would never change by itself. He decided to act as though the relationship he wanted with Daniel actually existed already. He would follow Gandhi's advice, "Be the change you want to see."

Frank began to greet Daniel every morning with hearty good spirits, as he would a good friend. He made sure to seek him out at the end of the day and say good night. He always asked how Daniel and his family were doing.

Daniel usually responded with silence or some self-deprecating remark. At least he didn't lash out angrily or sarcastically.

Feeling more confident, Frank expanded his remarks to include statements about how much he genuinely admired Daniel's strong technical skills and unfailing good judgment. Eventually, he began to say to others in front of Daniel that he liked working with him, which in fact he did.

One week, perhaps three months after Frank began his new approach, he was out with the flu. Daniel called every day to see how he was doing. Shortly after Frank returned, Daniel introduced him to someone new at the office as his "partner." Daniel continued to call everything as he saw it, but he began to trust Frank and stopped double-checking his work. The two of them completed their assignment well before the deadline.

What happened was simple: Frank took responsibility for the relationship. He reached out to Daniel. He treated him as he believed Daniel wanted to be treated, not as he treated others, beginning with a few tentative steps to test Daniel's reaction.

It's what we call the "Platinum Rule": Treat others as *they* want to be treated. (As opposed to the Golden Rule: Treat others as *you* want to be treated.)

Leaders especially need to reach out

Actively reaching out is a critical skill for leaders, especially those leaders who hold formal positions of authority. The reason is simple human nature: Many people are reluctant to approach someone in a position of power.

That poor fellow in Mike's Pastry shop probably felt he was putting himself on the line when he said, "Let me buy you guys a cannoli."

Perhaps people are afraid of somehow displeasing or upsetting the powerful leader. Perhaps it's social reluctance to disturb someone supposedly "higher" than they are. Whatever the reason, it's a fact of life. Anyone who's been in a formal leadership position knows how difficult it is to obtain real information about what's going on. Few people spontaneously approach a leader and provide unsolicited information or opinion. Those who do are often considered "pushy" or "forward."

In the same way, those who want some connection with the leader will usually wait for the leader to make the contact. That's the practical reason leaders have to reach out to others. Human connections won't get made unless they do.

But there's an even deeper reason. How eager are you to commit yourself—your heart, your mind, your sweat—to a distant authority figure with whom you feel no connection? Probably not much. Formal authority—giving someone a paycheck—will get simple obedience. Only leadership—reaching out and connecting with people on their terms—can capture hearts and minds.

It has to do, we believe, with the basic human need to be recognized. All of us want to feel that those we follow see us, hear us, know us, and value us. That sense of being seen, heard, known, and valued can only rise from a relationship. And a relationship will arise in the vast majority of cases because the leader has initiated it.

"Let me buy *you* a cannoli."

Actors must find the heart of a character

Empathy is the inner skill that allows an actor to understand what a character feels and why that character acts as he does. Most actors begin by researching the characters they play in order to understand them fully.

Oscar winner Robert De Niro is famous for the lengths to which he goes to understand his roles and get inside the minds of his characters. To play boxer Jake La Motta in *Raging Bull*, he put on thirty pounds and spent a year learning to box. He learned to play the jazz saxophone for *New York, New York*. He wore custom-made silk underwear for *The Untouchables*, though it would never be seen onscreen.

Beyond the appearance, speech, and mannerisms of his characters, he learns what drives them from the inside, what makes them tick. He spent weeks with steelworkers in the Ohio Valley to prepare for *The Deer Hunter*. For his film, *The Fan,* in which he plays an obsessive who stalks and terrorizes celebrities, De Niro went to Gavin De Becker, an expert on such people. By the time he was done reviewing case files, listening to taped interrogations, and meeting with knife salesmen (his character sells knives in the film), De Niro understood not only how such criminals behave but also what drives them internally. "He grasped that stalkers aren't starstruck or shy," said De Becker, "they're grandiose. They feel they deserve fame." That insight obviously changed the way De Niro played the role.

Besides empathizing with the characters they play, actors must also be skilled at listening, both to the literal words spoken by other characters and, especially, for the meaning with which other characters invest those words. The subtext affects the way the words are spoken and is a key way actors create authentic connections between their characters—what actors call a "truthful" performance. Leaders can learn from the tools, techniques, and practices that help actors create authentic, truthful connections. Paradoxically, those skilled at imitating others may know most about real relationships.

CHAPTER 4

Reaching Out and Empathy

It's the great gift of human beings that we have this power of empathy. We can all feel like Elliott when E.T. died. We can all cry for each other. We can all sense a mysterious connection to each other. And that's good. If there's hope for the future of us all, it lies in that. And it happens that actors can evoke that event between hearts. And when they do—well, if I'm in the audience, it makes me feel bigger. Enhanced. Even by the most tragic thing. I'm drawn out of my own life into someone else's life, and yet suddenly I myself feel more alive! I'm pulled out of what I do every day into something larger and more lasting, into humanity. That's what an actor can do.
                                          Meryl Streep, Oscar winner

LATE IN THE DAY, MARVIN SLIPPED INTO ROBERTA'S CRAMPED OFFICE and wearily eased his lanky frame into her one guest chair.

"So," he said. "Tell me where we are. What happened today?" He seemed upset and frustrated.

"What do you think happened?" Roberta asked.

"I think we blew up all the company's plans, everything I've been working on for years. These people had to question everything. Don't they want to know what I know?" Marvin said. "I've been working on wave-bending for years. They haven't. I spent hours getting ready. You know. You helped me. Market analyses, projections, vision, product plans, strategies, target markets, roll-out timelines."

Marvin was CEO of SonicPlus Inc., a three-year-old startup. He'd developed some proprietary technology—called "wave-bending"—that reproduced high-fidelity sound from tiny speakers. The first product, a radio as small as a paperback novel, was just out and already selling well.

He had used an initial round of funding to bring the radio to market. Its success led to a second round only a few months earlier, to be used for rapid expansion into a range of new products: laptop computers, PDAs, hearing aids, earplugs equal to the best headphones.

In the past several years Marvin had spent most of his time and his own money bringing the wave-bending technology this far. In spite of the money he'd raised, he, his wife, and two sons still had everything they owned invested in SonicPlus. He'd recently filled out his management team, adding three senior people to help expand his product line. For the first time the experience and expertise of others at SonicPlus could actually complement his own.

Only that morning, Marvin had held his first planning meeting with his new team.

Marvin passed out copies of his charts at the start of the meeting. Watching in irritation as people began to flip ahead through the pages, he said, "Guys, don't read ahead, okay? Spoils the dramatic ending. We'll get to everything in good order."

Things went downhill from there. A couple of people in the group spent the morning arguing with everything he said about technology and the marketplace, while the others sat in glum silence. Over lunch, the new people argued among themselves about projections and channel conflict. After lunch, Marvin presented his strategic plans. Again, some disagreed with everything he said (or so it seemed to him), while others watched, unhappily, and said nothing. Everyone seemed to take the attitude, "Not *my* plans."

The meeting ended because they ran out of time, not because they'd reached agreement.

"*You* feel awful," Roberta said. "How do you think *they* feel?"

Marvin had no idea.

Roberta chuckled at his confusion. She'd worked with him in a large high-tech company and had been with him at SonicPlus from the beginning. She handled all the people and organizational parts of the business he hated. He always sought her advice because she was completely candid with him. Her gray hair and soft, maternal face masked a pretty tough spirit.

"My guess is, they don't feel great either," she said.

"They don't?"

"Well, let's see. They just joined a company with an exciting new technology, thinking they're going to be part of the team leading the company. But today the boss gave them their marching orders. Being high-level flunkies wasn't exactly what they had in mind. I'm surprised they were as polite as they were."

"But I know more than they do! I've been working on this for years."

"Come on, Marvin. Put yourself in their shoes. Would you buy into someone else's plan? Arguing was their way of getting on board. You would have done the exact same thing."

To "see feelingly"

In one of Shakespeare's great tragedies, *King Lear*, there is a character, Gloucester, a powerful nobleman, who cannot distinguish the false love of one son from the true love of a second son. His false son betrays him, and his enemies gouge out his eyes and leave him to wander the world a blind, broken man. Yet as he wanders, he begins to "see" the truth of things, including the true love of his other son. Near the end of the play, King Lear says to Gloucester, "You have no eyes in your head, yet you see how this world goes." To which Gloucester replies, "I see it feelingly."

We don't know a better definition of empathy. Blinded, Gloucester learned to see the world through other people's eyes. So great, then, was his ability to "see" that he said of his days before losing his eyes, "I stumbled when I saw."

Empathy did not come naturally to Marvin. He was an entrepreneur, accustomed to playing both captain and conceiver roles. When the stakes were high and he thought he knew more than anyone else, it was difficult for him to look at the world through anyone's eyes but his own.

Get the best from people you lead

The failed planning meeting was not the first time that Marvin's unwillingness or inability to understand the feelings of others had sabotaged him.

In the early days of SonicPlus, he had put together a small organization but still spent much of his time outside the office, raising money. So when he did go to the office, he used his limited time carefully. Task-oriented by nature, he became task-obsessed. Each day he knew exactly what he had to accomplish and he focused on that.

Finally, Roberta went to him to say she was tired of replacing employees. She was hearing loud and clear that people felt diminished by his behavior. He barely seemed to have the time of day for them, unless he needed something. They felt taken for granted. And because he apparently thought so little of them, they were less willing to help him. They did their jobs but felt no more commitment to him than he seemingly felt to them. When something better came along, they left.

"But I'm nice to people," Marvin had protested to Roberta.

"I can give you an example," Roberta had responded. "Your mother's been sick for a month. Every day I hear people ask you how she is, and I can tell you appreciate them asking. All right? Two weeks ago, you know my son left college because of his grades. You know that because I took a morning off to go get him, and you know I'm worried about him because I said so. Not once have you asked how he's doing or how I'm doing. Why is that?"

To Marvin's credit, Roberta's question embarrassed him. He had no good answer. He could have said her problems weren't related to work, but he had the sense not to say that because it would have meant, "I don't care about you," and that's not at all how he felt.

With Roberta's help, Marvin had begun to treat the staff differently, but until the chaos of the planning meeting, he had considered it hand-holding and thought only junior people needed it.

Now he realized it was more than hand-holding. It was a key part of leading people at all levels.

"If you don't treat these people differently," Roberta told him, "they're going to lose heart and leave."

Roberta reminded Marvin how he'd felt years earlier in his career when she knew he'd worked for a boss who gave him no latitude.

"You left," she said, "You couldn't stand it." Marvin hated to be compared with the worst boss he'd ever had, but he could see Roberta's point.

Empathy makes the difference

There's no mystery here. All of us want to be seen, heard, and known by others, particularly by those important in our lives— friends, family, teachers, bosses, leaders. And when we're recognized in this way, our motivation and commitment go up.

More than a few leaders have insisted on leading from a lofty distance, based on their authority and expertise. You probably know, based on your own experience, why that doesn't work. Most people have had at least one boss they seldom saw, except in scheduled meetings or on formal occasions. He or she never came around to talk to you or your colleagues, didn't know you at all, paid little attention to you, and never recognized or acknowledged you and your feelings.

How does that make you feel?

Now, recall an occasion when your boss recognized and understood you. Perhaps he or she came to you in the middle of a backbreaking project and asked, "Are *you* doing all right? Are you getting what you need? Are *you* holding up?"

It makes a difference, doesn't it?

When you know and acknowledge your people and their feelings, they feel more motivated, work more productively, and they're more likely to stay, even if the going gets tough.

You might think that to play captain or conceiver roles, you don't need much empathy. But, as you saw with Marvin, a good idea and strong vision presented authoritatively aren't enough. Talented people don't just roll over. Even a captain handing out orders will do better by considering how each person or group wants to hear the orders.

Daniel Goleman, author of the groundbreaking book, *Emotional Intelligence,* reports in his latest book, *Primal Leadership* (with coauthors Richard Boyatzis and Annie McKee):

> *Empathy is the sine qua non of all social effectiveness in working life. Empathetic people are superb at recognizing and meeting the needs of clients, customers, or subordinates. They seem approachable, wanting to hear what people have to say. They listen carefully, picking up on what people are truly concerned about, and they respond on the mark. Accordingly, empathy is key to retaining talent. Leaders have always needed empathy to develop and keep good people, but whenever there is a war for talent, the stakes are higher. Of all the factors in a company's control, tuned-out, dissonant leaders are one of the main reasons that talented people leave—and take the company's knowledge with them.*

Actors and empathy

How can Russell Crowe convince you he's a Roman general and warrior in *Gladiator*, and then the next night convince you, in *A Beautiful Mind*, that he's a mathematical genius going mad? If you saw only one movie, the similarities between the character and Russell Crowe the person might seem so strong that you think Crowe simply plays himself. But a gladiator and mathematical genius? In fact, he played these roles so convincingly that he received an Oscar for one and a nomination for the other.

The only way an actor can portray such different characters convincingly is by getting inside each character and understanding what makes that character tick. The actor must understand not only how a character walks and talks, but how he thinks and feels.

Kenneth Branagh, Oscar-nominated actor for *Henry V*, took the extraordinary step of talking to Prince Charles, in preparation for the role.

> *[Henry's] loneliness is intense and his hurt at the various betray-*
> *als and losses is very acute. I asked Prince Charles whether the*
> *various newspaper betrayals of events, dramatic and mundane,*
> *had changed him. Yes, it had, profoundly. And it had, as I sus-*
> *pected was true of Henry, produced an extraordinary melancholy.*
> *It was a sadness that could either produce bitterness or a more*
> *useful but painful wisdom, and Prince Charles had clearly devel-*
> *oped the latter. . . .*
> *This confirmed what I felt I should try to convey in Henry. I*
> *didn't wish to present Henry as a tortured martyr, but I did feel*
> *strongly that a complex psychological portrait had been set up by*
> *Shakespeare which included guilt, doubt and self-questioning.*
> *Prince Charles's comments were immensely helpful. . . .*

Understanding the character's thoughts and feelings is only the first step. To become that person, the actor must first understand . . . and then look inside himself for an emotional connection with the character.

James Earl Jones, acclaimed stage, film, and TV actor, once played Lennie in John Steinbeck's play, *Of Mice and Men.*

> *Lennie was a gentle brute with a hulking physical presence. I*
> *spent some time at a center for the mentally disabled to try for a*
> *better understanding of how Lennie would look at the world. . . .*
> *I once actually took certain psychological tests dressed as Lennie*
> *and responding as I thought Lennie would. The psychology gradu-*
> *ate student administering the tests had no idea that I was an ac-*
> *tor playing a role. In fact, when he saw the results, he told his*
> *professor that they should have me committed before I did some-*
> *thing violent!*

Jones touched on an approach actors often take to understand a character they're going to play. They learn enough of the character and his circumstances—even inventing appropriate background detail, if necessary—to be able to imagine themselves in the same circumstances. It's called the "Magic If" approach in which actors ask themselves, "If I had the same background as the character and now found myself in the same situation, how would I feel?" In this way actors strive to get inside the skin of their characters.

Lessons for leaders

Leaders don't do what actors do. They don't try to portray characters other than themselves. But the goal here isn't for leaders to emulate actors. It's to learn from their practices. So what can leaders learn about empathy from those who take empathy all the way?

From our background in the theater and working with businesses, we believe the experience of actors suggests three guidelines about empathy for leaders.

1. Know what makes your people tick.

2. Make the link to your own feelings.

3. You can empathize with anyone.

Empathy guideline #1:
Know what makes your people tick

People often misunderstand the nature of empathy. It does not consist of warm feelings held in general for all of humanity. It only exists when one individual understands the specific thoughts and feelings of another.

In our workshops we conduct empathy-building exercises. The power of this approach became clear in one of the first team-building programs we conducted.

It was a workshop for a team that had existed many years. The team was split between New York and Dallas and met in person once a quarter. Between quarterly meetings, individual members worked together and often met. The team leader who arranged for the workshop told us, "I've inherited this team and it's completely dysfunctional. Two members haven't talked to each other in seven years. Either we fix this or I blow up the team."

We asked participants to pair off, share one defining moment, and acknowledge each other's strengths and values. We knew this exercise might be our only chance for a breakthrough with the two team members who wouldn't talk to each other.

One, Allen, was a tall, introverted man in his fifties from New York. The other, Bobbie, was a much younger motorcycle enthusiast from Dallas. We asked them to pair up and they both refused. We tried every rational argument. Finally we pleaded, "Do it for us. Just go off together. What happens, happens. If you don't talk, that's fine." They agreed, very reluctantly.

When they returned, we could see a difference in their faces. They shared their experience with us. Allen's eyes filled up as he spoke and it took several minutes for him to finish. "I had no idea until today," he said, "that seven years ago Bobbie was fighting cancer. He wouldn't let anybody know, because he didn't want to deal with it with everybody." For two years, Bobbie's illness and his decision not to talk about it caused all kinds of behaviors that were off-putting. He missed meetings and deadlines, didn't return phone calls, often didn't seem to care, was volatile, hard to work with. "I misinterpreted it all at that time," said Allen, who talked about Bobbie's courage. "I respect that he didn't want people worried about him, and didn't want to talk about it all the time. I respect his self-reliance." At the time, though, Allen had become so furious he stopped talking to Bobbie, who responded by not talking to Allen.

Bobbie talked about Allen and was equally moved. He applauded Allen's patience in putting up with his behavior as long as he did. Bobbie owned that he had been difficult and that he wasn't sure he had made the right choice in keeping silent. Now he understood why Allen had stopped talking to him.

We've found that members of high-performing teams consistently exhibit a high level of empathy for each other. So, as leader, you need to know what makes the people around you tick. What made them who they are? What do they care about?

You don't need the level of detailed knowledge actors require. You don't have to re-create the character. You only need enough information to understand the person.

Empathy guideline #2:
Make the link to your own feelings

It's worth distinguishing here between *empathy* and *sympathy*.

Sympathy is sorrow or sadness you feel for someone. The key word is "for," because sympathy involves some distance between you and the other person.

On the other hand, empathy can be any feeling, ranging from grief to joy, that you share with someone else. Instead of feeling *for* someone, it involves feeling *with* them. Making this link requires that you find in yourself the same feelings the other person is feeling. If they feel a strong sense of failure, you must find in yourself the same feeling. If they feel frustration, you must find frustration in yourself as well. Empathy requires you to connect with your own feelings and your own interior life.

In our experience with many business managers, we often find they've locked up their feelings. Or, perhaps, they leave them home every day. If you do this, you won't be able to empathize, and if you cannot empathize, you won't be able to create real, human relationships with your coworkers.

Early in her acting training, Belle bumped into this problem.

In class one day the instructor asked one of us to talk about a very painful experience he'd had. The rest of us were to empathize with him—to feel his feeling inside us. Everyone else in the class was able to connect with his pain and cry with him, but I couldn't. At first I couldn't, wouldn't, find pain within me like the pain he expressed, but then I recalled my parents' divorce. When I was able to connect that feeling of loss in my own life to the loss the other student was describing, then I could experience his pain and could cry with him.

Belle couldn't cry at first because she was unwilling to connect with her own feelings. Not long after his disastrous planning meeting, Marvin saw his older son, John, off to college in a city far away. That afternoon, Marvin found his younger son, eight-year-old Teddy, crying in his room. Marvin reminded Teddy that John would be home for Thanksgiving, for Christmas, and New Year's, for term break . . . he reeled off all the times Teddy would see his brother.

Still, Teddy was inconsolable. After a little while, Marvin grew impatient. He almost dragged Teddy out for an ice-cream cone, always the antidote for sadness in the past. But something stopped him.

As he sat with Teddy, Marvin remembered years earlier when his older brother had left home and how he'd felt more than just sad. Marvin had realized his brother was truly gone, that he'd moved out into the world. Marvin realized Teddy was feeling the same thing. No matter how many times John visited, John's life had moved on, and Teddy's life would never again be full of his big brother. Nor would Marvin's life be the same—his son had moved on. This was grief over a loss that no ice-cream cone could fix. The two of them sat in Teddy's dark room holding hands and grieving this new void in their family.

When it's difficult to make the connection

Feelings are complex things and all of us have different feelings swirling around inside us. Some of these feelings can get in the way of empathy. Recall the last time someone came to you angry and upset, and blamed you for some problem.

This is the acid test of your ability to empathize. Could you immediately recognize the other person's feelings and connect with them?

You'd be a candidate for sainthood if you always could. It's difficult in those circumstances—especially if the person's claims are unfair or a surprise—not to react at first with anger, fear, or guilt. All of these feelings will block your efforts to find an empathetic link.

How about your ability to empathize in the middle of a fight? This is certainly another time empathy gets complicated. In the middle of a conflict or a tough negotiation, you may find it impossible to empathize, or you may feel it will weaken your resolution if you put yourself in the other side's shoes. It's almost impossible to empathize when you're thinking, "I'm right, I have to show that I'm right." But experts on conflict and negotiation say these moments are exactly when empathy is needed most. A successful settlement can't be reached unless you see the world through the other side's eyes.

Now consider this. If someone you lead feels a strong sense of failure at the end of a project, you must find similar feelings inside yourself, in order to empathize. But your own feelings of failure may be uncomfortable for you. They may be hard for you to accept, or even recognize. As with Belle's memories of her parents' divorce, your feelings may be painful for you to dredge up. Marvin didn't want to go back and remember his experience with his micromanager boss; it would imply he was now acting the same way. And Marvin's memories of when his older brother left home were still painful to him. So he resisted, as would we all.

In Chapter 2 we told the story of Meredith Monk, the performance artist who began to experience overwhelming feelings of fear when she performed. At first she struggled against these feelings, to no avail. Nothing worked, until she, like the Buddhist saint, simply invited the demons in. Then they disappeared.

If you struggle with anger, fear, guilt, or any other feeling that blocks your efforts to empathize, accept those feelings as they are. Bring a sense of kindness to them. Be comfortable with them. Don't push them away. You can't be generous with others without being generous with yourself first.

Empathy guideline #3:
You can empathize with anyone

This is the hardest lesson to learn and put into practice.

It's far easier to empathize with someone you like. It's easy to make a connection between something you admire in someone else and some virtue you perceive in yourself.

But what happens when you must connect with someone you dislike or fear or don't respect, or with a feeling you simply cannot understand?

Suppose you are trying to develop someone who has real difficulty leading a team meeting. Part of you may feel, "That's ridiculous. It's not so hard to lead a meeting. What's the big problem?"

In that case, you must reach deep down inside and imagine for yourself what conditions would make it difficult for you to lead a meeting. What would you have to go through in order to be that kind of person? Or think of something else that does frighten you. Perhaps writing reports, or doing highly quantitative analysis is your weak spot, and every time you have to write a report or do analysis, you break out in a cold sweat. Find something. When you've found that, use it to feel empathy. That will allow you to work with that person appropriately, without condescension.

When we coach people, they sometimes mention a colleague they simply can't empathize with. We always ask, "Is there something that you do admire them for? One quality?"

They usually come up with something. Then we say, "Anything else?" And they can always come up with something else. Once they've done that, they say, "Yes, I can connect with them around those things."

Occasionally, they'll say, "There's absolutely nothing about this person I can connect with." Then we give them homework. We say, "Over the next week, when you're around that person, look only for things that you like and respect about them. Then come back and report at least three things that you found. They can be minute things, but three things." This exercise always shifts their attitude.

Keep in mind that the point of connection need not be a virtue. It may be a fault or a weakness. Or, you can reconceive a weakness into a strength.

Ben Kingsley, the well-known British stage actor who won an Oscar for his lead role in *Gandhi*, recalled a lesson he learned:

I was fortunate enough to be a part of a legendary production directed by Peter Brook of A Midsummer Night's Dream *in 1970. I was playing Demetrius—and I rather underestimated Demetrius. I thought he was a silly adolescent lover, and Peter Brook said, "No. No. No. No! You'll never get there. You'll never get there unless you find something in this young man that is greater than that part of you and that you really aspire toward and admire." And I realized, of course, that Demetrius was not this silly adolescent. He was a man so driven by love that he was not afraid to make a total fool of himself. That was very releasing.*

In the end, though, empathy doesn't involve finding what you like in someone else. It involves finding the humanity in someone else, even in their weakness, and connecting that humanity with your own.

We delivered a pro-bono program for a Boston-area nonprofit. We were taking a group through an empathy exercise. An African-American business owner in her late fifties exchanged stories with a Latino teenage boy, who had been involved in gangs. They returned from their discussion startled to have found so many similarities between their lives, values, and goals. In the exercise debrief, the teenager burst out, "We're the same person!"

As Alan Arkin, the actor nominated for an Oscar for *The Russians are Coming! The Russians are Coming!* and known for his role in *Catch-22*, said:

Each one of us has the seeds of absolutely everything within us. Anybody who has studied acting for any length of time knows that. Sooner or later, if you identify enough with the part, you find that part in you, be it an axe murderer, be it any aberration under the sun, any elevated state under the sun you want to think of. We have the seeds of that within us.

Anthony Sher, known for roles in the movies *Shakespeare in Love* and *Mrs. Brown*, played Richard III, a character so evil he is said to be one of Shakespeare's few characters without redeeming qualities. Sher struggled to find some connection with Richard III:

It taught me that human beings are very complicated, and that we are very vulnerable, and we are mixtures of things. There is Richard III inside me . . . and there are other characters, and being judgmental about people or about characters doesn't seem to be a realistic way of approaching humanity. Because they're not strangers, these people who do awful things, they're just us, they're aspects of us.

You can empathize with anyone because there is some part of everyone in you.

Empathy helps produce results

In case all this sounds a little too soft, you should be aware of an accumulating and compelling body of evidence that links a leader's emotional skills, especially empathy, with the hard results produced by the leader's group.

Daniel Goleman, the author of *Emotional Intelligence* has reported on some of that research. A study of over thirty-eight thousand leaders and their organizations, done by consulting firm Hay/McBer, found that leadership styles that rely heavily on empathy tended to create a more positive company climate (how employees feel about the company), and a positive company climate is a major driver of positive company results. According to this research, the less empathetic leadership styles ultimately detracted from results. In sum, empathetic leadership is a major determinant of how people feel about the organization, and how they feel is a key driver of hard results.

However, empathy alone is only a first, though crucial, step.

In our workshops we frequently ask a participant to role-play a difficult conversation or meeting. But instead of playing herself, we ask her to play the other person. It usually opens her eyes.

One participant, a manager in a consulting company, told of his struggle with a young woman, a new consultant, who showed great promise. She couldn't accept any criticism, even constructive, without breaking into tears. The manager thought he'd tried everything and had become angry and impatient. Another review session with her was coming up soon, and he fully expected more tears. We asked him to take the role of the woman and role-play their discussion.

The first time he simply said what he thought she *should* say. We pressed him harder to put himself inside her head. The second role-play was a little better. The third time, he got it.

"She's terrified," he said. "To her, every criticism means she's failing, and she's terrified of failing."

His insight came from remembering times, particularly in his childhood, when he'd felt as she did now. He realized at those times he'd been scared to death.

That's empathy. But what should this manager do with it? How should he behave toward the young woman based on it?

That's the subject of Chapter 5.

Reaching Out and Empathy

Empathy guideline #1:	Know what makes your people tick

Magic If

Purpose:	To Empathize or see another's point of view

To better understand a role, actors learn enough about the character and his situation to be able to imagine themselves in the same circumstances. Often they must invent details of their character's past, creating a story with which they can empathize. It's called the "Magic If" approach: "If I had the same background as the character and now found myself in the same situation, how would I feel?" You can use the same approach to practice empathy in your role as a leader:

Exercise:	■ Think about someone with whom you want to empathize. It could be a boss, colleague, or team member.

■ Take a piece of paper, turn it sideways, and with a pen divide it into four quadrants, labeled as follows:

- "Work"—for this person's work life, responsibilities, problems, etc.

- "Home"—for this person's home/family life, responsibilities, problems, etc.

- "Past"—for this person's history, especially what personal struggles, difficulties, or tragedies they may have encountered.

- "Dreams"—for this person's hopes, dreams, goals, and aspirations.

■ Give yourself about three minutes per quadrant to fill in as much information as you can.

■ When you are done writing, read what you wrote aloud,

imagining that you are this person, that what you're reading is about your own life (you may need to insert the word "I" or "my" in each sentence).

- How does this make you feel? Does it increase your empathy? Could you imagine reacting to this person differently in future?

| Empathy guideline #2: | Make the link to your own feelings |

Advanced Empathy

| Purpose: | To Empathize when strong feelings are present |

| Practice: | - Next time someone comes into your office with a problem that clearly has an emotional component to it, try this practice. |

- First, just listen until he or she has had a chance to share the entire situation. Be sure to affirm nonverbally and, if necessary, paraphrase to clarify understanding. Refrain from interrupting or offering suggestions of any kind.

- When you're listening, your main task is to identify with what the speaker is going through. Then notice if you feel any feelings as they are speaking. If so, notice where they are located in the body. Especially look for feelings of sadness, anger, humiliation, anxiety, fear, frustration, envy, shame, guilt, despair. Typical locations in the body for these emotions are belly, chest, shoulders, neck, arms, fists, throat, jaws, and upper back.

- When they finish speaking, empathize with their problem, including any emotion you felt while they spoke. For example, "I felt disappointment when you spoke about how your team had let you down. I can sense how frustrating this is for you."

- When you ground the comments in your own experience, the empathy is much more specific and credible. After this you can move to asking open-ended questions and eventually to problem-solving.

Empathy guideline #3:	Empathize with anyone

Three Things You Appreciate

Purpose: To deal with a colleague or team member with whom you simply cannot empathize

Practice:
■ Collect "empathy material":

- Try asking yourself: "Is there something that I do admire him for? One quality?" Often you'll be able to think of two or three. Write them down.

- Over the course of a week, when you're around that person, look only for things that you like and respect about him. Then write down at least three things that you found.

- Make some form of sign or display containing the three most important things you discovered. Post it somewhere so that you will see it every day. (If you are concerned about others seeing it, you can put it somewhere only you will see, such as in your car, or at home next to your bed.)

- Notice how your attitude and behavior toward this person begins to shift.

- One further step, for the brave at heart: Take this person to lunch and share with him what it is you appreciate about him.

Empathy in Conflict: Dealing with Challenging Conversations

Purpose: To handle difficult interactions where empathy feels impossible

Practice: Proactive Empathy. Before talking to someone with whom you are having a conflict, try answering the following:

- What do you think the other person's feelings are around this conflict?

  - What do you think the other person's needs are around this conflict?

  - What can you offer that will respond to their needs and feelings without sacrificing your own needs?

CHAPTER 5

Reaching Out and
Making Connections

*The more I am known by those I want to follow me and the more I know
them, the greater will be our ability to do great things together.*

David Pottruck, CEO, Charles Schwab

*What we go to the theater for is to celebrate the connections between us;
the connectedness, the universality (among) all of us.*

Christopher Reeve, accomplished stage actor,
best known for the *Superman* films

SEAN KAVANAGH, OUR CEO AT THE ARIEL GROUP, TELLS THIS STORY
about his father, John.

*Growing up in working-class Liverpool, England, without a col-
lege education, my dad, John Kavanagh, began his career as a
stand-up comedian working vaudeville theaters in the north of
England. He joined Phillips Petroleum as a salesman in 1965.*

*In 1977 he was named managing director of Phillips Petro-
leum Europe Africa with headquarters in Brussels, Belgium. He
was the first ever European managing director in the history of
Phillips, an American company, and he went on to become the
highest ranking non-American ever.*

*Belgium is a country with two languages, French and Flem-
ish. The Flemish Belgians lived in the north of the country and,
though they constituted the majority of the population and increasingly the lion's share of the economic wealth, they felt like
the country's underdogs. The French-speaking southern Belgians*

were historically the ruling elite. Though they no longer held the economic power they once had, they still held many positions of authority in government at that time, a fact resented by the Flemish and a cause for political and social strife in the country.

Most American executives at Phillips had learned a smattering of French in school and some of them took a refresher course to improve their ability to order food in French restaurants. My father was not much different. He could get by in stilted French but neither he nor any of his predecessors had ever bothered to learn a word of Flemish. This was curious because 75 percent of the Phillips workforce were Flemish and their manufacturing plants were in Antwerp, a Flemish town.

It was traditional to hold a Christmas party every year for the staff and spouses and the managing director usually made a brief speech and a toast. In prior years some of the executives mumbled through a few words in French in their attempt to "relate to the locals."

Without telling anyone, my father had his Flemish administrative assistant, Annie Guericks, translate a holiday message into Flemish and record it on an audio tape so that he could listen to it in his car and learn it by heart.

He approached the stage at the 1978 Christmas party, wished everyone a Merry Christmas in English and then launched into his memorized Flemish text. I'll never forget this. He didn't get more than a few words into the speech before the entire room of two hundred people leapt to their feet, roaring their approval, applauding and banging on the table. Never before had they been paid this kind of respect. In fact the prior attempts at relating to them had been insulting because they were done in French and not Flemish.

This simple act helped engender a loyalty and team spirit that lasted for years.

Empathy felt **and** expressed

Relationships are built on empathy, but empathy requires more than seeing and feeling. Empathy requires expression. John Kavanagh, the son of Irish Catholics who'd moved to England, could not only empathize with his workers' feelings about their Flemish identity, he was able to communicate that empathy in a clear and public way.

That is the focus of this chapter—what you do to communicate and act upon empathy. Think of it as shining the spotlight on others.

Empathy may be expressed in dramatic ways, like John Kavanagh's Christmas speech in Flemish. More often it's small, day-to-day things. Recall Marvin in the early days of SonicPlus, when he came to the office each day so pressed for time he focused entirely on the work he had to accomplish. As a result, his staff members came to feel ignored and devalued by him. Without any connection with their leader, they felt little loyalty and many left as better offers came along.

Roberta, who carried the burden of finding new staff members, convinced Marvin to spend time each day with the people in the office, to chat about what they were working on or about their lives in general. So Marvin would inquire of people about how they were doing and how their work was going. Roberta would let him know when something was happening—a birthday or illness, for example—that he could mention or ask about. Sure, much of it was small talk, but it wasn't of small importance. The necessity and power of these simple actions became clear to Marvin only after he saw the consequences of not doing them.

There's growing evidence that leadership plays a crucial role in retaining employees. A recent article from the American Society for Training and Development said, "Leaders, and their skill in creating a culture of retention, are emerging as the key in why people stay and what usually drives them away." The article cited a study by the Gallup Organization and was based on interviews with one million employees and eighty thousand managers, which concluded, "People leave managers, not companies. If you have a turnover problem, look first to your managers."

We often work with people as they first step into leadership roles. For many of them, expressing empathy hardly seems a crucial component of the leader's tool kit they're trying to develop. They're preoccupied by the more obvious work of a leader—setting direction, clarifying goals and priorities, keeping people focused, telling people what to do, and making sure everyone is pulling together.

We've observed that the longer people serve in leadership roles, the more they realize the importance of building relationships. They come to see this ability as vitally important for success. We often have to convince younger leaders of that truth. But we never have to convince experienced leaders, many of whom have told us of the pleasure they've learned to take in that part of their work.

We talked to Jane Alexander, a Tony and Emmy award–winning stage, film, and television actress who went on to head the National Endowment for the Arts (NEA), which funnels federal money to arts groups around the country. It was a new kind of role for her but one in which she found her people skills from acting served her well. She said:

> *Taking over a staff of close to three hundred people and being responsible for a budget of $174.5 million was pretty scary to me. What I discovered when I got there was it was really about people. It's always all about people.*

Jane frequently had to deal with congressmen, senators, and federal officials who held differing views about the NEA; some opposed any use of government money for the arts. Whatever their opinions, she reached out and built relationships with everyone. It paid off. She told this story, which took place when the Republicans, led by Senator Jesse Helms, were trying to dismantle the NEA:

> *There was a Republican senator from Utah named Robert Bennett. He believed in the arts, but he wasn't convinced of the NEA. I kept connecting with him personally and talking to him about*

it. I kept making the point, this isn't about big symphonies as much as it's about small little arts groups of one sort or another in small communities all across America. Then, one day, he was in the mountains in Utah, in a public park, and there was a little music ensemble playing. He sat down and it was so beautiful and he read that it was brought to them from the NEA. He came back and said, "I understand now. I've had an epiphany." From then on, he was practically my biggest supporter.

Rules for building empathetic relationships

We've developed three rules that we believe capture the essence of building empathetic relationships. They are:

1. Listen to build relationships.

2. Acknowledge the person.

3. Share yourself.

Any leader who follows these rules will foster the kind of positive work climate that contributes so strongly to good results.

Reaching out rule #1: Listen to build relationships

Acting illustrates the fundamental importance of listening. Tony award–winning stage and film actress Cherry Jones develops a new character by working with and listening to her fellow actors.

I usually only read a play once or twice before I go into a rehearsal process, because I want it to be fresh and new. . . . At the first read-through, I want to hear what the other actors are finding. . . . I can then be free to connect with my fellow actors and take from them, because it's all about listening in the moment to what is being given by the other actor.

In the early days of The Ariel Group, a large U.S. management consulting company hired us to work with consultants rising into management. These thirty-year-olds had gone to top business schools, where they'd honed their superb analytical skills. Then they'd succeeded in consulting work by applying those skills to their clients' business problems. However, as they rose to the level where supervising other people and developing relationships with clients became significant parts of their work, their analytical skills not only diminished in overall importance but, in many cases, became obstacles to building the kind of relationships they now needed.

As we worked with them and observed them with others, it became clear that they used listening, and interacting with others in general, for one primary purpose: *problem-solving*. As they listened, their minds focused on finding, defining, and analyzing the speaker's problem. Once they had enough information to understand and resolve the problem, they would present their solution. That was what they did well and, for them, that was what relationships were all about. In extreme cases, it was as though these people had problem-solving pit bulls in their brains, and they spent all their time looking for opportunities to unleash the pit bulls. That approach had been rewarding so far, and many of them saw no need to change.

Marvin was in the same spot. As he worked, or even chatted, with others, he'd explain how to cure a cold, fix a car, even patch up a broken engagement—along with business advice, of course. It's not that his advice was misguided. But, like the young consultants, it was all he had to offer.

Here's the trouble: problem-solving alone not only fails to create good relationships, it's anathema to them. It creates a me-you orientation and implies "I'm going to fix your problem, which obviously you haven't been able to fix." It does nothing to create a sense of "us."

Don't get us wrong. The world needs problem-solvers, and we applaud people with strong skills in that department. When we call it a "pit bull," we're referring only to the worst cases. But whether the problem solver in your brain is a pit bull or a Pekingese, you need to muzzle it at the beginning of a conversation and let it loose only when problem-solving can be done as part of an established relationship.

Listen for subtext

That problem-solving part of your brain can be so domineering when you listen to someone else talk that you can't simply turn it off. To stop it from taking over, you have to give it something different to do.

Instead of listening for problems to solve, listen for subtext, the meaning and especially the emotion communicated beneath the spoken words. Rarely do people mean only what their words alone mean.

Actors listen for subtext. The variety of ways actors can create and respond to subtext explains how four actors can play the role of Hamlet and create four versions of Hamlet—for example, tragic, angry, crazy, and guileless. All say the same words but with different meanings—subtext—attached.

In Arthur Miller's *Death of a Salesman*, the audience knows Willy Loman's glory days—if, in fact, they were ever glorious—have passed him by. But Willy can't admit that. He can't face the fact he's getting old and feeble. He's lost his power and his sense of himself. His customers no longer respect him. He's making no money. As the facts of his life become more and more obvious to all around him, he retreats into desperate bravado.

He tells his sons, for example, "Be liked and you'll never want. Take me for instance. I never have to wait in line to see a buyer. 'Willy Loman is here!' That's all they have to know, and I go right through."

Biff, his son who's heard all this before, plays along, "Did you knock them dead, Pop?"

Willy: "Knocked 'em cold in Providence, slaughtered 'em in Boston."

In a sense Willy's deluded and frightened enough that he means literally what he says. But the context of the play makes clear another meaning, a cry, beneath his literal words: *Love me even though I'm a failure. Love me for what I used to be, not what I am now.*

Subtext is always the real, emotional meaning of what's said, regardless of the literal words spoken. And it's what others hear and respond to on an emotional level. It's there, just under the surface, in virtually all conversations.

It's no surprise, then, that listening is a major part of an actor's training. Sanford Meisner, best known as a drama teacher whose students include Steve McQueen, Joel Grey, and Diane Keaton, devotes the first year of his three-year program primarily to listening and being present with another actor onstage.

Consider some business examples of subtext. When Marvin presented his plans for SonicPlus, the subtext of the negative responses he got was, "These are your plans, not ours. We want to be part of making the plans we implement." Or, when someone complains they're paid too little, they're probably complaining about not only the pay but also the job or the organization. They may be saying, "You don't pay me enough to put up with the inadequate equipment and tiny cubicles here, or the fact that all I ever hear is criticism, never praise."

At The Ariel Group, we asked our consultants to complete a form following each workshop they conducted. We needed to know how each workshop went—what worked, what didn't, any client comments, and so on. A senior consultant, one of our most accomplished and experienced people, objected vehemently. He said the form wouldn't capture what happened in the workshop and would take too much time. The strength of his opposition—he was actually angry—told us something else was going on. A little conversation uncovered the subtext of his objection. He was anxious that the form would make us bureaucratic (as he said, "McAriel Group") and, more important, eliminate a valued opportunity for him to talk to us about the work he'd done.

Be sensitive to the important communication that occurs on the level of subtext, because subtext is where the speaker reveals himself and what he values.

Listen for what moves and touches you

Finally, do more than simply catalog what you hear. Remember the empathy we discussed in the previous chapter? Find ways that you can connect yourself—*your* feelings, values, and strengths—with those you hear inside and behind the words of someone else. Ask yourself, "What's similar in my life?" Or, "What touches or moves me in what this person is saying?" Look for links and connections.

However, take care that the links you discover within yourself don't dominate your discussion. Kathy recently learned from a friend that his father was dying. To express her empathy, she mentioned that her father had died only a few years ago. Several minutes later she realized the entire conversation had shifted away from her friend's father to her experience with her father's death. Make the connection, if it's appropriate, but don't let the spotlight move off the other person.

Listen for values and strengths

Besides feelings, listen as well for the speaker's values and strengths. These can be personal or professional. Personal strengths might be *maturity, enthusiasm, willingness to change, courage, compassion.* Professional strengths might be *good judgment, risk-taking, results orientation, vision, networking skills.* Values include anything the speaker considers important or holds dear. They might include *achievement, contribution, creativity, fairness, excellence.*

Reaching Out rule #2:
Acknowledge the person

Express to the other person what you've heard in and beneath their words.

Acknowledge feelings, values, and strengths

We asked Marvin to listen as we described a business problem we faced and then to tell us what he heard *about us* in our description. We described the problem: An Ariel Group account manager handling a client of ours was succeeding well but beginning to antagonize a key contact. We wanted to keep the manager on the account but had to head off problems with that contact.

Marvin listened, asked a couple of questions, and said we probably had to change the account manager.

No, we said. Don't give us a solution. Tell us what you heard about us.

We described the problem again.

He listened and then told us what we had to tell the account manager to resolve the problem.

No, we said. That's another solution. What about us? Who are we? What can you tell from what we're saying?

It took several tries, but Marvin finally was able to shut off the brilliant problem-solving part of his brain and tell us what he heard. He heard *compassion* in our description of our account manager's problems. He identified some *frustration* and even *anger* in us at the demands of the client contact. At the same time, he heard how much we *valued our relationship* with the client, and how much we wanted to develop it further. Marvin felt it was a strength for us to be able to *balance* client needs with our concern for individuals.

We thanked him wholeheartedly for listening in a way that allowed him to identify who we were and what was on our minds that we hadn't expressed outright. We felt truly seen by him.

Suppose someone comes to your office to talk about a problem. The most basic step you can take beyond listening and summarizing the details of what you hear is a simple one: *Name the emotions, values, and strengths you hear.*

You might simply acknowledge their feelings by saying something like, "That sounds upsetting" or "That must be frustrating" or "I can tell how much you want everyone to be recognized for their contribution." That simple act will open a channel between the two of you.

When you're playing the role of the coach, your direct reports may come to you and want you to solve their problems. Paradoxically, this is when it's particularly important to build the relationship first and then go to problem-solving. You want to build the relationship so that they'll be open to your coaching, and to build their confidence so they begin solving problems more on their own.

For example, say one of your team leaders, John, barges into your office complaining about how Peter, another team leader, is grabbing all the credit for his team but only doing half the work. You could solve the problem by telling John to calm down and pledging to call Peter and sort it out. But, instead of going right into problem-solving mode, what if you started by empathizing with how upset John might be for having fought with Peter? You might say, "John, I can see that it took *courage* for you to bring up this issue. I can also see that you value *fairness*." Then you could ask him to list some options for solving the problem and begin to offer options yourself. By first acknowledging his strengths and his values, you build his confidence and your relationship.

We once visited the customer service operation of a leading international airline, known for its focus on customers. We observed as their highly trained people dealt with angry callers who wanted redress for some perceived wrong.

The people on the phones were trained to begin responding by repeating the problem back to the caller and then acknowledging the customer's feelings about the problem—anger, frustration, impatience, and so on. The acknowledgment was the turning point. It created a relationship between the two people—it put them, as the airline said, "on the same side of the table, so to speak, instead of sitting across the table from each other." Then the two of them could proceed to a resolution. (The airline, we noticed, was very generous with flight coupons for those it had genuinely inconvenienced.)

What works with an angry customer works with anyone. As we've said more than once, all of us want to be seen, heard, understood, and valued. The simple act of acknowledging feelings, values, and strengths is a simple but powerful way to do that.

Offer positive insights

An important way to acknowledge someone's values and strengths is to offer positive insights, based on what you hear the person say. When you listen deeply, you sometimes develop some understanding of who they are or what they want, and that understanding might be useful to them. Offering insight can lead them to see themselves in a new way, and can foster a stronger relationship between you.

Laticia, an executive in one of our workshops, who participated in a relationship-building exercise, described what she learned this way:

> *I have always felt that I have this very strong forward-moving energy that is very male, for a woman, and I have often felt uncomfortable about that. But after he heard my story, Bill [her partner] told me, "You know, Laticia, you have an amazing ability to use both the feminine and the masculine sides of yourself. You're really able to go fully forward and then at the same time build relationships and soften, and I have rarely seen someone do both sides like that." When he said that about me, it helped me reframe the way I thought about it. Instead of always thinking this is a bad thing and it's not very feminine, I was able to see that it was a valuable thing and that maybe it's a gift I have to be able to balance both sides.*

What Bill did for Laticia was to reframe the way she saw herself. He helped her see that a quality she feared was a liability, a fault, was instead a powerful and useful strength. It was the mutual act of deep listening that allowed Laticia to see herself in a new way. Alan Alda, star of the TV series *M*A*S*H*, put it this way: "Listening is being able to be changed by the other person."

How can you acknowledge people while managing their performance?

As these ideas come up in our workshops, worried participants often ask, "How can I listen and empathize and acknowledge someone if their performance isn't up to snuff? Doesn't all that imply I think they're fine and I like what they're doing? If I recognize people's feelings won't they take that for approval?"

Acknowledging an emotion, or value or strength, doesn't mean you agree with it or even that you think it's appropriate. If you think it's inappropriate or misplaced or exaggerated, there's nothing to prevent you from naming it and then going on to tell the person, "You may not be right" or "Maybe you should look at this in a different light. Let's get the job done and then figure out a better way to do it in the future."

Listening carefully and empathizing and acknowledging, in no way prevents you from commenting on a person's performance. You can recognize someone's frustration *and* tell them it's misplaced. In fact you can go on and tell them, if they don't resolve their frustration and produce more or better work, they will have to leave.

You may want to separate the times you're empathizing or acknowledging from the times you deliver hard messages, just to avoid any confusion, but there's nothing inconsistent between empathizing and hard messages.

In fact, when you create an honest relationship that includes careful listening, empathizing, and acknowledging, we think it's easier to be forthright about everything in the relationship, including the quality of a person's work.

As a manager, you must be clear about what you expect of people. They must get clear feedback about how they're doing. If their performance is below par, they deserve a chance, and help, to improve it. Then, if performance doesn't improve, they will understand why they must leave the job.

What could be behind people's questions about performance may be an odd dynamic we've sometimes noticed.

Let's say Bob isn't performing as he should. Mary, his boss, notices. Instead of raising the issue forthrightly (let's say Bob is touchy and Mary hates confrontation), the situation goes along with nothing said. Bob's performance slowly gets worse. Mary gets more frustrated. In fact, she gets angry at Bob, whom she hired in the first place. But, instead of finally confronting him while there's a chance to fix what's wrong, she turns against Bob as a person. She demonizes Bob. As someone described it, she has allowed the relationship to become "toxic." It's no longer just a performance problem with Bob. Now, in her mind, he's lazy, insensitive, incapable. Soon Mary will make him into a completely irredeemable ogre. Then she'll begin the bureaucratic process of documenting his performance, in preparation for giving him the boot. Hard feelings all around.

Wouldn't it have been better for Mary to develop the kind of forthright, supportive relationship we've been describing? If she had, she probably could have confronted him about his performance when it first began to slip. The ultimate outcome may still have been the same but no one would have had to suffer indignity and demoralization along the way. Terminating someone for performance, the worst and hopefully rare outcome, is never easy, but we make it harder than necessary by failing to establish open, forthright work relationships, characterized by listening, empathy, and acknowledgment.

An extreme example comes from Jack Welch, who in his unique way of managing, sent a note to Jeff Immelt, who went on to succeed him:

Jeff,
   I love you, and I know you can do better. But I'm going to take you out if you can't get it fixed.
   Jack

Reaching Out rule #3: Share yourself

One of the consultant managers we worked with was Betty, who did all the things we've discussed so far in reaching out to people. She empathized, she listened, she acknowledged. Yet she had difficulty coaching people, not because she was unwilling to help but because her people hesitated to share their weaknesses with her.

As we talked to her team, we discovered that Betty, for all her willingness to draw out and support others, never revealed anything about herself. In fact, she rarely talked about herself at all—how she felt, what she thought, her successes, her failures, her life, her past, her family, or friends. As one person put it, "She lives in the back of her mind."

We found that her unwillingness to share herself with others ultimately created an element of distrust. Since people didn't know her at all, they couldn't know if her expressions of support were genuine. They had no way of connecting with her. Most of all, they were reluctant to reveal their weaknesses for fear she would notice the deficiencies and evaluate them poorly. In the end, her unwillingness to open herself to others created a distance that reduced her effectiveness as a leader.

Any number of reasons are possible for Betty's withholding herself, but the one many people assumed was that she didn't find them worthy of knowing her. If you only create conditions for another person to be open with you, but don't open yourself back, then your behavior will begin to feel slightly patronizing and condescending.

Openness is critical for coaching

To coach someone successfully, a leader must create an environment in which it's safe for the person being coached to be vulnerable.

To overcome her team's apprehensions, Betty had to reveal her own needs. What she began to do, at the beginning of each new project, was openly share her own development needs with the new project team. She found this approach allowed team members to feel more comfortable with her and enabled them to share their own development needs with her. In the end, it helped her manage her projects much more effectively.

Vulnerability—reveal the chinks in your armor

Leaders like Betty fear others won't respect them if they reveal their faults. The problem is, it's difficult to form a relationship with a perfect person.

Actors know this. They must reveal some chink in the armor of the characters they play, because the audience cannot identify with a character without fault or vulnerability. At the same time they face the same problem leaders face: If the faults are too great, it will make them unappealing. What both the actor and the leader need is the paradoxical ability to assert power effectively and be vulnerable at the same time.

Marlon Brando managed to find this balance perfectly in *The Godfather*, as described by Anthony Sher:

> *Look how compassionate Brando is to that character of the God-father. In someone else's hands, another actor might be trying to say, "Look what a bastard this man is, look what a monster he is." Brando plays that, but he also plays him with this kind of weariness, and this sense almost of failure. This man has spent his life washing his hands in blood, and it has left him with his spirit scarred and mauled about. And he animates that, at the same time as having all the power and status of the man. It's astonishing. It's really the element of tragedy that he brings into the centre of that film which, I think, transports it way beyond what it could have been, to the level of something quite Shakespearean. The part is actually quite underwritten, but he brings such enormous vulnerability and melancholy to the part, that it takes the whole film onto quite another level.*

Most leaders aren't going to elevate the roles they play to the level of Shakespearean tragedy, but the point still applies. Vulnerability and power can go hand in hand.

About six months after Marvin expanded his leadership team at SonicPlus, he realized that Sam, who headed engineering and product development, had stopped talking about new product ideas and developments.

One day Marvin asked Sam why his ideas had dried up. He was shocked when Sam said he preferred to talk about ideas after they'd been thoroughly worked out and tested.

"But we need to talk about ideas at all stages," Marvin said.

The reason, Sam finally told him, was that Marvin usually responded to ideas with some variation of, "I already tried that and it didn't work" or, in so many words, "That's a dumb idea." Sam had learned that proposing ideas to Marvin was like asking for a poke in the eye. Sam was shocked to learn how much Marvin had enjoyed their idea discussions.

They resumed their discussion of ideas, but thereafter Marvin took greater care with his comments. If Sam was heading to a dead end, Marvin would coach him, rather than declare his idea useless. Marvin had to create a safe place for Sam to talk about his ideas, even though most of the ideas, like any stream of ideas, were ultimately worthless.

The key way Marvin encouraged Sam's creativity, however, was by telling stories of his own ideas, including both successes and failures. Like Sam, Marvin had had a long string of ideas during his career. Most had gone nowhere; some of the failures, he had to admit, he had pursued vigorously. In retrospect, some of them seemed spectacularly wrongheaded, like a solar-powered radio for joggers, and he shared those too.

Marvin's stories lightened his discussions with Sam and encouraged him to think of more ideas.

Tell stories about yourself

Stories are a powerful way to share yourself with others.

Aaron was one of the young, promising management consultants we worked with. Unfortunately, a series of problems, mostly out of his control, led to some problems for him with the client on a major engagement. At the end of the project, the engagement manager gave him a mixed review. He believed his career at the firm was over, just as he'd begun to want to stay longer.

The firm had a mentoring program in which partners met occasionally with younger consultants. Aaron was part of that program and in one of those meetings shortly after the problematic engagement ended, he found himself expressing his fears about his career.

The partner responded by telling the story of her own experience, years earlier, when she had irritated a client far more than

Aaron had. She also had gotten a mixed review, but she'd gone on to become partner and head of one of the firm's most successful practice areas.

It was a simple story, compelling only for its relevance to Aaron's fear. Yet there was probably no way for the partner to respond that could have been more encouraging and useful to Aaron.

The story allowed the partner to convey a complex set of messages without telling Aaron what to do. It told him it was possible to flub up and recover. It was believable because it actually happened. It was far more powerful than any opinion the partner could have offered. Though it was brief, it offered some hints for what Aaron could do to help his own recovery, like openly acknowledging and owning the problems, asking for assistance in developing the skills to avoid future problems, and quick success on another project.

Storytelling is such an effective tool for leaders that we'll return to it in later chapters. We mention it here because it's an effective way of acknowledging and endorsing the listener, while revealing the vulnerability of the storyteller.

Marvin's stories about his own failures and lost causes probably did more than anything else to encourage Sam to talk about all his ideas.

The real turning point in their relationship, however, occurred when they found themselves on the same long flight. It was the first time they spent several hours together.

They talked first about technical matters but soon passed on to other topics. They talked about children and family. Somehow they got on the topic of first jobs as engineers just out of college and it turned out they both had worked overseas in large consumer electronics companies. They told funny stories of adjusting to different cultures.

Without planning to, Marvin found himself telling a story he hadn't even told to most of his friends. In college he'd been a good enough sprinter to compete in the state championships. As he nervously awaited the final race, in a stadium filled with ten thousand people, he warmed up, pulled off his track suit, and stepped into his assigned racing lane. The sprinter next to him looked him over and said, "You always race that way?"

Marvin looked down and discovered he'd pulled off his shorts with his tracksuit and was standing there in his racing top and jockstrap.

Sam laughed until he cried. Then he told Marvin his experience one day as a boxer in grade school. His shorts were too large and so his mother tightened them with a big safety pin. Every time his opponent hit him in the gut, the pin let go and his shorts fell down.

The trip was a turning point in their relationship and their ability to work together productively and trustingly.

Find common ground

What Marvin and Sam did was find common ground. They identified their common humanity, all the things they share beneath the superficial differences. They discovered times and places where they'd experienced the same emotions, the same challenges and successes.

In a sense, finding that common ground is what reaching out is about. It's as Christopher Reeve says of the theater:

The differences between human beings are much less than we think. Underneath all the flak that we send out—the social conditioning, the education, the regionalisms, whatever it is that makes us behave on the surface in certain ways—underneath that, the core humanity is so universal, that when you plug into it, that's where the power of theater comes from.

Empathy—How personal should you get?

We believe it is possible, even necessary, to develop human relationships with all those you lead. No leader should hang up his or her humanity when they walk in the office each day.

However, it does raise the question: How personal should you get? We're not suggesting that everyone who works with you should be your friend. None of this is about friendship. It's about working together toward a common goal.

Obviously, you need to use good judgment as to what you share of yourself, and what you hope others will share with you. There is a difference between someone's personal world and his private world. You have no right to anything in his private world, and how much of his personal world he reveals should be entirely up to him.

One ground rule we've found helpful is to share yourself first, in stages, and then see how others respond. If they choose not to respond in kind, that's their choice. But finding this balance should not deter you from reaching out to create human relationships with those you lead.

One day while Marvin was away from the office, a terrible accident occurred among some construction workers working on the SonicPlus building. Everyone inside the building heard the shouts and crash as a three-story scaffolding collapsed. Two workers were badly hurt and a third died before help could arrive.

When Marvin returned late in the day, he found everyone gone. Roberta had sent them home and left a note for Marvin about what happened. That evening Marvin called everyone at home to make sure they were all right and to let them talk about the experience.

The accident had nothing to do with work, but Marvin understood the impact it would have on everyone. He knew how it would have shocked him. So he reached out to connect with each person.

That, we maintain, is as crucial a part of leadership as setting direction, clarifying goals, keeping people focused, telling people what to do, and making sure everyone is pulling together.

Indeed, the rest may not work very well without it.

Reaching Out and Making Connections

Reaching Out rule #1:	Listen to build relationships

Listening

Purpose:	To build relationships before jumping to problem-solving.
Practice:	Next time someone comes into your office with an issue or problem, listen for:

■ *What Moves and Touches You.* What did she say that moved or touched you? What, in particular, did you respond to emotionally, from your own experience?

■ *Values and Strengths.* What personal or work-related values did you hear in what she shared? What personal strengths or positive qualities were implicit in what she said or how she said it?

Afterward, reflect on how this listening affected the quality of your interaction. Did it change the experience for you? Do you think it might have had an impact on your relationship with this person?

Reaching Out rule #2:	Acknowledge the person

Naming Emotions, Strengths, and Values

Purpose:	To acknowledge the person so he or she feels seen, heard, and known
Practice:	Acknowledging means to express to the other person

what you've heard in and beneath their words, instead of just "solving the problem." Try these three practices with everyone who enters your office:

- The basics: listen carefully, and, as appropriate, reflect back by paraphrasing what you heard. (It's important neither to overdo this nor to do it robotically.)

- Name the emotions, values, and strengths you heard in what they said. Pay attention to phrasing things in such a way as to show your respect and empathy. (For example, when naming emotions, instead of saying "You sound angry—" which could put your visitor on the defensive— you might say something like "It sounds like this situation is creating some real tension for you.")

- Offer a positive insight or two—perspectives into who they are or what they need that are bigger than what they may see in themselves. Offering such insights can lead them to see themselves in a new, more helpful way, and can foster a stronger relationship between you.

- Here are some strengths and values that you might listen for and acknowledge:

Strengths	Values
Professional	■ Achievement
■ Communication	■ Contributing
■ Intellect	■ Creativity
■ Good Judgment	■ Growth
■ Creativity	■ Enjoyment
■ Track Record	■ Excellence
■ Results Orientation	■ Adventure
■ Technical Expertise	■ Integrity
	■ Making Work Fun
Personal	■ Mastery
■ Vision	■ Relationship
■ Courage	■ Kindness
■ Awareness	■ Community
■ Maturity	■ Teaching
■ Responsibility	■ Winning
■ Perspective	

Reaching
Out
rule #3:   Share yourself

Share Personal Stories

Purpose: To help someone who is shut down or feeling discon-
             nected

Practice: The right story about yourself can be the best way to
             connect with another person. It acknowledges the lis-
             tener and reveals the vulnerability of the storyteller.
             Sometimes, however, it's difficult to think of the perfect
             story on the spot that is relevant to the situation and
             builds the connection. We find that it is useful to:

■ Keep a journal specifically for stories.

   • Begin cataloguing stories from your life that shares
     something about who you are and reveals vulnerability.
     (If you remember, Marvin's stories about his failures did
     more than anything to encourage Sam to express his
     creative ideas.)

   • Record other people's stories that move you and
     resonate with your own life. This can jog your own
     memory.

■ Choose a personal story appropriate to the situation, and
  share it the next time someone is having difficulty
  opening up with you.

EXPRESSIVENESS

The ability to express feelings and emotion
appropriately by using all means of
expression—words, voice, body, face—
to deliver one congruent message

Introduction to Act III

When the Revolutionary War ended, the British didn't just pick up and go home, so American troops couldn't either. When Congress wouldn't pay them, officers in Newburgh, New York, stirred up a near rebellion. In a famous incident, General [George] Washington strode before the officers, started to read a statement, then fumbled in his pockets and pulled out reading glasses. The men had never seen him wear glasses before. Washington said, "I have already grown gray in the service of my country, and now I am going blind." The officers were so moved by his speech that they rallied around him and abandoned the rebellion. Some historians will tell you Washington didn't really need those glasses—he was acting. And it was very effective theater. David Gergen

NOW DIRECTOR OF THE CENTER FOR PUBLIC LEADERSHIP AT THE KENnedy School, David Gergen was an advisor to Presidents Nixon, Ford, Reagan, and Clinton and helped each of them communicate the ideas and messages they wanted to deliver. In the *Harvard Business Review* interview from which the story above was taken, he went on to comment, "Washington's stagecraft worked because it came from an authentic core."

What Gergen called "stagecraft" we would simply call "communicating with all means at your disposal." Too many people think communicating is simply what you say, when in fact what you say is only one part of what you communicate.

Great leaders are great communicators

Leaders communicate, and great leaders communicate exceptionally well.

Think back to the list of leaders with presence we mentioned at the start of the book. Martin Luther King, Jr., Winston Churchill, Eleanor Roosevelt, Alfred P. Sloan, and others like them, were all notable for their ability to communicate. They were able to express a vision, a powerful message, to those they led.

The heart of communication, of course, is the ability to express oneself. It's no surprise then, that expressiveness is one of the key elements of Leadership Presence.

Recognized even by his detractors as "The Great Communicator," President Reagan used to go on national television and, as he spoke, pull out of his pocket and read letters from common citizens. This too, said Gergen, was "theatrics, but it was honest. He really did share the writers' concerns and the audience sensed that."

Leaders communicate with those they lead by using every means at their disposal to express themselves dynamically and authentically.

Not every leader must be a great orator, able to move thousands with their words. But they must be able to express themselves in ways that motivate and inspire others to do the right things, to work hard, to sacrifice, to work for something higher than their personal interests.

To accomplish these ends, leaders must above all be able to express emotions and touch the feelings of listeners. Washington's talk to the officers in Newburgh was about loyalty and patriotism and perseverance. The letters President Reagan read were more than recitations of facts and figures.

The ability to express yourself is crucial to each of the leadership roles we first discussed in Chapter 3. The captain must express authoritatively a direction or goal or purpose. The conceiver must express a compelling vision of the future. The coach must express herself in a way that's clear, supportive, and motivating. And the collaborator must express himself in a way that aligns the individual's needs and goals with those of the group. Without an ability to express her- or himself compellingly, all of these leaders will fail.

In the Introduction to Act II on reaching out, we commented that the skills of that element would be particularly useful for natural captains and conceivers who needed to play the roles of coaches and collaborators more authentically. Now, in Act III, natural coaches or collaborators, who want to enhance their ability to play the roles of conceiver and captain, will find the techniques and skills of expressiveness particularly useful.

The importance of all means of expression

Albert Mehrabian, a social scientist who worked at UCLA and MIT, studied the elements of expression and how they affected the impact of individual communication. In one of his books, *Silent Messages,* he reported the results of a study in which businesspeople were evaluated by listeners in three areas: the words they said, the tone of their voice (meaning the *way* they spoke—pitch, volume, warmth, etc.), and their body language.

Surprisingly, the most important factor in determining the impact of an overall message was body language—how the speakers looked, whether they appeared confident, grounded, and sure of themselves. The second most powerful was tone of voice. Did the voice, for example, radiate confidence and clarity? The least important determinant of the impact of communication was the actual words the speakers said.

We worked for years with a consulting firm helping the consultants become more credible with their clients. The consultants would spend hours getting their PowerPoint slides right. On these slides, they outlined their logic, the words they said in their client presentations. Our goal was to help them allocate their preparation time. They spent perhaps 99 percent of their time on what they were going to say and 1 percent on how they were going to say it. We wanted them to spend at least 25 percent of their time on expression.

Even that wouldn't come close to what Mehrabian found. He discovered that the words (content) accounted for only 7 percent of the speaker's impact. The voice—tone, pitch, etc.—accounted for 38 percent, and body language for an astounding 55 percent. If you're not thinking of using every tool of expression at your command, you're probably falling far short as an effective communicator. You should be thinking about how you can use all those tools—words, voice, body, including what Gergen called stagecraft or theatrics—to communicate a coherent, powerful message.

That's exactly what good actors do

The expressive dimension of the PRES model is the one most closely tied to the theater. Actors spend literally hours each day stretching and strengthening their voices, bodies, and emotions. They know that the bulk of what an audience soaks in from any performance is not the spoken words themselves, but the emotional thrust, the intention and energy level of the performer. Am I committed to what I'm saying? What mood am I setting here? Is my posture confident, my voice clear and colorful? Do I have your attention? What feelings am I trying to convey?

As TV and screen icon Danny Kaye once said, "All that matters is what you feel when you say the words." The expression of emotion and the arousal of feelings are two areas in which leaders can learn much from actors.

Next time you're watching a movie on television, mute the sound for a few seconds and watch how the actors use their bodies. Poor actors simply stand around, unless they're performing some specific physical action. Good actors communicate with their bodies all the time—the way they move expresses anger or anxiety or happiness or confusion without saying a word. Their bodies reveal and illuminate the characters they're playing. When you turn the sound back on, listen to how actors use their voices to express themselves, beyond the actual words they speak. It all produces a single congruent expression of character.

Michael Cunningham wrote the novel, *The Hours,* which was made into a movie with Academy award–winner Meryl Streep. Like most authors, he wondered how the star and moviemakers would translate his written words to the screen. After seeing the movie, he wrote:

> *Ms. Streep's Clarissa [the character she plays] is stunningly complex, in part because she creates a whole person out of movements, expressions and inflections. When she says to Louis . . . an old friend who's dropped in unexpectedly, "But I never see you," the line has a singsong quality. It rises steadily to the word "see," then drops to the "you." It is offhand and girlish, venomous, haggard. And when she finally begins to lose her desperate composure there's a moment—a half-moment, you miss it if you blink—when she literally loses her balance, tips over to the left, and immediately rights herself. If there's a way to do things like that on paper, I haven't found it.*

Perhaps now you can appreciate what President Reagan meant when he once commented, "There have been times when I've wondered in this office how you could do this job if you hadn't been an actor." In a sense, he was simply repeating President Franklin Roosevelt's remark to Orson Welles that the two of them were, at that time, the best actors in America.

It doesn't have to do with pretending. It has to do with expressing yourself clearly and honestly, using congruently every means and tool at your command.

Are these just "presentation skills?"

We hope by now you understand how far beyond "presentation skills" these ideas go. Certainly what we're talking about includes the ability to make a compelling, engaging presentation. Such an occasion is often the reason we're first called in to work with leaders.

But expressiveness is much more than that. It's about how you express yourself every day, moment by moment, in every inter-action, including one-on-one meetings, gatherings with a small team, or before large audiences.

Expressiveness builds on the previous parts of the PRES model of Leadership Presence. Being present, which has to do with bringing all of yourself to whatever occasion you're in, concerns your mind and heart. It's the basis for everything that follows. Then we discussed reaching out to another person or group of people and establishing a connection through empathy. Now, in Act III, we're talking about how you extend beyond reaching out to express your vision, message, or direction.

CHAPTER 6

Emotion Drives Expressiveness

Great leaders move us. They ignite our passion and inspire the best in us. When we try to explain why they are so effective, we speak of strategy, vision, or powerful ideas. But the reality is much more primal. Great leadership works through the emotions. . . . even if they get everything else just right, if leaders fail in this primal task of driving emotions in the right direction, nothing they do will work as well as it should or could.   Daniel Goleman, Richard Boyatzis, Annie McKee

WE'RE OFTEN CALLED IN TO HELP AN EXECUTIVE COMMUNICATE A critical message to his or her entire organization. Richard, the executive director of a national nonprofit organization was about to kick off a major reorganization and he needed the full commitment and flexible support of everyone in his organization. He anticipated some resistance but he accepted responsibility for getting everyone on board. We first met with him one morning and chatted about his plans for the organization. Tall and distinguished—if you'd put in a call to central casting for an executive type, he's what you would have gotten—he couldn't have been more charming or lively or funny. Better yet, he was articulate. He talked about the consequences if the organization didn't change. He talked about the current economy and its impact on his plans. He talked about the challenges other nonprofits were facing and their need for private sector partners. He had his story down cold, and it was totally convincing because he believed it deeply and passionately himself.

We're pretty tough customers, because we've heard more of these stories than most people, but as we sat around the conference table in his office, Richard had us ready to storm the barricades with him. In fact, we began to wonder why we were there. What did he need from us?

It turned out he was going to address a group of regional directors that morning. They were exactly the people he had to convince if his reorganization was going to work at all. So we asked to sit in and watch him present the message he had just delivered to us so eloquently and convincingly.

We took a seat at the rear of the amphitheater-style meeting room, where about fifty directors had been attending a workshop, and waited to see how this charismatic guy would inspire this group.

He rose to speak, but before he said a word, his hands dove for his pockets, his shoulders slumped, his facial muscles went dead, and he glued himself behind the podium. "I'm tremendously excited," he began in a monotone, "about the new direction this organization is heading in." Then he droned through the rest of his presentation as though he were reading the phone book.

We wanted to run down and shake him. The engaging, enthusiastic leader we'd first met was gone. In his place, in front of these once-eager directors whose wholehearted support he desperately needed, stood a "tremendously excited" sack of flour.

At the end, he answered some perfunctory questions, received a round of polite applause, and left.

"What happened?" we asked as soon as we had him alone.

Our question surprised him. He admitted to some nervousness; even with all his experience, making a presentation was still a little uncomfortable for him. But that didn't explain the problem. As we have seen, accomplished actors often feel stage fright before a performance and then perform magnificently.

Do leaders express feelings?

More conversation uncovered the real culprit. He was the victim of a misconception that still plagues many in organizations: the notion of the leader as an aloof authority, above it all, cool, calm, dispassionate, always in control, swayed only by careful reasoning based on hard data.

According to this misconception, leaders don't show emotion.

Why? We hear lots of reasons. It's unbecoming. It undermines authority. It reveals a lack of control—someone who feels something too strongly can't be trusted to be rational. It reveals weakness. For men, it reveals something unmasculine. For women, it says they're not tough enough. The reasons go on and on.

We have a simple reaction to that: It's a cop-out. Many people use this excuse to avoid expressing emotion even when it's entirely appropriate. We're convinced, after working with thousands of leaders on exactly this issue, that this misconception—leaders shouldn't show emotion—makes them far less effective than they could be.

The reason is simple. All human interaction is full of emotion, even at work. You can ignore it, but it's there. Emotion is wrapped around every human activity. Without emotion, nothing is worth doing. We wouldn't get up in the morning. We wouldn't work hard. We wouldn't care.

Some of you may remember the business world of only a few years ago, when the philosophy was: Leave your feelings and your personal life at the door when you come to work. Of course, work never really functioned that way, even then, but it was an excuse for leaders to avoid dealing with feelings, their own or those of people working for them.

Leaders' moods matter

Fortunately, that philosophy has begun to change. As we saw in the last two chapters, the role of emotional maturity in leadership is crucial. Success in life and leadership probably depends more on emotional skills, including the ability to recognize and express emotion, than it does on traditional IQ. Possessing this ability will make a leader more effective and set the emotional tone and energy level of the whole organization.

As Daniel Goleman ended an article in the *Harvard Business Review*:

Taken as a whole, the message sent by neurological, psychological, and organizational research is startling in its clarity. Emotional leadership is the spark that ignites a company's performance, creating a bonfire of success or a landscape of ashes.

There's also growing recognition that leaders must engage people's emotions in order to foster successful corporate change. John Kotter, professor emeritus at Harvard and an expert on leadership, says in his book, *The Heart of Change,* "In highly successful change efforts, people find ways to help others see the problems or solutions in ways that influence emotions, not just thought."

In Chapters 4 and 5 we discussed the need for the leader to empathize—to create real relationships with others by recognizing and connecting with their feelings. For many leaders that's hard enough. Now we're saying leaders must go even further; they must express their own emotions publicly.

The reason that's important will be clear if we go back to Richard's droning speech to those unfortunate directors. What was he trying to accomplish?

What he needed, and completely failed to get, was the most important emotion of all for leaders: *authentic excitement.* It's the emotion leaders tell us they want most in their people. But in our experience, genuine, heartfelt excitement is the emotion most often missing in organizations.

When Richard finished his talk, the room was emotionally dead. The energy and anticipation that had greeted him had leaked out, like air from a leaking tire. By the time he got through talking to all the leaders in his nonprofit, he would be driving his organization on four flat tires.

Is that what he wanted? Of course not. He wanted excitement, an intense commitment to move ahead with his change program, starting then and there.

What he got was no emotional energy at all. Why? *Because he put none in.* He expressed no emotion and that's exactly what he got back.

No one can *tell* people to be excited.

Leaders are responsible for the energy level

What we can tell you is what we told Richard and what we tell all leaders.

You, as leader, are responsible for the energy level—the level of authentic excitement—in your organization.

We get mixed reactions when we say this. You may think that's not in your job description. Maybe no one's ever told you that before. Or you don't think your boss would hold you responsible for it. We agree, it's probably an idea you haven't heard before and you need to think about it.

But when you've thought about it, we suspect you'll come to agree. The link between excitement and commitment and results is not hard to grasp.

A former comedian who was directing Belle in a comedic cabaret show told her a valuable lesson he'd learned in his early days on the comedy circuit:

> *When I first started out, I'd schlep onstage with a tentative attitude, using my first few jokes to test the water, hoping for approval. But an audience doesn't want that responsibility. They don't want to take care of you. They want you to take care of them, to walk out there with an attitude that says, Get ready to laugh, people, because this is going to be the funniest damn show in the history of humor.*

Maureen Stapleton, the highly respected character actress and Oscar winner for the 1981 film *Reds*, said something similar about stage acting:

> *If you have a big part, you have to be sure your energy level is high. It's a new audience every night. You can't say on Thursday,*

"Oh, you should have caught me Monday. I was in good shape then."

Kenneth Jay, now a successful financial services executive, trained extensively as an actor before acting several seasons with a renowned Shakespeare repertory theater company. He talked about his own approach to leadership, and said he had been surprised to learn that business leadership required some of the same role-playing as acting.

I had to find parts of myself I didn't normally stress, because the (leadership) role is not natural to me. It requires a more outgoing, a bigger personality than what I'm used to. I tend to use more volume when I'm leading. I feel like I have to be more "on" than I am at home. Because in order to be a leader, people have to follow, and they don't follow people unless there's a reason to. You have got to have energy. Energy creates the gravitational pull. . . .

What we tell leaders next usually elicits a stronger reaction, or at least more discussion. It's the first of three guidelines we've developed for leaders around the expression of feelings.

1. Generate excitement by expressing emotion.

2. Express *authentic* emotion.

3. Use passionate purpose to invest your words and actions with authentic feeling.

Expressing emotion guideline #1: Generate excitement by expressing emotion.

You, as leader, arouse emotional energy by expressing emotion yourself, by personally investing the work with appropriate and authentic feeling.
Everyone knows from simple life experience that expressed enthusiasm usually generates an enthusiastic reply, or that anger

sparks anger. So, after some thought, most people agree with this guideline. But it often makes them uncomfortable.

It can be uncomfortable—but the results are worth it

We were called in to work with Jack, the head of one of the major divisions of a worldwide financial services firm. The structure of his twenty-five-thousand-person firm required that the twenty-two hundred worldwide partners every four years elect a CEO. Jack was putting himself up for the top post and some of his closest colleagues had advised him to get some help.

In particular, he wanted to prepare for his "elect me" presentation at the firm's annual meeting. Jack was running on a platform of globalization. Though the firm was truly international, with offices in over forty countries, those offices had historically operated as fairly autonomous units. The problem with such an organization emerged when the firm's big international clients wanted to work seamlessly with the firm around the world. Policies and operations needed to be more standardized from office to office—for everything from office software to strategic positioning. Everyone in the firm agreed on the need, and the opportunity, but the history and inertia of autonomy were still strong. The firm needed a strong leader to make the necessary changes, and Jack planned to present himself as that leader. He was running against two other candidates, including the incumbent, whose directive style hadn't accomplished much.

We met Jack one fall afternoon in his New York office. Of medium height, with thinning brown hair, Jack was, by his own description, a "quiet Southern boy." He was pleasant and soft-spoken, quietly charming and witty, but those latter qualities became apparent only as you spent time with him and he got to know you. To most people and to a large audience, he revealed very little of himself. At our first meeting, Jack expressed some qualms about working with us. He said he recognized his need to be more expressive, particularly when speaking to large groups. However, he said, it was important in working with us that he remain in his "comfort zone." Uh-oh, we thought. He's in for a surprise. The first thing we usually do with a client like him is ask him to move outside his comfort zone. It's the only way to become more expressive.

The reason we push people outside their comfort zones is that many of them, and this included Jack, are just uncomfortable expressing emotions, period.

Perhaps you're one of those people.

Maybe you learned, as you came of age, to "stifle yourself," as Archie Bunker used to tell his wife. At school, at church, at temple, in interactions with friends, you learned not to laugh or cry. And when you got to work, "outbursts" of feeling were definitely discouraged.

You probably discovered very early that expressing feelings makes you vulnerable. When you reveal to others what you want or don't want, like or don't like, you give them power over you and your happiness. They might withhold something you want or force on you what you hate. Safer, you learned, to keep your inner feelings to yourself.

Especially for women

Expressing emotion in public can present special problems for women. It plays into the stereotype that women are "weak," or "flighty," and can't manage their feelings.

We were invited to work at a large engineering company where most of the employees had previously worked for the military or in science. It was a very male culture.

Florence, the first woman ever to be made a senior vice president at this company, was speaking to two hundred of her colleagues. She was the only woman. It was her first talk to the company. In describing the honor she felt at being named to her position, she told the story of how her mother had always encouraged her. Unfortunately, her mother had died recently without ever knowing of her daughter's promotion. At this point, Florence started to cry and there was a very awkward moment. She actually lost control.

We taught a workshop soon after and all in the workshop who had been there told us about it. They said the whole room had been electric, as people waited to see what would happen.

Instead of becoming flustered, Florence just took the moment and allowed herself to cry. She got her Kleenex out, she blew her nose, she put herself back together. Then she said,

> I want you all to know that this is going to be part of my leadership style. I am going to bring my emotions and that is going to be part of how I lead, and I think it's going to add something sorely missed in our culture. I hope you will appreciate it.

She finished her talk and she got a standing ovation. In the workshop a couple weeks later the men were all telling us how much they had learned from Florence, how much respect they had for her, and how excited they were about what she was going to bring to the leadership of the company.

If you own your emotion and feel totally comfortable with it, then you will be fine. In fact, it can make you, the leader, whether female or male, even more powerful.

Wait a minute . . .

At this point, you may already be out of your comfort zone. People, you might say, can't all run around expressing all their feelings all the time. That would be chaos. We agree. So let us be clear about what we mean here.

We do not advocate either the free expression of destructive emotion or the destructive expression of any emotion. For example, anger needs to find some means of expression, but the right means is rarely an outburst of rage. There are better, and ultimately positive, ways to express those kinds of strong, difficult feelings.

We do advocate the expression and evocation of emotions that deepen our bonds with others, help others in some way, or reveal our humanity and vulnerability. Such emotions are hardly limited to positive ones. Anger, frustration, and pain *properly expressed* can ultimately draw us closer to one another.

In the same way, no effective leader is free to express emotion indiscriminately. The reason is simple. Your moods have enormous impact on those you lead. Kenneth Jay, the successful financial services executive who trained as an actor, discovered this the way most of us learn it, through experience. He said,

> *I'm not allowed to have bad moods at work. You can't. If you're in a leadership role and your mood is bad, you will bring the team down. Your every emotional wavelength is picked up and reverberated amongst those you work with.*

Karin, an executive at one of our client companies, told us a similar story.

> *The company had gone through a year of rapid reorganization. I was running two divisions and after the first set of changes, I found myself running only one of them. It was a bigger division than it had been. Still, you know, it felt like a step down. Then, in the second set of changes, I came out running a smaller division than anything before. I wasn't happy about that. In fact, I went into a funk about it. But I realized I couldn't show my feelings to my people because that would only discourage them. I had to come to terms with the changes before I could say or show anything to anybody.*

Because the expression of emotion is such a powerful tool for leaders, it must be used carefully. That's why we don't advocate the expression of any and all feelings, regardless of consequences. We do advocate the clear expression by leaders of authentic and appropriate emotion. It's too powerful a tool not to use. But use it thoughtfully.

Expressing emotion guideline #2:
Express **authentic** emotion

When leaders express emotion, the emotion must be authentic in every way. It must be genuine and true, real and appropriate for the occasion.

Actors don't pretend feelings. That's a misconception. They may pretend to be a character, but they bring real feelings of their own to each character they play. Kenneth Branagh appeared in Ibsen's *Ghosts* with the legendary British actress Dame Judi Dench, who won an Oscar for *Shakespeare in Love*. Commenting on her "delight" in laughter, he went on to say,

> *She seemed able to embrace every emotion wholeheartedly. There is an amazing, childlike quality in her acting which allows her to cry or laugh with the full abandon of a child.*

Contrary to stereotype, though many beginning actors may be naturally loud and outgoing, they are rarely born with an innate ability to express authentic feelings. When they first approach the craft of acting, they struggle with the same self-censorship and fear of exposing themselves we all have.

Much of modern acting rests on the belief that an actor should find and express from inside himself an authentic emotion appropriate to the scene he is playing. We mentioned Stanislavsky earlier, but this idea actually goes far back in history. There is a story of the famous Greek actor Polus more than two thousand years ago, whose son had died tragically. To play a scene in Sophocles' *Electra*, in which he must mourn the death of a brother, Polus carried onstage the urn containing his real son's ashes. It was a perfect example of what we now call "emotional memory"—the memory of a powerful event in the actor's past that is used to elicit an authentic emotion in a performance.

Why would an actor subject himself to such grief, like pressing on a wound? For the same reason we tell leaders they must express feeling if they want those they lead to have positive feelings about their work: *The only way to elicit emotion—whether from an audience or a work group—is to express authentic emotion.*

Jack, our financial services client who was having difficulty being expressive, participated in a workshop we ran for senior managers in his firm. We often ask coaching clients to do this. A workshop, with its small group of supportive colleagues, can be an ideal and safe place to try out new behaviors. We ask workshop participants to make presentations in which we strongly encourage them to express themselves with more feeling than they would normally.

Jack simply could not loosen up. No matter how the others in his group tried to help him, every time he stood up to make a presentation, his face turned wooden, his body stiffened, his voice went flat. He seemed unable to change, no matter how much he genuinely wanted to. Something held him back.

That evening, we happened to walk through the hotel lobby where we saw Jack talking on the phone. He had a big smile on his face, his eyebrows bounced up and down, his hand waved. We confess we moved closer so we could hear his voice. There was a lilt in it. He was doing everything we'd tried so hard to get him to do in the workshop.

When he was done, we apologized for listening and asked him who he had been talking to. He said he'd been saying good night to his kids, who were five and eight years old.

We suggested he imagine the next morning that he was speaking to his kids when he spoke to the group. He did, and it not only instantly transformed his presentation but it upped his energy and vitality in all his presentations after that.

This little substitution exercise worked for Jack because it put him in touch with his feelings in a new context. Did he thereafter have to think of his children every time he gave a talk? Not at all. Thinking of his kids gave him access to feelings in a situation where he'd been conditioned for decades to tamp down emotion.

At first, he felt he'd gone way over the top, but his colleagues in the workshop assured him he'd remained credible and been more engaging too. The experience opened the door to his feelings for good and after that he rarely had to use the substitution again.

Positive emotions are not the only ones you can and should express. For example, we had a client once from a large energy company who needed to tell his team about a reorganization involving numerous layoffs. He felt deeply troubled, but he was determined to project a positive attitude. We asked him if his work group was likely to be so positive about the news. "Are you kidding?" he asked. So we encouraged him, instead, to show his own fears and be "real." Relieved of the burden of expressing feelings he didn't possess, he stepped in front of his team and let his pain and disappointment show, along with his genuine determination to move ahead positively. He fielded the emotions of his people— anger and grief in particular—and responded honestly with his own feelings. If he had just mouthed what his people perceived as the party line, he would have alienated everyone. But showing authentic emotion built a deeper bond of trust between him and his team. It increased his credibility and allowed them all to go forward constructively.

Passionate purpose

People sometimes tell us the work they do just doesn't merit much emotion. What should they do in that case?

It's an important question because, remember, the emotional response of the audience hangs on the emotional intensity of the leader. If you put no emotional energy in, you'll get none back.

Actors have a method for taking what may appear to be an everyday task and investing it with heightened emotion. When an actor approaches a scene, he never says, "I'm going to feel sad here." Or happy or angry or any other emotion. As Jack Nicholson, screen legend and three-time Oscar winner, said,

I go in knowing [my character] wants this, and the environment is that, and this is how he's going to approach his problem, and I

try to make it even more important than it would be to the char-
acter, and that creates feeling. Whatever feeling trying to achieve
those ends creates, that's the emotion.

In other words, the actor identifies what the character wants.
What is the character's goal or intention or purpose? That purpose—
what we call the character's passionate purpose—is what creates
the emotion he will express.

Madeleine Homan, the professionally trained actor, now a vice
president of a prominent training and coaching firm, has this to
say about passionate purpose:

If you look at an animal and they're moving, they are moving for
a reason. You don't move for no reason ever, under any circum-
stances. You may forget why you went to the kitchen, but you
went there for a reason. You stand up for a reason. Lazy actors,
and I've been one, neglect to understand the action or the reason
behind every action. If you rub your face, it's because you have an
itch, or because you're worried about your mascara and how you
look, and what that does is build layers of complexity and makes
things really interesting. I think as a leader the parallel is that
you have to have a clear picture of where you're going. If you're
putting one foot in front of the other for a reason, what is it? A lot
of leaders are just vaguely wandering in the general direction of
something unclear. Then they wonder why their employees are
lackadaisical.

Expressing emotion guideline #3:
Invest passionate purpose into
your words and actions

Here's how you can apply passionate purpose to your work:

Every time you want to communicate a message of any kind,
identify your intention or purpose by naming it with a specific verb.

Most of the time, when we ask a businessperson to do this, say
in a presentation or a memo they must write, he will say his in-

tention is to "impart information," or to "explain" or "announce" something. An actor might say his character's intention is to "ask" or to "tell."

Unfortunately, for both business leader and actor, if the purpose is merely to impart information or to explain something, or to ask or tell, the resulting expression will be flat and dull. Why? Because those intentions or purposes spark no energy or passion or tension. Instead of naming your purpose with some dry, colorless verb, you must find another verb that contains and expresses more emotional intensity.

You must find your passionate purpose.

To help you do that, here's a list of some verbs. You can start with a list like this but ultimately all of us should have our own list of verbs that particularly excite us.

Admonish	Console	Frustrate	Promise
Alert	Dazzle	Gloat	Reassure
Amaze	Defend	Heal	Shake up
Amuse	Disempower	Humor	Shame
Appease	Divert	Hypnotize	Surprise
Assure	Embrace	Implore	Tantalize
Attack	Enliven	Impress	Tease
Beseech	Entice	Inspire	Threaten
Calm	Excite	Intoxicate	Warn
Cajole	Fight	Motivate	Welcome
Challenge	Flatter	Placate	Win over
Chide	Forgive	Plead	Woo

Aren't these verbs more powerful, more interesting, more energized than "inform" or "announce?" Of course they are. They're full of life and passion and meaning. There's nothing dull or humdrum about them. Each one indicates some supreme effort against some opponent. Tension! Drama! Conflict!

When you do this, you're doing exactly what actors do. Scene by scene, moment by moment, they keep drama compelling by showing their characters striving against some kind of opposition or inertia. Whenever characters in a scene stop trying to change one another and simply begin exchanging information, the play skids to a stop. No passion, no struggle, no emotional intensity, no energy.

Every human exchange—every meeting, every presentation, every memo, every serious conversation—can be thought about in a way that reveals needs and desires, real or potential conflicts.

If you want to invest what you do with more emotion, you must ask yourself the same questions an actor asks: What am I fighting for? What do others want? What are the obstacles? Then use your answers to select the appropriate verb that captures your passionate purpose.

As we worked with Jack, we focused on helping him prepare for his firm's coming annual meeting of worldwide partners and the election for CEO. It was the highest-profile, highest-stakes presentation he had ever made. He was asking the firm's leaders to change the way they worked, to give up some cherished autonomy, even to make personal changes like moving to a different city, and he was asking them to anoint him the one who would lead them down that difficult road.

We asked Jack about his purpose in this crucial meeting. His first answer was the one we typically get. He had great difficulty thinking of a goal beyond "informing" people. He believed that if everyone understood the situation, they'd come along. At least that was how he'd always approached his presentations in the past. If the facts are known, he thought, the solution will be obvious.

We suggested that perhaps there was a more energizing purpose than "to inform." He tried on such passionate purposes as "excite" and "motivate." Slowly, he realized that to lead his people to a new global vision, one that involved personal change for many in the group, he himself would have to show some willingness to change—actually *show* it, not just talk about it. He finally decided his passionate purpose for that meeting was twofold: first, to *excite* his managers about global opportunities, and second, to *demonstrate himself* the kind of personal change he was asking all those people to make. It was a gutsy decision, because if it didn't work, especially the second part, he might look foolish. Yet it fit exactly the twofold message he wanted to deliver: "We have to go truly global and I'm the guy to lead us there."

Jack accepted the risk. Passionate purpose galvanized him. No more "I want to stay in my comfort zone." He was ready to do whatever it took.

No communication needs to be dull. Every meeting, presentation, memo, or conversation represents an opportunity to change minds in some way. If that's not the case, why make the presentation or write the memo? Your task is to identify the change desired, or the problem to be overcome, and invest it with passionate purpose.

Consider how passionate purpose might work in these normally mundane situations:

- The routine handoff of a project to another department becomes an opportunity to *placate* that department after a problem caused by your group last week forced the people there to do extra work. (*Hand off* becomes *placate*.)

- Your group is debriefing at the end of a difficult but successful project. The temptation will be to identify the problems, but you mustn't forget to *celebrate* the achievements too. (*Debrief* expands to *celebrate*.)

- You're initiating some change in work process. Normally you would begin by explaining the need for change. Instead, you could *warn* the group about the future and what will happen if things remain the same. (*Explain* becomes *warn*.)

Here's the final piece of encouragement we give leaders about expressing emotion: *Passionate purpose is the key to finding and expressing your emotion in the workplace. It will work as well for you as it does for an actor onstage.*

So now you're ready. You've got your passionate purpose. You're excited, energized, eager to change the world, or at least your corner of it. In Chapter 7 we'll talk about how to express your passionate purpose in a congruent and compelling way.

Emotion Drives Expressiveness

Expressing emotion guide- line #1:	Generate excitement by expressing emotion

Read to a Child

Purpose:	To find energy and expressiveness
Exercise:	Pick your favorite storybook from childhood and read it aloud to a child. (You can also do this with a story or fairy tale you know by heart—don't be afraid to embellish it with your imagination.) Emphasize the different emotions in the story. For example, as the story's narrator, and when playing different characters, use the range of your voice to express happiness, sadness, fear, rage, etc. Also make sure these emotions come through in your facial expression and body language too.

Expressing emotion guide- line #2:	Express *authentic* emotion

"Missing" Emotions

Purpose:	To have a repertoire of authentic emotional responses
Practice:	Read through the list of emotions that follows. Put a check next to the ones you naturally express or those that are habitual for you. Circle three to six you'd like to express more often—either at home or in your leadership role. Find an opportunity to express those "missing" emotions over the next week (it helps to make

some kind of sign or reminder for yourself that you will see every day). What do you notice happening when you add these emotions to your repertoire?

Missing Emotions

Afraid	Confused	Grateful	Lively	Solemn
Aggressive	Delighted	Greedy	Longing	Spirited
Amazed	Delirious	Happy	Low	Strong
Amused	Disappointed	Hopeful	Merry	Surprised
Astonished	Empowered	Humble	Passionate	Tender
Awed	Energized	Hurt	Peaceful	Thrilled
Calm	Enthusiastic	Impressed	Playful	Unsettled
Cheerful	Expectant	Inspired	Relieved	Upset
Compassionate	Frightened	Irate	Remorseful	Vulnerable
Competitive	Frustrated	Irritated	Scared	Warm
Concerned	Fulfilled	Joyful	Selfish	Yearning
Confident	Furious	Liberated	Sincere	

Expressing emotion guideline #3: Invest passionate purpose into your words and actions

Passionate Purpose

Purpose: To improve dead or boring presentations and meetings

Practice: Here's a powerful process to use when preparing for any presentation:

- Answer the following questions: What is your overarching objective? That is, in what way are you trying to change your audience? It sometimes helps to fill in the following blanks: "When my audience gets up from my presentation, I want them to feel _____ and do_____." For example: To feel inspired to mobilize their divisions around this new change initiative.

- Take a look at your presentation outline, script, or slides. Find the transitions in your presentation. Using a pencil, divide your presentation into sections. For a short presentation, you may just have a few. (As a rule of thumb, it's good to have a change every three minutes or so to reengage your audience—more often if possible.)

- Using the list of passionate purpose verbs on page 151, assign a distinct passionate purpose to each section of your presentation. For example, you may wish to start your presentation by "welcoming" your audience, then "shaking them up," then "enticing" them, etc. Choose words that excite your own passion for your presentation.

- Try giving your presentation out loud or with a trusted colleague or family member. Make sure to vary your energy, speed, voice, and body language to match each passionate purpose. Really try to achieve your overarching goal, using the passionate purposes as tools for having a direct effect on your audience.

Once you deliver the presentation, get some feedback about how it was received. Try to get specific feedback on your vocal and physical presence, as well as the effect you had on your audience.

CHAPTER 7

Expressiveness Using Voice, Body, and Story

There is a vitality, a life force,
an energy, a quickening that is translated
through you into action.
And because there is only one you in all time, this expression is unique.

Martha Graham

THE DAY OF JACK'S PRESENTATION TO HIS FIRM'S ANNUAL MEETING finally arrived. His was the first presentation of the first day. It would set the tone for the whole three-day affair. He had rehearsed several times, including two full dress rehearsals. The only thing he couldn't rehearse was presenting in front of all twenty-two hundred live partners.

The night before, after Jack had finished his rehearsal in the cold and empty hotel ballroom where plenary sessions would be held, we'd encouraged him to spend some time walking around the hall thinking—even saying aloud—"This is my concert hall! This is my space!" It's a common actor's technique. At first Jack was reluctant. "Too many people around," he'd protested.

Though the cavernous ballroom was empty, many technicians and others were finishing the stage and other preparations for the meeting the next morning. With our assurance that they'd seen stranger behavior, he did as we suggested, ending twenty minutes later onstage practically bellowing, "This is my space!"

We smiled at how far this mild-mannered, soft-spoken "Southern boy" had come. Jack's plan was to start at the podium with presidential teleprompters (the kind that let him read text off clear glass screens while appearing to look at the audience) and then move on from there. Starting at the podium, where he'd delivered every other presentation he'd ever made, was a conscious decision. It let him start in a comfortable place. In fact, the whole presentation could be given from the podium, though that wasn't the plan. The plan was to abandon the podium after ten minutes and present in ways completely new for him and his company. The question was, what would he actually do once he stood there in front of all those partners?

He came onstage and, instead of walking to the podium, he stepped to the front of the stage and stood alone, silent. A hush fell over the vast room. "Before I begin," he said, "I have to know something. How many of you had trouble with those high-tech shower faucets the hotel put in? It took me fifteen minutes to figure the darn things out." He raised his hand with a big smile and waited. It was an electric moment because it was risky. What if he was the only person who'd had trouble?

We knew he'd succeeded when the audience responded with a burst of laughter. Slowly, hands began to sprout, until at least half the audience admitted near defeat by a faucet. Jack had known that before he launched into his message he needed to break the ice a little, to connect in a lighthearted way, to perhaps show a little of his own vulnerability or humanity.

Then he went to the podium and began his rehearsed talk, the laughter and good spirits still echoing through the hall.

His twofold goal emerged quickly and clearly. First, going global: *Enormous opportunities await us if we truly go global. And enormous dangers if we refuse or fail.*

He created an overarching metaphor by telling the story of how the railroad system developed in the western United States in the late 1800s and early 1900s. At first there had been a maze of local and regional railroads only haphazardly connected. Then a few pioneers had had the foresight and ability to weld those autonomous units into an interconnected system that met customers' needs far better and improved business for the railroad owners. The analogy with his vision for this international financial services firm was clear.

Now the second part of his message: *Elect me CEO. I'm the guy who can take us global.*

Jack left the podium and went—actually he almost ran, he was so full of energy—into the audience. It was the beginning of his second passionate purpose. He was demonstrating a willingness to move out of his "comfort zone" and to make personal change. Video cameras around the hall projected his image on a huge on-stage screen as he moved around the audience with a wireless mike in his hand.

He interviewed partners—their images flashed on the huge screen—from local offices already taking some of the steps needed to go global. These partners described what they had done and the results they'd gotten. Jack acknowledged their foresight and endorsed them and the steps they'd taken. "You see," he said to the entire group, "we've already begun. We have the expertise. We can do this."

Back onstage, Jack told a story from his boyhood of going to the local YMCA for swimming lessons. He and his classmates stood hesitantly by the side of the pool, as the instructor urged them into the water. Finally, Jack jumped in, and when he did, everyone else followed. It was his first lesson in leadership, he said. "Some of you have already jumped in. Now I'm jumping in. I hope and expect all of you will follow. The water's great!"

Then, the final and perhaps biggest stretch of all, he recited a short speech full of life and energy adapted from Shakespeare's *Tempest*:

> *Be not afeared.*
> *The world is full of enormous opportunities,*
> *Changes and challenges*
> *That give delight and hurt not.*

"I want you all to recite it with me," he called out, as he ran out into the audience again to recite it with them. The words appeared on the onstage screen. All twenty-two hundred partners read them out loud.

"What?!" he called out. "I can't hear you! Do it again!"

All twenty-two hundred of these stolid partners read out the words again.

"That's better!" he said. "Much better. But not good enough. We'll never make it that way. Again!"

He made them read the words five times until all twenty-two hundred people were on their feet bellowing the words with all their hearts. The applause at the end lasted a full five minutes and would have gone longer if Jack himself hadn't ended it.

When he was done, the hall was awake with energy and Jack had accomplished his twofold mission: He'd made clear his global vision for the firm. And, in demonstrating the kind of personal change and risk-taking that vision required, he'd also shown he was the fellow who could take them all where they needed to go.

His presentation ended with a Q and A session with the audience. He handled several questions easily and convincingly. Then, someone said, "Jack, I understand you've been using a personal coach. Is that correct?" The audience caught its breath. The implication was, "Do you need a personal coach because you're weak?" Everyone wondered how he would answer. This is the kind of small but crucial moment that tests a leader.

With a big smile, he said, "That's absolutely correct. In fact, she's right here at the third table. A lot of what you just saw and heard was due to her help." He paused for a moment, then said, "Many of you know I haven't relished giving speeches and presentations all these years. I thought it would be smart to get some help for this one. It's helped me step out of my comfort zone and I recommend it for all of you."

Someone there later commented on "the authenticity of Jack's gesture of telling the truth. This was a real leadership moment, a moment of honesty and openness. It deeply enhanced (Jack's) stature and effectiveness as a leader."

Afterward, a crowd stormed the podium to congratulate Jack. Everyone had seen his past presentations and knew what a leap he'd made to unleash his voice and energy and movement for this one. Many of them said they were ready to follow his lead. At the election a day later, Jack won the top spot by a large margin. Passionate purpose had opened the door for him to communicate in a dynamic, compelling way.

Three rules for Expressiveness

From our experience in the theater and working with scores of executives like Jack, we've identified three Expressiveness rules:

1. Conquer your fear of overexpression.

2. Use your voice and body congruently.

3. Tell stories to unleash your Expressiveness.

Expressiveness rule #1: Conquer your fear of overexpression

It took a lot of work with Jack, but he was able to overcome one of the biggest obstacles we find among businesspeople when it comes to self-presentation: The fear of overexpression.

Most all of us fear being overly expressive, being tagged "flamboyant." In most businesses, that's not a good reputation.

Think of regulating your expressive power as you would turn a dial on your stereo. You probably think of actors as a full ten on that dial, in terms of their expressive power. Think of Robin Williams, who can be so flamboyant and "big" sometimes.

We're not saying you should go all the way to ten—that's for yelling "Look out!" when you see someone in the path of a speeding car. But we suspect you're probably setting your own dial between one and three in your business communication. We're suggesting that a three to seven is a better range. Even one-on-one, when you should turn the dial down a bit, you probably want to be at a three or four. Unless you're in adversarial negotiations, you want to let your emotions read on your face, and in your eyes and body. And when you're in a group you should be going up to a five or six or seven, so that everyone can see what your face and body are communicating.

An actor adjusts her expressiveness dial in the same way when performing onstage versus performing in front of a camera. The stage actor must be much "bigger" with her expressions. She must literally throw them fifty or one hundred feet or more, all the way to the person in the last row. On camera, however, she must work with smaller expressions and gestures because the camera is much closer and more intimate. To use the Expressiveness needed onstage when performing to a camera would seem so over the top and dramatic as to appear phony.

Proper expression requires more than turning the dial up or down. As you move along that leadership spectrum from "responsive" to "assertive," you'll need to become more or less expressive. Generally, the more assertive you need to be, the fuller (not the same as simply louder) your expressiveness needs to be. Thus, captains and conceivers tend to be "bigger" in their Expressiveness than coaches or collaborators.

Steve Chambers, our former television actor-turned-executive vice president, brought to business an adaptable Expressiveness that he attributes to his acting training.

> I was senior marketing executive, and then I was given sales too. For my first meeting with the entire sales group, I thought very hard about what that group needed from me. Salespeople are generals. They dictate. That's what they expect. Without thinking, I would have gone in and done a "Steve Chambers," the way I am in marketing, which is my more natural style—incredibly empathetic, a problem solver, motivating people the way I want to be motivated. But that's not what the salespeople needed or expected. For them I had to be the new sheriff in town. I needed a little edge, a little "prove it to me" attitude. They talk about sales strategy, but there's a lot less strategy in selling than in marketing. They needed to be talked to the way they would talk. So I created a mantra for them—"We close business"—and my voice and face said I meant business.

If you want to become more expressive, to become more assertive, you must be willing to experiment with letting go of habitual patterns and levels of expression—holding your body or using your voice a certain way. You will need to take a leap of faith and experiment with other patterns and levels to see what kind of feedback you get. In fact, don't rely on random comments from others. Enlist the active help of a friend to give you feedback as you try new modes of expression.

It happens over and over in our workshops, when we ask businesspeople to turn up the dial by releasing themselves from some comfortable habit (like hanging onto a podium or speaking softly with a smile all the time). They feel wildly uncomfortable. They're sure they've made fools of themselves. They're amazed when they hear from their workshop colleagues not only that they were perfectly normal, but that they were much more effective.

All we ask here is that you consider giving up your own habits of restraint. If you're like the thousands of businesspeople we've observed, those habits probably haven't served you very well.

Expressiveness rule #2:
Use your voice and body **congruently**

A big problem we find time and again with businesspeople is the problem we saw with Richard at the beginning of Chapter 6. When he spoke to that group of directors, he said he was "tremendously excited," but his voice and body communicated a different message—in fact, it conveyed the exact opposite.

He wasn't congruent.

Congruence

All of us communicate in many ways simultaneously. Your spoken words communicate something. But as you say them, your voice itself—its pitch, tone, and so on—communicates something as well. Your face and body convey messages too. Problems arise when these different means of expression send different messages simultaneously. If you think listeners should pay attention only to what you say, you're asking them to deny the wisdom of eons of human evolution. Survival depends on the ability to "read" the facial expression and body language of others. That probably explains the results of Albert Mehrabian's research into the powerful effect of messages conveyed by face, body, and voice.

The way to communicate most powerfully is to use all these means of expression *congruently*, so they all communicate the same message.

The price of incongruence is loss of credibility. We're convinced it's the reason so many leaders we see come across as insincere and artificial. Their voices say one thing, but their bodies or voices or facial expressions say something else. How can you trust someone who seems to be saying different things at the same time?

Some years ago, the CEO of a struggling major airline made a videotape, shown to all employees, in which he asked for their help in keeping the airline flying. In the video he said, "I want to ask you to help me today. I know this is difficult, but I want to ask you to consider a pay cut." Unfortunately, he made the videotape in what looked like a fairly plush executive office. As he spoke he leaned against a desk with a nervous smile on his face. Even though his words expressed urgency, his casual voice and body seemed to say, "Not a big deal." The employees refused to take a cut and the airline went out of business. We're not saying it was all because of that video, but the CEO certainly didn't help himself with it. That's the negative power of *in*congruence.

Congruence is yet another compelling reason for passionate purpose. If you believe deeply in what you're communicating, and you allow your passion to express itself, it will almost automatically align all your means of expression.

Actors train intensively

Actors practice for years to gain full control over every facet of communication. They learn to create whole characters virtually without speaking a word.

Kenneth Branagh conveys humorously a sense of what actors

go through in their training. He describes a voice class he took at the Royal Academy of Dramatic Arts in England. He had just delivered a speech by Hotspur from *Henry IV*, Part I, for which he'd given Hotspur a stutter—"For he made me m-m-m-mad!"

> *Palmer [the voice teacher] said, "Marvelous, absolutely super, tremendous grasp of that. A couple of reservations."*
>
> *Here it was. The iron fist in the velvet glove.*
>
> *"Horrendously stiff jaw there, Ken. That'll lose you all vocal flexibility if you're not careful. You've got to work on that sibilant 's.' Also those dark 'l's are letting you down badly. Don't want to be just a regional actor, do we? The hollow back really is a problem. It's affecting your rib control and contributing to that annoying sailor's roll you've developed. I think also if you can even out those vowel sounds, you'll do yourself a favour. Can't have kings sounding like peasants, can we?"*

What can you do?

How can someone like you, who has never been trained, learn to use your voice and your body to express what you're saying?

We don't assume you can undertake years of study and practice, but there are some things you *can* do. There are simple techniques you can practice without professional guidance. Besides, simply being aware of certain concepts and possibilities can help you begin to expand your Expressiveness.

Relax (again!) Katharine Hepburn discovered how important learning to relax was early in her career.

> *I lost my voice and would get very hoarse whenever I played a part which was fast and loud. It was agony. . . . I think that I was so excited by life and living and my future that I was simply wound up so tight I didn't—couldn't—relax.*

Relaxation is crucial for being present, for empathy, and now, for self-expression. Recall the airline CEO whose videotape we described a moment ago. His palpable tension forced a nervous smile that undermined his urgent message. That's exactly what nervousness does. It can make the messages you're sending via voice, words, and body seem incongruent and, consequently, insincere.

Before any situation in which you will express yourself, but particularly before such major events as presentations, do the relaxation exercises that you've found work best for you.

Certainly, you should do belly breathing. You should do whatever exercises help you get "out of your head" and "into your body."

As Jack sat just offstage waiting to begin his presentation, we knew he was focusing on his breath and alternately tensing and relaxing parts of his body. We knew what he was doing because we'd coached him to do it; it was part of a prepresentation ritual he'd worked out for himself. But the ritual wasn't obvious to anyone else.

When he went onstage he was "up" and energized, yet relaxed. We could tell by the way he lightly held the microphone. We've seen many presenters who grip it for dear life. And when he moved, he moved fluidly, as he would in his own office.

Variety is the spice of expression In all that follows, variety is a common thread. It used to be said that if you didn't vary your voice, your body, and virtually every aspect of expression in a presentation every six minutes or so, you'd lose your audience to boredom. We suspect it's even less now, maybe a couple of minutes.

Television and movies are edited much faster now; scenes and angles change more quickly. There's something new to see and hear all the time. Because of that, people have come to expect constant variety, and if they don't get it, they tune out. So you must not only use the different modes of expression available with your voice and body, but also vary them frequently.

To provide variety is a gift to your audience. It will satisfy their needs and help you communicate your passionate purpose more effectively.

Marry language to passion Your choice of words matters.

Playwrights and actors don't speak in dull, everyday language. Mark Anthony in Shakespeare's *Julius Caesar* didn't begin his great funeral oration with "Ladies and Gentlemen! May I have your attention?" Instead he said, "Friends! Romans! Countrymen! Lend me your ears!"

As James Earl Jones said,

> *A modern writer may be content to evoke a character's emotion. Shakespeare was never content until he found a character's passion. There is nothing more moving or powerful than the power of the Word when beautiful language is married to deep passion.*

Language that matches the intensity of your passionate purpose will have a double benefit: It will lift *your* energy as you speak it—try saying "Lend me your ears" in a monotone. And the right words will raise the hair on the necks of your audience.

You've surely had that experience. The right words on the right occasion gave you goose bumps. They made you tingle all over. Or cry. Or laugh. Heightened language can do that.

Most all of us lack the ability to write that kind of language ourselves, but there are still some things anyone can do.

- *Find appropriate quotes from great works of literature.* Turn to Shakespeare, Auden, Whitman, Thoreau, Emerson, and other great poets, writers, and playwrights. The Bible, especially the King James version. Other religious texts, such as the Talmud or the Bhagavad Gita. Great political orations—the Gettysburg Address, Churchill's famous World War II speeches ("Blood, toil, sweat, and tears"). The right words in the right order can have a magical effect.

- *Use vivid language, with metaphor and imagery.* Vivid language will generate a stronger response from your audience. Provide vivid detail—the "dusty" road, the "weighty" document—to paint a picture, create an image in the mind's eye of your audience. Use sensory description so people can see, smell, touch, taste, or hear what you're talking about. Use metaphor to make meaning memorable—winning was "sweet" and defeat "painful." Jack clarified his vision for his firm by using the growth of a coherent railway system in the American West as a metaphor.

■ *Speak plainly, clearly, and directly.* Many business leaders fill their speech with abstractions and jargon. Yet without exception the great speakers and actors move us with language plain, direct, concrete, and clear. They make no attempt to impress or confuse. "Lend me your ears!"

■ *Learn from great orators.* The speeches of Martin Luther King, Jr. illustrate these principles.

King was a preacher, and he and his audience had grown up in a rich tradition of biblical oratory. King first emerged as a civil rights leader through the power of his speeches. The seamstress Rosa Parks had refused to move to the back of a bus in Montgomery, Alabama. Her simple refusal had unleashed a protest and a boycott of city buses. King, a relatively unknown young minister then, was named president of the newly formed Montgomery Improvement Association, at the urging of his fellow minister, Ralph Abernathy.

King's first task, with very little time to prepare, was to deliver a major speech to the thousands of blacks participating in the bus boycott. He began by noting that all present were citizens and therefore entitled to certain privileges. He reviewed the series of events leading to the boycott. He recognized Rosa Parks for her integrity. Then King found his pace. He declared it was time for patience to become protest.

And you know, my friends, there comes a time when people get tired of being trampled over by the iron feet of oppression.

The crowd began to reply with loud and positive choral responses.

There comes a time when people get tired of being pushed out of the glittering sunlight of life's July, and left standing amidst the chill of an Alpine November. We are here because we are tired now.

The crowd was with him, rushing forward.

We are not wrong in what we are doing. . . . If we are wrong—the Supreme Court of this nation is wrong. . . . If we are wrong, God Almighty is wrong.

The crowd roared in response.

King's biographer, Taylor Branch, described that moment: "The boycott was on. King would work on his timing but his oratory had just made him forever a public figure. In the few short minutes of his first political address, a power of communion emerged from him that would speak inexorably to strangers who would both love and revile him, like all prophets."

Vocal variety What's the biggest problem you come across when you listen to someone? What drives you crazy? We bet it's someone speaking in a monotone. The speaker just drones on and on. Listeners stop listening.

The voice is an incredible instrument that allows a broad spectrum of expression. You'll probably never achieve the voice skills a trained actor possesses, but even being aware of the potential can help.

We talked to Kenneth Jay, our actor turned financial services executive, about how he uses his voice in business.

When you're speaking at a meeting, there are totally different rhythms and diction choices you make from a one-on-one, which is less formal and totally different. It's different with clients too. My voice tends to be bigger when I'm with clients. It's intuitive. There are word choices that I make when I'm with clients that are very specific. I tend to exaggerate the pitch and musical line of my voice when I am with clients. I modulate enormously. I start and I stop. I change rhythms. These are all ways to get people to notice and plug in. When I am more intimate it gets a little quieter, there are a lot more pauses and there is a lot less inflection.

In case you're tempted to think small changes in the voice don't make a difference, here's a story from Maureen Stapleton.

We'd been running about four months or something [in Plaza Suite], and there was one laugh that was huge. It was built in, it was solid, it was there all the time, and one night I didn't get it. Gone! I was stunned. George C. Scott, who was the leading man, and I tried everything. He tried helping me; I tried every which way but I couldn't get it back. So I called Mike Nichols, our director, and I said, "Mike, I don't know what to do. I've tried everything. I lost the laugh on whatever the line was that's surefire, and I can't get it back. Would you please come and watch and tell me what to do?" So Mike did; he came back after the first act (and) said, "Take the second half of the sentence an octave lower." Okay, that sounds very technical, which it was. The next night I took the last half of the sentence an octave lower, and back came the laugh like gangbusters.

- **Vary your pitch:** You can make your voice high, like a violin, or low, like a cello. In Western culture, a lower pitch usually conveys authority, gravitas, and self-confidence.

- **Vary your volume:** Some people naturally speak more loudly, and others speak more softly. Both can be effective—assuming, obviously, you can be heard—but vary the volume for emphasis.

- **Vary your speed:** Some talk fast. Others talk slowly. Varying your speed can serve to emphasize something important.

- **Add warmth:** People like to hear a warm, rich voice, as opposed to a nasal twang. Think of James Earl Jones' voice; it's both deep and warm. You can find this quality when you yawn and speak at the same time.

- **Use pauses:** Pay attention to effective speakers. You'll notice they're not afraid to make a point and then say nothing for a second or two. It underlines the point and conveys a strong sense of conviction.

When we describe all these features of the voice, they can sound mechanical and even manipulative. But that's not how they're used. Actors learn and practice all these techniques and many more until they become automatic. And that's the point—to make the voice an instrument of marvelous variety that can effortlessly and unconsciously play whatever music your passionate purpose dictates. No actor, when performing, thinks, "Now I'm going to make my voice bigger and warmer." He simply does it because it's right for his character and the situation.

James Earl Jones explained it by telling a story about Ty Cobb.

"You have about forty different ways of sliding," people used to say to Ty Cobb. "How do you decide which way to slide?"

"I don't think about it, I just slide," he answered.

So it is with an actor's voice. You hope you have worked so hard for so long that you don't have to become self-conscious and think about it. You just use it organically, as the instrument of your art.

Body language Next time you're in a public place, like a shopping mall or some large event, watch how people move. See if you can tell anything about them—their mood, physical condition, personality—by the way they move. We bet you can tell a lot. When you're meeting a friend or loved one, you know their frame of mind just by seeing the way they move. They don't have to say a thing.

Michael Cunningham wrote about the way Nicole Kidman used her body (as well as a prosthetic nose) in her Oscar-winning portrayal of Virginia Woolf in the movie based on his book, *The Hours*:

I met Ms. Kidman, talked to her briefly about Woolf, and was asked if I'd like to see her in the Nose, which was the first I'd heard about Ms. Kidman appearing in any nose other than her own. She was escorted to the makeup room, from which she emerged an hour later as another person entirely. Not only was her face unrecognizable, but her stance had changed. She held her head more sternly; she set her shoulders slightly forward, as if trying to conceal the fact that she expected, at any moment, a blow from behind.

There are many ways all of us "speak" with our bodies. By standing erect, head up, you communicate confidence. Your feelings play across your face. You lift your arms, for example, to emphasize a rise in sales. You move around as you speak to a group, approaching the group, entering its space, to emphasize a point and establish a closer bond. You use eye contact to connect with another person.

Take up space It's common to hear someone with presence described as "taking up space," meaning they seem to occupy more space than their simple physical size would warrant. In fact, it has little to do with physical size and more to do with how they think of themselves as they move around the space.

You can try it yourself. First, think of yourself as solidly grounded, connected to the earth, though able to move. Then, think of yourself as literally taking up more physical space than your body actually requires. Imagine you're much larger than you really are. Imagine you're walking through the room with your arms extended wide. Imagine you're a king or queen, someone of enormous authority. Imagine you're in your own home, greeting and welcoming the people around you.

It will help to have visited the room where you'll speak and made yourself comfortable with it. You might even do what Jack did—walk around the empty room, thinking and saying, "This is my space."

All these exercises, and others like them, will give your confidence in your bearing, and that's the secret of taking up space.

Taking space can be overdone, as a funny story by actor-businessman Kenneth Jay illustrates.

I've got a guy who's a transactor, who is very passionate about what he does. All he wants to do is go out there and close deals. We were in a meeting with a tough risk manager and my deal guy got very passionate. He was getting resistance from the risk manager, so he stood up on a chair and said, "It's insane if you don't see my point."

Unfortunately, the risk manager reacted badly to the dealmaker's dramatic gesture. Kenneth had to call a break in the meeting and have a talk with his dealmaker. There may be situations where standing on a chair might help. This wasn't one of them. Use your judgment.

Expressive rule #3:
Tell stories to unleash your Expressiveness

Ever notice what happens when someone tells a story? The speaker's voice, face, and whole body come alive. The audience comes alive too, pulled forward in their seats, each listener eager to hear what happens next. It's a universal response.

Storytelling can help you naturally express yourselves congruently. Stories help you automatically pull together every means of expression and compensate for any lack of formal training in voice and body movement.

At a meeting Kathy once attended in Boston, where the audience was at least 75 percent Republican, the first speaker was a leading Democrat, Senator Edward Kennedy.

I looked around the room as Kennedy began speaking, and the expression on most faces seemed to say, "Oh God, do I have to listen to him one more time?" But Kennedy started his speech with a story and immediately you could feel the energy in the room change. For twenty minutes he told story after story, each with a clear point. He had the audience laughing and rapt at the same time. At the end he received an enthusiastic ovation and left the audience excited and energized. The next speaker was a Republican congressman who opened his talk with a graph and proceeded to show one chart after another and spoke of nothing but dry facts and figures. After a few minutes of that, many attendees began reading their manuals and others went looking for coffee. Some even did the dreaded F-to-F (forehead to Formica). Only a few— clearly diehard Republicans—visibly tried to pay attention. The energy and enthusiasm in the room had completely evaporated. At that moment I knew that storytelling should be at the heart of our work.

Acting and theater come from storytelling. The first actors were bards, storytellers, who began acting out the characters in the stories they were telling. Eventually, different actors played different characters and storytelling evolved into acting.

Stories help you express emotion in two ways:

First, they give you permission to take on roles, speak in the voices of characters, laugh, cry, shout, whisper. Heightened expression is almost expected when you tell a good story.

Second, stories generate emotional responses from your audience. Just as stories let you ham it up a little, they give listeners permission to respond outright. Tears roll down cheeks. Faces get red with anger, eyes light up with delight.

Stories lift both speaker and audience into the realm of full-bodied life and feelings. *They touch both the heart and the head.*

Conceivers and coaches, in particular, will find storytelling a valuable tool. Stories are an ideal means for the conceiver to paint a vivid picture of the future as it can be in the conceiver's vision. A story can bring that vision to life and make it real.

Once, we were working with Gary, a vice president of marketing for a major petroleum company whose charge was to upgrade the convenience stores linked to the company's gas stations. The company brought in an Australian consulting firm, the Sydney Group, which had a lot of expertise in this area. Unfortunately, Gary's team felt it knew the U.S. market better than anyone else and didn't need help, and so it refused to connect with the Australian people. Gary decided he had to get a personal message across. We asked him if there was ever a time in his life when he'd been kept out and ignored. There was and he told that story to his people.

> *My family moved around a lot, and when I was eleven years old we moved to a new town. I loved baseball, and I went to the baseball field where there was always a pickup game and I sat there waiting to be picked for the game. Nobody picked me. I just sat there. The next day I went back and again, nobody picked me. I went back again. They ignored me again, like I didn't exist. I was totally crushed and almost didn't go back the next day, but I did. Finally somebody picked me. You know what? I hit a home run for that team.*
>
> *Well, the Sydney Group is feeling like I did, sitting on that bench, out in the cold. Nobody is using their talent. They know some things we don't know. Why don't we let them hit a home run for us?*

It helped Gary's team take the first step toward accepting the new group.

How Kenneth Jay handled his dealmaker, the one who'd stood up on his chair, is a good example of telling a personal story as a coach. Kenneth called a break in the meeting and took his negotiator aside. But he didn't criticize him because the guy immediately said, "I screwed up. I couldn't help it. I'm not very good at reading these situations." Instead, Kenneth said,

> *It's really hard when you're the one that's happening to, because you feel like you're out of control. What's the first rule of holes? If you find yourself in one, stop digging. It's very difficult to do. I know this because I have a tendency to always want to win an argument, and that's because I have two brothers. Growing up, it was always about competition and getting airtime and never losing an argument. Every night at dinner the three of us and our father had these take-no-prisoners, never-say-die arguments. I still have trouble giving in. So I know when you're in the middle of it, you can't stop digging sometimes. So in the future, keep checking with me, not verbally, just watch me and take your cue from me.*

Kenneth's story about himself and his weakness probably did more to help the negotiator learn than any lecture or admonition could.

Whatever kind of story you tell, the key requirement is that you make it dramatic. You always want the listeners asking, "What happens next?" Get into the story as fast as you can—we call it "vertical takeoff"—by eliminating as many preliminaries as possible. Then build the suspense and don't give away the ending until the end.

Since most stories are told orally, here are some features of effective storytelling that can help your stories come alive.

- *Present tense:* "It's 1982 and I'm standing in front of an angry board of directors." This is more important when telling a story in person than on the printed page, because, when done live, the present tense adds an air of immediacy. Experiment. See if it helps enliven your story.

- *Bullet phrases:* It's better to use punchy, brief, even incomplete sentences. It will help you raise the energy level of your telling, give pace to the story, make it easier for listeners to comprehend, and help you avoid those awful "ah's" and "um's" that can punctuate long spoken sentences.

- *Descriptive/sensory language:* Use words that evoke sounds, sights, tastes, and smells. They help the reader experience the story along with you, and they are words you can highlight with your voice as you speak.

- *Variety in voice, face, and body:* A reminder of what we said earlier—vary the volume and tone of your voice, and let the emotion show on your face and in the way you move and hold your body.

You want to draw your audience into the story. Capture the mood and feeling of what's happening. Don't give the ending away. The question, "What happened next?" is usually what keeps the listener interested.

A colleague of ours once worked with a major maker of massive earthmoving machinery. Its technology was outdated, its manufacturing too costly, and its competitors backed by parent companies with deep pockets. Its stock price had dropped steadily for three years. Once an industry leader, it was struggling to stay alive. The new CEO, whom everyone knew as Buck, called the company's top four hundred managers to St. Louis, its home office, and spoke to them all in a large hotel ballroom.

He began by explaining "the company troubles," which everyone knew about. Then he told them what needed to be done—"a new way of doing business." There was nothing new in what he said; one way or the other they'd all heard it more than once in the previous six months.

Then, something triggered a memory in Buck's mind, and he began to tell a story of the day he joined the company twenty-five years earlier.

It's 1975 and I'm a green M.E. (mechanical engineer). They give me a problem nobody else could fix. They figure I'll break my pick on it too. It's a problem with a critical mechanical linkage on the old Model 472. For six months that machine is my entire life. I'm sure I'm going to fail. I'm gonna be canned. I'm waking up every night at 3 A.M. I'm chewing my fingernails down to stubs. Then one day at a meeting, we start talking about some other damn thing and it's like the solution just walks in and introduces itself. There it is.

When he recalled in that big hotel ballroom how much he had wanted to help the company back then, and how deeply he still cared, Buck's voice broke and he had to stop talking for several moments. Buck was a big, burly metal-bender and that room was full of big, burly metal-benders. According to our colleague, there wasn't a dry eye in the place.

Later, everyone would remember that incident as the moment

something changed. Departments decided to work out their differences. Resistance to new technology began to melt. Management began to see labor as a partner instead of an adversary.

Hard work turned the company around, but that story and the moment of authentic emotion it released was, by all accounts, the bolt of lightning that first energized the process of change.

Buck didn't plan what he did. It happened. Fortunately, he had all the expressive tools needed to communicate what he felt and what he wanted everyone else in that room to feel about the company. He probably hadn't explicitly identified his passionate purpose beforehand, but it was there nonetheless. It was to reveal to everyone there the depths of his feeling for their company and its future. Because his actions came out of something so deeply and genuinely felt, they were real and authentic.

Develop the willingness and the skills to express yourself fully, and when your passionate purpose needs expression, you will be able to communicate it without thinking.

Expressiveness Using Voice, Body, and Story

Expres- siveness rule #1:	Conquer your fear of overexpression

Heightened Language

Purpose:	To spice up dry, technical, or mundane language
Exercise:	In his 1963 "I have a dream" speech, Martin Luther King, Jr. used poetic imagery and the language of metaphor to convey powerful ideas. For example, instead of merely saying "I hope that one day blacks and whites will get along," Dr. King said:

> *I have a dream*
> *that one day on the red hills of Georgia*
> *the sons of former slaves*
> *and the sons of former slave owners*
> *will be able to sit down together*
> *at the table of brotherhood.*

In the same way, you can use heightened language to inspire your audience, to lead them in a call to action. For this exercise, find these three things:

1. A poem that you love

2. A favorite quote

3. A metaphor (such as King's "table of brotherhood")

See if you can include all three of these elements in your next presentation or meeting. Make sure to get feedback afterward. Did they think you were overly poetic or expressive? What was the effect that using more dramatic language had on the audience?

Expres-siveness rule #2:	Use your voice and body congruently

Vocal Variety

Purpose: To break out of the monotone trap

Exercise: We have all had the experience of sitting in a meeting while the speaker is droning on and on (and on and on!) in a monotone. And nothing puts your audience to sleep faster. Here are a couple of exercises to break free from the monotone trap:

■ Practice Bringing a Story to Life. In the last chapter, you practiced expressing emotions by reading a story to a child. This time, take the same story, and practice vocal variety, using the chart on page 184. You can practice by yourself first, and then by reading aloud to a child. Notice the effect of varying pitch, speed, and volume—how does each contribute to raising or lowering the dramatic tension and engaging your audience? How does changing the warmth of your voice affect how the different characters come across? Does the child stop paying attention when you pause, or does a pause create more suspense?

■ Extra Help. If you're having trouble with certain aspects of vocal variety, try these coaching tips:

• Pitch—Go as high and low as you can. You may never go this far in a business presentation, but it's great practice to do it when reading to a child. If you're reading the part of a princess, allow your voice to go up into squeaky falsetto. An evil character can have a low, rumbly, gravelly voice. Practicing this way will open up greater flexibility in your voice. Singing in the shower or in your car can help too.

- Warmth—Yawn! On a big inhalation, open your mouth as wide as you can, stretch the back of your throat, and allow the soft palate (the fleshy rear portion of the roof of your mouth) to expand. This creates maximum space in your mouth and throat. Then, on the out breath, say "Aaaahhhh!" on a big sigh of relief. If you put your hand on your chest while you do this, you'll feel some real vibration. This is called chest resonance. Try speaking words using this voice. Find a story with a dragon, ogre, or monster, and give it this "yawn voice." Then, try toning the effect down, just keeping the feeling of warmth, without the big volume.

- Pauses—We tend to think that pauses are bad, "dead air," and that our audience will think we've lost it. In fact, your audience *needs* pauses to process what you're saying. Experiment with the difference between using lots of short pauses, versus taking a long pause only now and then. Short pauses, which can create a natural feeling, are opportunities for you to breathe, and provide time for your message to sink in. The strategic use of a long pause—particularly in the middle of a sentence—can create real suspense, and even bring your audience back if they've been tuning out.

- Apply Vocal Variety. Now take a business presentation and deliver it with vocal variety. You can do this by yourself, first—you may wish to record your voice and listen to it afterward. See how much variety you can use before it begins to sound like too much. Get a friend to listen and comment. A couple of specifics to focus on:

- Bullets—Notice how using vocal variety can help you vary the sound of items on a list. For example, if you have three bullets on a slide, see what happens if you subtly change the delivery so that the first bullet is slow and low, the second is high and fast, and the third is warm and with pauses. Make sure your vocal choices are congruent with the meaning of your words. The audience will not realize you're doing this—all they'll notice is that you are a more engaging speaker and they'll be much more likely to remember your points.

- Big Picture—Vocal variety can also help differentiate the different parts of your presentation. The contents of one slide can be made to sound different from the next. The beginning of the talk can have a completely different quality from what follows. Experiment—how can you use vocal variety to give your conclusion more dramatic impact and weight?

Vocal Variety

←	What Can Change	→
deep/low bass tenor	Pitch	high alto soprano
soft	Volume	loud
slow	Speed	fast
yawn (chest resonance)	Warmth	nasal twang (face resonance)
many and/or long pauses	Pauses	no pauses

Body Language

Purpose: To improve static presence or address fear of using body and space

Exercises and Practices: Body language is something actors and business leaders know and use fluently. Try these approaches for better understanding and using your body congruently:

- Become Aware. Next time you're in a public place, like a shopping mall or some large event, watch how people move. See if you can tell anything about them—their mood, physical condition, personality—by the way they walk and hold themselves. When you meet a friend or loved one, and have a chance to see them move, try to guess their frame of mind before they say a word.

- Posture. People with presence tend to hold themselves erect. If you slouch and let your shoulders round in, it communicates a lack of confidence. However, correcting bad posture involves more than "standing up straight." To correct years of bad posture may take considerable effort and the help of a teacher or coach. We often recommend Pilates training to get your body strong so it can release your shoulders and help you stand up straighter. Tai chi, martial arts, Alexander Technique, or yoga can help too.

- Facial Expression. Some people prefer a poker face, one that reveals nothing about their state of mind. While we recognize there are some situations when a poker face might be useful, in general you will connect with others better if you allow your face to reveal what you feel. Just as you can mirror someone else's voice, you can mirror their facial expressions. Facial mirroring says, "I understand you." There's nothing more supportive for a public speaker, as we know from our own experience, than to look out at an audience and see facial expressions that say, "We're with you." Try doing this in your next team or one-on-one meeting.

- Gesture. Notice how others use their arms and hands when they talk. Some people, some entire cultures, favor great expression. Others prefer to be more self-contained. There are appropriate times for both approaches, but in general you'll communicate better if you use gestures that are congruent with what you're saying. If you're talking about a rise in sales, lift up an arm. If you're talking about expanding an operation, extend your arms wide. Again, notice what others do, including professional speakers or television personalities, and pay attention to what you think works well.

- Movement. This applies in particular when you're standing and speaking to a group:
  - Use the Space. Walking, especially in combination with pausing, can be a powerful combination. Make an

important point, then pause, and while pausing, move to a different position. Then begin speaking again. (It's usually not a good idea to talk while moving.) If you're telling a story, let the different locations on your stage represent different locations in the story (e.g., home and office) and move to those locations when the story changes scenes.

- Distance. Moving can change the energy level in the room. If you stand far from the audience—at the podium, for example—that's a safe, low-energy place for you in relation to the audience. But if you move toward the audience, you create a more intimate connection. And, if it's physically possible, moving right up to or into the audience will pick up the energy level in the room enormously.

- Wake-up Call. Whenever you enter someone else's space—an individual's or an audience's—you create a moment of high potential, even danger. Will you call on someone? What do you want? What are you going to do? People wake up when the speaker approaches. Be aware of that dynamic and use it to add energy and emphasis to your message.

■ Taking Up Space. Some people seem to take up more space in a room than their physical size alone would justify. These exercises will give increased confidence to your bearing:

- Grounding. Walk around in an empty room. Think of yourself as solidly grounded, with your center of gravity not in your chest but in your pelvis where your legs and hips connect. Think of yourself as solidly connected to the earth.

- Expanding. Then, think of yourself as literally taking up more physical space than your body actually requires. Imagine you're much larger than you really are. Walk through the room with your arms extended wide. Imagine you're a king or queen, someone of enormous authority, because people usually give such figures a lot of space. Imagine you are in your own home, greeting and welcoming the people around you. We know one fellow who imagined he was a general with enormous epaulets extending out from his shoulders.

- *Owning.* Go into the room where you'll speak and make yourself comfortable with it beforehand. You might even do what Jack did—walk around the empty space, thinking and saying, "This is my space." Don't be shy—this technique really works!

∎ Eye Contact. We've saved one of the most important means of body expression for last—the eyes.

- Eye contact when you're expressing yourself is critical—without maintaining eye contact, you risk losing the attention of a listener. It's just as important in a meeting or presentation as in a one-on-one. In our experience, speakers make two major errors. First, they want to include everyone and so their eyes shift much too rapidly around the room. Or even worse, they speak to the back of the room. Second, they focus too much on looking at the materials they're presenting, whether it's a speech in front of them or a slide projected on a screen. In both cases, they haven't used their eyes to connect with the audience. Some antidotes:

  o If the group is fairly small, be sure to establish eye contact for several seconds with each person in the group at least once in the meeting.

  o Throughout your talk, speak to individuals, one at a time, never to some blank spot between people or to the piece of paper in your hand.

  o A good rule is to maintain eye contact with one person for an entire thought. Then move to another person for the next thought. Move from person to person that way, rather than going back to the same person all the time.

  o If the group is large, you cannot literally connect with everyone in the room. Fortunately, you don't need to. The people in the back of the room will feel connected if they see you connecting with audience members near the front. Be sure to divide your time between people on one side and people on the other side.

Congruency

Purpose: To address insincerity, lack of credibility, or lack of trust

Practice: A great tool for noticing congruence versus incongruence is voicemail. By taking the body out of the equation, we can focus specifically on the quality of the voice, and how it matches—or contradicts—the content of the message:

- Become a connoisseur of incoming messages—does the caller's delivery really match the text? Notice how speakers use changes in pitch, volume, tempo, enunciation, and vocal quality, to covey warmth, concern, humor, urgency, etc. Who does it really well? How can you emulate them?

- Listen to your own outgoing message, and critique it for congruence. Then redo it as many times as necessary until it carries just the right tone you wish to convey.

Expres-   Tell stories to unleash your expressiveness
siveness
rule #3:

Storytelling

Purpose: To add dynamism to impersonal, dry, or technical presentations

Exercise: At the end of Chapter 5, we introduced an exercise of cataloguing stories from your life that would help you connect with others. In the same journal, you could also start recording stories that could be used in business presentations. Choose from the following types of stories.

Types of   ■ Personal: "When I was seventeen . . ."
Stories:

　　　　　　　■ Moments that made you who you are or that clarified your values

- Moments when you discovered your voice or leadership potential
- Personal Business: "When I was working at . . ."
  - Heroic moments—difficult but worthwhile struggles or extraordinary feats in business
  - Overcoming resistance to change
  - Learning experiences (moments of truth)
- Impersonal Business: "Jack Welch at GE . . ."
  - Dangerous mistakes in business
  - Stories of how your company has handled these things in past
  - Stories of how future could look: bright or dark
- Universal Myths or Fables: "You know the story of . . ."
  - The Trojan Horse
  - Sisyphus
  - The Tortoise and the Hare

Telling Stories with Drama

Purpose: To connect with your audience and engage them through stories

Practice:
- Review "Tips for Telling Stories with Drama," to follow. Choose three that would make the biggest difference in your storytelling.
- For your next presentation, include a story and apply the three tips you chose.
- Ask a colleague for feedback after your presentation.

Tips for Telling Stories with Drama:
- Reexperience the event. Do not lead up to the real story with a lot of runway time. Instead, begin in the middle of the action and use the present tense. Example: *"It is our second meeting with this client when, suddenly, someone says, 'Why not . . .' "* instead of *"We received a call from client A. We had one meeting that went fine. In our second meeting . . ."*
- Be succinct: Use bullet phrases and fewer "ands" to connect sentences. End each sentence with a verbal

period, a small pause. Example: *"We go through the report, page by page. Bill looks up at me suddenly. He says: 'Jim, we've done it. The work we've put in has finally paid off,' "* instead of *"We go through the report page by page and Bill looks up at me suddenly and says that we'd done it and the work we'd put in had finally paid off."*

- Use sensory images and descriptive language: Sensory images (*"marble conference table"* instead of *"conference table,"* *"ten-pound computer printout"* instead of *"computer printout"*) help people visualize the story. The above examples appeal to the sense of vision and touch (weight). You can also appeal to the senses of smell, hearing, and taste. Make sure to be selective with your use of images. One or two key images should be sufficient and will leave room for the listener to actively participate by contributing detail.

- Have a clear beginning, middle, and end: Tell the story from a "point of innocence," as if you don't know how it will end. Keep the listener waiting for the outcome. Example: *"We worked with a client whose costs of production were not competitive. We did X, Y, and Z. As a result, they were able to reduce costs by thirty percent,"* instead of *"We helped a client reduce costs by thirty percent. Here's how we did it. . . ."*

- Use vocal and physical variety: Whenever you have a different character in the story, use a different vocal tone and physical posture. If there is action in the story use gestures and deliberate movement to express that action. For example, if your *"costs have skyrocketed,"* let your hand move upward through space to illustrate your point.

SELF-KNOWING

The ability to accept yourself, to be
authentic, and to reflect your values in
your decisions and actions

Introduction to Act IV

This above all: To thine own self be true, and it must follow, as the night the day, thou canst not then be false to any man.

William Shakespeare, *Hamlet*

WE ALWAYS BEGIN OUR WORKSHOPS BY ASKING MANAGERS AND LEADERS what benefit they want from greater Leadership Presence.

We get many answers, but we hear one in particular over and over.

"I want to be more inspiring."

We hear this so often we've come to recognize it as a universal desire among those who lead others.

When we ask what it means, we hear that leaders want to go beyond "motivating." To motivate means to get others to do what you want, and that's important.

But people don't tell us they want to be "more motivating." They want to be more inspiring, and that's a different thing.

The literal meaning of inspire is "to breathe life into." In the story of Genesis, it is what God did to Adam and Eve when he created them in the Garden of Eden. It's come to have related but broader connotations, such as to "arouse" someone else, particularly to arouse something animating inside them, or to "enliven." But all the meanings come back to the notion of infusing others with life and energy and passion.

So inspiration goes far beyond motivation. We think of it this way: If "motivate" means to get others to do the *right* things, then "inspire" means to help others do *great* things.

Every leader should aspire to inspire.

P, R, and E aren't enough

It took us at The Ariel Group years of experience and learning to understand that inspiration—the ability to breathe life and purpose into others—is the ultimate promise and purpose of Leadership Presence.

When we began our work more than a decade ago, we focused on what are now the Being Present, Reaching Out, and Expressiveness elements of the PRES model. It was clear in our minds how important those actions and skills were for leaders, if they wanted to develop the kind of Leadership Presence that would make them more effective. But as we worked with hundreds and eventually thousands of leaders we gradually realized something was still missing, even when P, R, and E were in place. Leaders who were present, reached out, and were expressive often still lacked the kind of Leadership Presence—the ability to connect authentically with the hearts and minds of others in pursuit of some common goal—we were hoping to foster.

What they lacked, we finally realized, was that ability to be inspiring.

Fortunately, we now and then came across exceptions—leaders who could and did inspire others, both in our workshops and the workplace. We began to pay particular attention to them and what they did.

Self-knowing is the final ingredient of Leadership Presence

In our workshops we conducted exercises in which we asked participants to reflect on their experience and tell stories about themselves. We encouraged storytelling as a good way for leaders to reveal themselves, be authentic, and connect with others.

But after listening to hundreds of stories, we realized the most engaging and compelling—the most inspiring, in fact—were those in which a leader told of learning from personal experience. Most inspiring of all were stories of overcoming difficult challenges, even failure. In these stories leaders spoke of how an experience had shaped them. These compelling and inspiring stories were about the lessons the storyteller had learned about life and work.

We discovered that reflecting on experience and then telling stories not only helped a leader reveal herself and connect emotionally with an audience, they also helped her understand and then express those values, beliefs, and principles most important to her. Something about the experiences related and the lessons learned instilled in others a desire to ask more of themselves.

Inspiring leaders were those, we concluded, who knew themselves, who had distilled from their experiences lessons and principles that they felt deeply and intensely and which they could communicate to others. As a result, they seemed fully authentic: They seemed totally themselves, completely at ease with who they were, comfortable in their own skins.

The name we gave this quality was *Self-knowing*, which of course became the S in the PRES model. It was the missing ingredient of Leadership Presence.

When we put the whole model together, we realized that those leaders who were most inspirational could communicate who they were by using all the skills of Being Present, Reaching Out, and Expressing themselves fully. To the P, R, and E elements, they were bringing the S, their knowledge of themselves and what was important to them. In doing that, they truly were integrating seamlessly all the pieces into one totality, and that was Leadership Presence.

Acting and Self-knowing

Self-knowing is a theme that runs deep in acting. It is crucial if an actor is to find the heart of a character and inspire us with her portrayal. To bring authentic elements of herself to a role, the actor must know herself well enough to know which elements are and are not appropriate for that character. For each role there are parts of herself that simply won't apply.

That's the difference between a great actor and some Hollywood personality actors, who always seem to be playing themselves—because they bring all of themselves to every role. A great actor can portray a truly different character in every role because he understands the differences between the character he's playing and himself, and that understanding comes only from Self-knowing.

Self-knowing is a major part of most actor training programs. In many programs students spend the first segment, up to a full school year, focusing on it. In some programs, for example, every student is required to keep a journal for the first year, and every quarter a professor grades each student on what she's written in it.

Acting students begin to learn what Susan Sarandon, who won an Oscar for *Dead Man Walking*, said of her craft:

> *Acting forces me to be aware. . . . Just in terms of trying to work on yourself to stay an open, aware person who's trying to go towards some kind of humanity, it's an enforced work program.*

Self-knowing continues well beyond the formal training of young actors. It is the foundation of virtually every role an actor plays. Indeed, actors often view the roles they play as opportunities for self-exploration. As Laura Dern, who was nominated for an Academy Award for *Rambling Rose*, said:

> *I think every character I've played is someone who is trying to define herself for the first time. . . . I love exploring that part of myself—that place that feels so vulnerable—with all the people I've been lucky enough to play. The female characters I've played have to come to terms with their own identity and find their truest selves, as opposed to the sort of self that's been created for them or that they've created. That really fascinates me.*

Our experience as actors training and coaching executives led us to an important realization. *Just as actors can learn to be Self-*

knowing and can then bring that knowledge to their work, we discovered Self-knowing was a skill that leaders could develop and use as well. And when they used it in combination with Being Present, Reaching Out, and Expressiveness, they could achieve inspiring Leadership Presence.

Leaders stand for something

Eleanor Roosevelt, wife of President Franklin Roosevelt, consistently emerged from public opinion polls as the most esteemed American woman of the mid-twentieth century, and one of the most highly regarded and inspirational women in the world. Though born into a world of extraordinary privilege, she was admired by people of all races and classes. One columnist called her "the most influential woman of our times."

Two features stand out in her life: first, how comfortable she appeared to be with herself and, second, how clear and outspoken she was about her values and principles. This clarity was especially striking because many of her beliefs were not widely shared by society of the time. According to Howard Gardner, the Harvard psychologist who selected her as one of the subjects in his book *Leading Minds*, she "particularly cared about the dispossessed, the marginal, and the unentitled—blacks, inhabitants of the third world, young people, Jews, women."

She did more than speak. When the Daughters of the American Revolution refused in 1939 to let Marian Anderson, the black contralto, sing in Philadelphia's Constitution Hall because of her race, Roosevelt publicly resigned from that then-august organization. It was a step that might today seem little more than politically correct, but then it required great courage and created considerable comment.

Our experience with Ariel Group clients highlighted the crucial and inspirational role of values and authenticity in Leadership Presence.

Values are simply what you consider most important in life, as revealed not only by your claims and statements but also, especially, by your decisions and deeds. When we ask people "What are your values?" they sometimes have difficulty answering. But no one has trouble with the questions, "What's important to you?" or "What are you passionate about?" They're all the same thing.

Values, or guiding principles and beliefs, can range from the highest ethical and moral aspirations—for freedom and equality and justice, for example—to such basic requirements as safety and comfort. Values can be psychological states, such as closeness and community, or needs, like the desire to win or excel.

Every time you make a choice—when buying something in a store or deciding to take a new job or asking someone to be your spouse—you're reflecting your values, what's important to you.

So, in fact, all of us have dozens of values, if not more. But when we speak of values here we mean the few that are absolutely core to you, the ones around which you construct your life and make large, life-shaping decisions.

The reason values are critical is that they define you. To know you, to follow you, someone must know what's important to you. That's why values reside at the heart of Self-knowing and thus of Leadership Presence.

Without knowing a leader's values, those in the leader's group have no way of knowing or predicting what he or she will do. Without a clear set of values, clearly expressed and lived, a leader can only ask others to follow blindly, something most people rightly hesitate to do.

Authenticity—the hallmark of Self-knowing

Values, however, reside in the context of something broader. They are a central component of authenticity, and authenticity is the defining characteristic of a Self-knowing leader. "Authentic" is the word the world uses to describe someone who is Self-knowing.

- A Self-knowing leader accepts himself, including his limitations. The world sees him as secure and fully comfortable with himself; he never tries to be someone or something he's not.

- A Self-knowing leader possesses clear, explicit values, principles, and beliefs. An authentic leader speaks and lives these values congruently; there is no difference between what the authentic leader believes, says, and does.

- A Self-knowing leader connects personally with her work. It is an important expression of who she is and what's important to her. The authentic leader speaks of this connection between self and work and inspires others to create similar links. In this way she creates meaning for herself and those she leads by casting the work they all do in a context higher and richer than personal gain or goals.

Authenticity is crucial to leadership, for leaders cannot lead, cannot inspire others, without trust, and leaders create trust by being fully themselves, authentic, in the ways we just described.

All of us can be inspiring as leaders. Most of us won't have a public persona like Eleanor Roosevelt's. And most of us are unlikely to face a crisis in which we're asked to condone or support racial prejudice. But we will have to face different situations where remaining ourselves, fully authentic, will be difficult, and holding true to who we are and what we believe will make us inspiring to the people who work for us.

CHAPTER 8

Self-Knowing, Self-Reflection, and Explicit Values

"Know thyself," was the inscription over the Oracle at Delphi. And it is still the most difficult task any of us faces. But until you truly know yourself, strengths and weaknesses, know what you want to do and why you want to do it, you cannot succeed in any but the most superficial sense of the word. The leader never lies to himself. . . .

Warren Bennis, *On Becoming a Leader*

JOHN PERKINS FOUNDED A COMPANY CALLED INDEPENDENT POWER Systems (IPS) in the early 1980s. Its purpose was to build electric power plants that were environmentally friendly. In practical terms that meant plants that could burn coal without producing acid rain. Though many other companies were formed at the time for the same purpose, IPS was, in the end, the only company to succeed in demonstrating that such plants made economic sense.

Finding investors for IPS and then leading it to success required many arduous years for Perkins. As the other companies failed, he persisted, even against the advice of his own investors and colleagues. Why did he persevere and ultimately succeed?

Perkins told us he had grown up in two worlds. His father, a man of modest means, taught at a small private school in pastoral New England. One world was that of the wealthy students he knew there; it was a world that valued material success. The other was the world of rural New England, which fascinated him with its Native American history, culture, and values. He explored that world further in the Peace Corps after college when he worked with native cultures in South America. From this experience he developed a strong sense of the need for sustainable economic development. Following the Peace Corps he went to work for a Boston-based international consulting firm.

> *We traveled all over the world and what we did was look at what would happen to the economy, let's say of Indonesia, if the World Bank invested a billion dollars there. What would be the results if they put that money into a harbor, as opposed to the utility grid, as opposed to a highway into the jungle?*

Excelling at this work, Perkins became the youngest partner in the firm. Yet his success troubled him. He came to believe the large projects he helped develop around the world did not, in fact, foster sustainable development. He believed the burden of debt placed on the countries reduced the resources they could devote to the health and education of their people. He agonized over what to do for a long time.

It was important to him that he was a fifth great-nephew of Thomas Paine, the American revolutionary who wrote the famous words that roused American colonists: "These are times that try men's souls. The summer soldier and the sunshine patriot will, in this crisis, shrink from the service of their country. . . ."

> *I went back to Tom Paine [said Perkins], and I kept thinking, what the hell would Tom Paine do in a situation like this? It was pretty clear to me. Tom Paine would be opposed to what I was doing.*

After years of soul-searching, Perkins finally decided to leave the consulting company. He became an independent consultant. One day he realized that new technology was on the verge of producing electricity in ways both economical and environmentally friendly. That was when he founded Independent Power Systems, and eventually found a way of reducing pollution from coal-fired power plants.

In one of those instances of poetic justice, Perkins did well by doing good. He eventually sold his company, making his investors a sevenfold return on their money. Because his company's success demonstrated the feasibility of a better approach, Congress passed laws forbidding power companies from building new plants that burned coal in a way that produced acid rain.

The answer to our original question—why did Perkins persevere?—now seems clear. *Values.* The importance he attached to sustainable development, which the native cultures he'd studied expressed as "thinking seven generations" into the future, allowed him to keep going when all others gave up. IPS expressed a deep belief Perkins had struggled a long time to clarify and was unwilling to compromise.

Leaders need explicit values

Everyone has values. Perhaps you think of them as the principles or beliefs that guide you. Values are nothing more than your sense of what's important to you. You use them every day to make choices large and small. You may not be able to express your values or principles explicitly, because they often operate just below the level of conscious thought, but they're still there. Only when you face a particularly tough choice might you expressly think about what you "really want"—that is, your values.

For leaders, however, we've found that's not enough. Leaders need explicit values. Individual contributors have values but it's less important for them to express their values clearly and explicitly. More is required of leaders, for these reasons:

1. Followers want to know. They constantly scrutinize their leaders' words and actions, to figure out how the leaders think and what they want.

2. Leaders must go beyond simply making sure work gets done. That's what supervisors and managers do, while leaders motivate and inspire and energize. Explicit values

play an important role in the critical process of moving people beyond the simple accomplishment of the task at hand.

3. And finally, as leaders take charge of larger and larger groups of people, they can no longer rely on their actions alone to express what they believe and want. They need to start speaking their values in clear, unmistakable terms.

The benefits of explicit values

Explicit values provide several benefits for leaders, which the well-known case of poisoned Tylenol capsules can illuminate.

In 1982 seven people died from taking cyanide-filled capsules found in bottles of Tylenol. As best anyone could ever tell, the deadly capsules had been added to only a few bottles after they had left the hands of Johnson & Johnson, Tylenol's maker. Public trust in the safety of the best-selling painkiller evaporated overnight. It was a crisis—the makings of a complete disaster for the company—because Tylenol was such a significant portion of J & J's sales and profits.

Nothing like this had ever happened before. What the company should do was far from clear. Johnson & Johnson might simply have hunkered down in a defensive posture of "not our fault" and waited for the storm to blow over.

That's not what the company did. Led by its head, James Burke, Johnson & Johnson responded quickly and proactively. Burke believed in "putting the public first." He was convinced the continued success of Tylenol hinged on public trust and confidence. He also believed in playing things absolutely straight, in being honest and candid.

J & J removed the entire stock of Tylenol from store shelves throughout the country and accepted returns from customers, taking back a total of 31 million bottles at an overall cost of more than $100 million. Because it acted so swiftly and decisively, Tylenol regained 95 percent of its dominant market share within three months following the recall and enhanced its reputation for purity and trustworthiness.

Given the outcome, the company's response seemed obvious. But the right response—the one Burke chose—was far from clear in the heat of battle. When Burke appeared on *60 Minutes* to defend J & J in the midst of the crisis, it was against the advice of his head of public relations, who angrily told him his decision to appear was the worst decision a company executive had ever made. In fact, Burke said afterward, "Only one person here supported what I was doing."

It was ultimately Burke's explicit values—putting the public first and playing it straight and honest—that were instrumental in saving Tylenol.

Having clear, explicit values can help you make better decisions in hard situations. They can help you make difficult decisions in less time than you otherwise would need. And basing decisions on values—what you deeply believe to be important—can help you make decisions with greater confidence and peace of mind.

Clear, explicit values may help you make the right decision, but they don't necessarily make hard decisions easy. Being profitable was certainly one of Burke's values too, and giving up $100 million was not easy to do. Yet it almost certainly was the right decision. Most dilemmas don't require choosing between good and evil. Those decisions are usually easy. They require instead a choice between good and good, between one value and another—in Tylenol's case, between profits and the long-term good of the brand.

Look for values in your life stories

In our work over ten years with leaders, we've found an effective way to identify values explicitly. We discovered that personal stories were not only an effective way to communicate better, but they were also a powerful tool that could help leaders identify the basic principles and beliefs most important to them.

The stories we heard were often of challenges leaders had faced and mastered—the failed project, the lost job, the strained relationship with a child, an illness—that allowed them to connect with what they truly stood for and what was most important to them. The lesson we learned from this experience was simple: The way to define or clarify your own values is by reflecting on your own experience, the choices you've made, the difficulties you've faced and overcome.

In our experience, business leaders often hesitate to spend time in self-reflection. It doesn't seem productive to them, and they fear it won't accomplish anything directly. But as we gave leaders in our workshops the opportunity to reflect on and talk about their life-shaping experiences, they began to understand the fundamental importance of self-reflection. It is the road to Self-knowing—and ultimately inspiring Leadership Presence.

One of the key exercises we use with clients and in workshops is the River of Life. It embodies a powerful, intuitive metaphor—the idea that the present flows out of the past and that understanding the past can help you understand the present and prepare for the future. In the River of Life exercise, you identify the pivotal experiences, both affirming and challenging, that have led you to be the person you are now. Then, you pair off and describe them to a partner.

A participant in a workshop, Arthur, told the following story:

When I was a teenager, my brother and I started to fight all the time and I didn't know how to deal with it. Our parents were no help. We were constantly at each other's throats. His anger at me was preventing me from doing what I wanted to do. So I cut him out of my life and didn't speak to him or deal with him until I got out of college.

Arthur and his brother finally reconciled. The painful, years-long estrangement taught Arthur a powerful lesson: the value of working through conflict and not allowing it to poison an important relationship. As a leader that lesson has led him to institute in his organization a clear process for dealing with conflict. He has people trained in conflict resolution and he constantly asks people to express conflicting points of view.

In the River of Life, after you describe to a partner the important milestones in your life, your partner responds by saying what he or she heard as your strengths and values. This part of the exercise can provide great insight, because others are often able to see in you what you cannot see in yourself.

Rosalie managed a back-office department for a large bank. She attended one of our workshops and participated in the River of Life exercise. After reflecting on the major events, decisions, and people that made her who she was, she and a partner exchanged stories.

Rosalie described how her father had abandoned her and her mother when she was very young and how she and her mother had struggled to survive. Her mother had toiled through an endless succession of menial jobs, and they had moved from apartment to apartment, never settling anywhere. When Rosalie finished, her partner said, "So what's most important to you is stability. You'll do almost anything to keep your life and the world around you stable."

It was a revelation to Rosalie. As soon as she heard the word "stability," she knew that was what she valued most. But until that moment she'd never identified this value so simply and explicitly.

It was the beginning of freedom to change. Having that insight was like opening a door in a wall, which until then had blocked her ability to do or be anything different.

She realized she had chosen to work in her organization—the back office of a bank where important transactions were recorded and processed—because it valued stability almost as highly as she did. That was good. It helped explain why she did her work so well and found it satisfying. Not so good, she realized, was that her need for stability could often make her rigid and unwilling to accept anything new—like some changes the bank's IT department had wanted to make in her operation. Her need for stability also drove her to place unreasonable demands on employees, colleagues, and friends. Now she could begin to understand the tension that sometimes existed between her and others. She didn't want to change and she didn't want others to change either. Rosalie left the workshop determined to explore how this one value, stability, had both enriched and limited her life. She said:

> I've always been ambitious too, and I've never felt my job used all my talents. But I've always been afraid a higher position would be more chaotic and I'd have less control. So I've never tried for something more, and that's frustrating for me.

Knowing herself and understanding her need for stability has given her freedom to make more thoughtful decisions and to make tradeoffs among her conflicting values. Rosalie's epiphany demonstrates the power of self-reflection and of sharing the fruit of that reflection with others. Each of us is largely defined by what we consider important. We cannot know ourselves, or make ourselves known to others, until we understand our own values through some form of self-reflection. When we know ourselves, we can begin to make positive, practical changes in our work lives.

Acting and self-reflection

Like a leader, an actor must dig deeply into her own life experience to bring meaning and authenticity to a character she's playing. As Hume Cronyn, Tony Award winner of the Lifetime Achievement Award, said:

> If an actor isn't constantly aware from the time he's very young, he will not build up a bank of experience . . . on which he can draw later. From that point of view, going inward is terribly important.

Kathy's experience preparing for her first role after she completed actor training illustrates one approach actors take.

I played Laura in The Glass Menagerie. *To prepare for that I started keeping my own journal in the voice of Laura. Every day I would write in her voice, about her life, what she felt. Then I would spend some time writing a few pages in my voice about the differences between the way I would approach a situation and the way she would. In order to do that, I had to know myself. At the same time, the process of working on that role and keeping that in-depth journal was a step in the continuing process of Self-knowing for me.*

Every actor has his own approach. Anthony Hopkins, renowned stage and film actor, best known for his Oscar-award–winning role in *Silence of the Lambs*, likes to take long drives through the American West. We know from our own experience that the big sky and vast, open landscape can create a state of mind in which ideas, thoughts, and memories bubble up without conscious effort. Connections are made, insights revealed, that no amount of logical thought could produce.

Each performance offers an actor the opportunity to think about how she will choose to portray her character. It's common for actors to solicit notes and comments from fellow cast members and the director, to make sure their portrayals align with the text, their characters, other actors, the director's conception, and the feelings and expectations of the audience. It's a way of reflecting on their performance. Leaders can seek out similar kinds of commentary.

Understanding your values will allow these core beliefs to shine through in your words and actions as a leader, just as they shine through in a credible and powerful acting performance.

Guidelines for making values explicit

Based on our experience helping leaders identify what's most important to them, we've developed three guidelines that can help you make your own values more explicit.

1. Pursue some regular process of self-reflection.

2. Write down your personal leadership values.

3. Speak your leadership values.

Explicit values guideline #1:
Pursue some regular process of self-reflection

Most people, we've observed, reflect on life and experience only when a dilemma forces them to make a choice. It's not something they do regularly. That's why self-reflective leaders often employ some device, process, or conscious, specific way of reviewing their experience and learning from it. They don't wait for a crisis.

In addition to our exercises, such as River of Life, we often suggest these conscious steps: Think about your heroes and heroines, notice what inspires you in them. Think about your strengths and how others view them. Think about your emerging strengths, the things you're working on improving. We also suggest leaders think symbolically. What symbolizes your aspirations? Are you a knight on horseback who charges in and solves problems? Are you a wise grandfather in a rocking chair who's more a listener than a problem-solver?

Over time, you will discover what works best for you. Nigel Morris, president and COO of Capital One, the eighteen thousand-employee credit card bank, mentions two simple but effective approaches he uses.

On the way in to work in the morning, I am much more focused on the tasks I have to do. Voicemail. Call this person. Do this transaction. But on the way home, I reflect much more on things like—How did I show up as a human being today? Did I show up as Attila the Hun, brutalizing people, or did I show up decent and caring about the organization? You might get a voicemail from me after that, which says, "You know what, I might have been a bit abrupt with you today, but let me tell you what I really care about. . . . Why don't you give that a bit of thought and let's get back together."

Morris is also an inveterate note-taker. He writes in a hardbound journal he carries with him throughout his day. Periodically he goes back and reviews notes taken earlier.

I looked back at my notes a year ago and realized just how piti-fully naïve I was. So, one year from now, I will look at what I am doing now, and I will say, "Gosh, you were so naïve, Nigel." I think that if I continue to believe I was naïve twelve months ago, I'm probably learning.

Another approach many use is to get away regularly—a change of physical perspective often prompts self-reflection. Many of us have had real insights about work when cruising on a sailboat, or relaxing in a mountain cabin.

Yet another approach is consciously choosing a role model to emulate. That person may be someone in your life whom you ad-mire. It may be a historical figure you know only through reading and research. Reflecting on such people can enrich your examina-tion of yourself and your experience.

When she was a partner at Boston Consulting Group, one of the leading international strategic consulting firms, Barbara Berke made a habit of reflecting about others and learning from them.

When taking on a new challenge, I think about what I value in people who have faced similar situations. One of the things I learned from John Clarkeson, BCG's CEO for twelve years, was that giving many people platforms for leadership has the power-ful effect of releasing tremendous energy and commitment from multiple points across a far-flung and diverse organization. I was fortunate to know John well enough to have some insight into what he did and how he did it. I've learned a lot from my part-ners and have always tried to bring that learning into how I ap-proach my work. I'm always trying to tap into and learn from other people's value systems.

Explicit values guideline #2:
Write down your personal leadership values

To make the most of what they learn from self-reflection, we encourage leaders to write down the values they've uncovered in a leadership values statement. What we do here comes from our work with leadership credos began with Professor Michael Fenlon at Columbia Business School and the Columbia Senior Executives Program (CSEP). Mike's definition of the credo includes three parts: who I am as a leader, where we're going, including strategic priorities, and the shared beliefs and behaviors required to get there . . . expressed in a way that engages the hearts and minds of others. In this book, we focus on "who I am as a leader." These are the beliefs you will take from job to job and organization to organization. They are the bedrock of your Self-knowing.

Writing down your values is important because all of us can make the mistake of assuming something clear to us is equally clear to others. You may think your actions speak for themselves, but that's always a dangerous assumption to make. Writing out your leadership values will make speaking them far simpler. It will make what you say more consistent over time, and help you choose language that touches and engages others.

A simple two-step process

Writing your leadership values statement is a simple two-step process that flows out of the reflective practices we've already described. Based on self-reflection, you should:

1. Identify the three to five values, principles or beliefs most important to you as a leader. These might include such values as "keeping my commitments" or "developing people's capabilities" or "integrity and honesty."

2. For each of these core values, recall a story that defines and illustrates that value for you. The story is very im-

portant because it shows the value in practice and grounds it in tangible reality. Write out a simple version of the story for each value.

John G., a division manager for a telecommunications company, wrote this for his value of work-life balance:

My first son was born on a Wednesday. I had planned to take the following week off to help bring him home. The following Monday, I got a call at home telling me I had to come in to the office for the kickoff of one of the biggest projects in the company's history. Wanting to continue to be successful and do my best, I went.

We proceeded to work six to seven days a week for the next six months. When I did get home, my son was always asleep. I missed him very much, but believed this was a great opportunity and it would be better for all of us in the end.

At the "conclusion" of the project, we had a team celebration.

We were told, "Thank you all for your hard work. You should be very proud of yourselves. But there's much yet to be done and we can't slow down now."

I thought to myself, "What did I do? I just missed the first six months of my son's life and now we're expected to continue like this. Sure, he'll never remember, but what about when he gets older? Kids need you in their time, not yours. Is this really the way I want to live?"

So I juggle. I juggle many balls. I juggle my job, my friends, my family, and my other commitments.

If I drop my friends, I will apologize. They will understand.

If I drop my job, I can find another one.

If I drop my commitments, I can make up for it.

But I cannot drop my family, because that ball is made of glass. It is the most fragile and, if ever shattered, would be impossible to repair.

Geoff Nicholson, a financial manager for Telstra, a large Australian telecommunications company, drew one of his leadership values from his experience as a serious runner. It was his way of capturing his value of making a difference, always striving and competing, but in a constructive rather than destructive way.

Let's run hard, learn from each other, and test ourselves to the limit.

Herb Elliott, who won the fifteen-thousand meter gold medal at the 1960 Olympics, said, "I ran at first to remorselessly beat everyone I possibly could." He said that because his coach, Percy Wells Cerutty, drove into him a hatred of opponents, a secret, lonely training schedule, and an overpowering sense of destiny to win. Percy preached this message for success in sport and in life.

As a young boy I soaked up the Gospel preached by Percy Wells Cerutty. For years I told myself about my Destiny. But for years I struggled. I was consumed by my failure to achieve my Destiny. I found I could not hate with passion. And I struggled to enjoy something I loved, running.

Then I met and trained with Ron Clarke and his mates. Clarke at one stage held every world record from two miles to twenty-five thousand meters. His philosophy was radically different, and ridiculed by Cerutty. . . . However his philosophy was one of enjoying the running, sharing training ideas with mates, and having fun testing one another in races. Sure, he was intensely competitive in the races. But he also saw them just as tests, just as benchmarks of the greater game, another way of enjoying running. . . .

I contrasted the philosophies of Cerutty and Clarke. Clarke's made more sense to me. As I grew and each time I looked at some new challenge it was very appealing to recognize it as part of the game, just another test, another benchmark to measure progress.

Now I love to take on lots of challenges. The more, the better. Challenges and accomplishments are my life. One can't achieve without always striving ahead and failing, striving ahead again and failing.

These values statements communicate not only the values themselves but also, through the stories, the conviction of the speakers. By itself, the bare statement of a leadership value can seem bland or commonplace. The purpose of stories is to bring the statement to life.

Your values don't have to be new, fresh, different, or innovative. They do have to be what you believe deeply, what matters passionately to you. As you write each down, ask yourself: Do you believe in it heart and soul? Do you, will you, truly live your life as a leader around it? Can you say it and live it authentically? Your level of commitment to your values, not their originality, is what counts.

Explicit values guideline #3: Speak your leadership values

We encourage leaders we coach to find settings and situations in which they can appropriately express their values clearly and explicitly. A setting may be a group meeting, large or small, an orientation for new employees, a meeting with a new team, or a one-on-one meeting with a new team member.

Some situations virtually cry out for values to be expressed, such as gatherings where key decisions are made or thorny issues discussed, coaching sessions, annual meetings, off-sites, and planning sessions. These are all occasions when it's both appropriate and useful to speak aloud what you consider most important, as an individual and as an organization.

Perhaps you're reluctant to repeat your values. You think you've told everyone and there's no need to say again what you believe. What's that old saying? You have to tell people something five times before they even begin to hear you.

Be sure to tell stories that embody your values. Like John G., who talked about juggling the many parts of his life, tell stories of where your values came from, the formative experiences that shaped your passion and commitment to a core principle or belief.

As Noel Tichy, the leadership expert, has said:

It's critical that leaders condense their own career experience into those magical moments of personal transition—moments when something major happened to them and a major learning evolved from it. Such career (or life) transition points are teachable moments. Leaders need only extract the wisdom from such experiences, and pass it along.

Stories work so well because they engage the heart *and* the mind, and because they help people make changes in their behavior. They do this in the simplest, clearest way possible—by *demonstrating* the right behavior. They show rather than tell, and that's a key source of their power.

In fact, don't limit yourself to one story per value, simply because that's the minimum we've suggested for your leadership values statement. Find more. Look for stories in the people and day-to-day work of your group that illustrate your leadership values. Find them anywhere you can.

John Clarkeson, former CEO of Boston Consulting Group, often told the story of crew chief Wagner Dodge and a group of fifteen "smokejumpers" during a Montana forest fire in 1949.

Dodge and his men parachuted into a place called Mann Gulch to get ahead of the fire. Suddenly the wind picked up, and the fire jumped a river. It came at them so fast they couldn't outrun it. Dodge had an idea. If they lit a little fire and let it burn ahead of them, then they could lie down in the burned area left by their fire and let the main fire burn around them. Dodge lit the fire and jumped into the burned patch, motioning his men to follow him. But his men ignored him and ran up the gulch. A wet towel wrapped around his head, his body pressed to the charred ground, Dodge survived the flames that passed over him only seconds later. All but two of his men died.

Clarkeson used to tell the story to make a simple point. If you're the leader and you're right, but nobody follows you, you're a failure. You can't succeed without the trust and confidence of your people. They won't follow if you haven't established credibility with them. And you can do that only by revealing yourself to them—who you are and what you believe—so they can learn to trust and respect you before the crisis occurs. Establishing that trust and credibility, so crucial to becoming an inspiring leader, requires you as leader to be clear and outspoken about what you believe. But that's only a crucial first step. Our experience tells us inspiring leadership requires both explicit values *and* values lived.

In the next chapter we'll look at the critical importance of expressing your values in action. Then we'll set leadership values, principles, and beliefs in a broader context. We'll look at how values form a key element of what every leader with Leadership Presence must have—that elusive but crucial quality known as authenticity.

Self-Knowing, Self-Reflection, and Explicit Values

Explicit values guideline #1:	Pursue some regular process of self-reflection

Life as a Journey: Discovering Values through Self-Reflection

Purpose:	To get clear on one's values or purpose

Exercise:	Leaders making a difference in the worlds of business and politics consistently take the time to reflect on themselves, their lives, and those core values that make them who they are. One of the most powerful approaches we know to taking this inward journey is a process we call the *River of Life*.

Creating Your River:	■ Find a quiet time and space to work where you won't be interrupted for at least twenty minutes. *Tip: Although this can be done with normal paper and pen, we recommend using a large sheet of flipchart paper and some colored markers. You can spread out on the floor, or tape your paper to the wall.*
	■ Before you begin, take a moment to relax, breathe, and be present. Imagine that you are on retreat, and have all the time in the world.
	■ Draw a river on the piece of paper winding from the lower left corner to the upper right corner. Label the lower left "Birth" and the upper right "The Present." *Tip: Get creative! Break the rules! When you draw your river, let its shape and features represent what's special about your life. We've seen swamps, bridges, waterfalls, forked rivers, circular rivers, etc. Don't strive for artistic perfection—improvise and surprise yourself.*

- Cast your mind back over your life. Draw islands in the river, each representing places you've lived, key people you've known or who've influenced you, and any other "landmarks" along the river of your life (e.g., key companies, projects, etc.). *Tip: Have fun with this—use different colors, symbols, etc.*

- Along each side of the river, add tributaries representing challenging and affirming moments from your life. Think of those events, decisions, choices, and turning points that taught you something, that made a lasting impact on who you are. *Tip: Draw affirming tributaries in green on the left side of the river, and challenging ones in red on the right side. Write a key word or symbol to remind you what each one represents.*

- Take a few minutes to look back over your river, adding any missing details. Make sure the river really captures every aspect of your life: family, work, spirituality, other life pursuits.

Exploring Your River:

- Note Your insights. In your journal, write about what insights you have while looking back over your river:
  - What patterns or trends do you notice?
  - What experiences and people were especially significant?
  - How do you relate these to how your values have formed over time? Make a list of your core personal and leadership values.
  - How would you relate what you see in your river to the approach you take as a leader?

- Advanced River Work. Attach another piece of paper above the first, and extend your river into the future:
  - What do you envision happening, in your own life, your family, your organization, and on the planet?
  - What key choices or decisions lie ahead? Where would you like to be in five or ten years?
  - What would change in your future if you could consistently live your leadership values? What would change in your organization if those values were expressed and lived by others?

Rituals of Self-Reflection

Purpose: To proactively create time to reflect

Practice: Instead of waiting for a crisis, self-knowing leaders regularly and systematically review their experience, distilling what there is to learn. In addition to the River of Life, we recommend using one or more of these approaches on a regular basis:

- Take Notes. Keep a journal of your thoughts and feelings, particularly for insights regarding your own behavior, challenges you are facing, and how you see your path of growth and learning.

- Retreat. Get away regularly—a change of physical perspective often prompts self-reflection, particularly in moments of quiet, amidst the beauty of nature. Even a mindful stroll around a local pond or park can prompt deep insight.

- Study Others. Consciously choose a role model to emulate—someone in your life whom you admire, or a historical figure. Reflecting on other people and what makes them successful (or what limits them) can enrich your examination of yourself and your own experience.

- Clear the Mind. When the mind is still, like a clear pool, we can better see our own reflection. Find a ritual that works for you. Yoga, tai chi, meditation, breathing and relaxation exercises (see Chapter 2), and physical exercise such as walking or jogging are all ways to calm and center the mind for deeper self-reflection.

Explicit values guideline #2:   Write down your personal leadership values

Compose Your Leadership Values Statement

Purpose: To get clear about what you stand for or what's important to you

Exercise: Find a quiet place where you won't be interrupted, and free write in your journal on the following themes. Do not strive for perfection. Feel free to improvise, make mistakes, and surprise yourself:

- "Who I Am." What are the beliefs, principles, and values you believe are essential for effective leadership?

  - Start by brainstorming, and then narrow the list down to three or four key values you feel express your own deepest truth about who you want to be.

  - For each of those items, jot down a key event or story from your life that illustrates that principle or value—how you learned it, what happened when you did not apply it, or how it led to success—in a personal or business situation. (For source material, have your River of Life handy.)

  - Everything you've written is the raw material for your leadership values statement. Let it sit for a while—wait a week or so. Then go back and read it once again, underlining those parts you feel are most vital, that speak to your passion for leadership and the success of your organization.

- Writing Your Values Statement. Imagine you are addressing an audience or team within your organization. Drawing from what you underlined above, create a rough outline of your leadership values statement. Remember that your goal is to engage their hearts as well as their minds. For this outline, limit yourself to enough material for a five-minute presentation. You will need to be selective!

Here is one possible structure of a leadership values statement we have found useful. Do not limit yourself to this—let your creativity and passion inform your writing:

1. Context. "As we kick off this new project, I wanted to welcome you to the team and give you a broader picture of why we are here. . . ."
2. Values. "There are three values/principles that I am operat-

ing from in my role as the leader of this group: A, B, and C. . . ."

3. **Story.** "Let me share a personal story. The year is 1992. I am coaching a soccer team in my local community. . . ."

4. **Teaching Point/Business Message.** "This story illustrates an underlying issue that is facing us in our work over the next six months on this project with Company X. . . ."

5. **Conclusion.** "Therefore, these three values/principles will be important to us: A, B, and C."

Explicit values guideline #3:	Speak your leadership values

Deliver Your Leadership Values Statement

Purpose: To create clarity and inspire those you lead

Practice: In order to speak your leadership values as you live them, "in a way that engages the hearts and minds of others," it is crucial to pick the right time and setting. We encourage leaders we coach to find settings and situations in which they can appropriately express their values. These are occasions when it's both appropriate and useful to speak about what you consider most important, as an individual and as an organization.

- Pick one of the following settings to deliver your leadership values statement:
  - An orientation for new employees
  - A meeting with a new team
  - A one-on-one meeting with a new team member
  - An annual meeting
  - A meeting where key decisions are made or thorny issues discussed
  - A coaching session

- A team off-site or planning session
- Or any group meeting, large or small

∎ The first time out, keep your leadership values statement succinct—five to seven minutes is ideal. Make sure to include at least two or three personal stories to illustrate your points, and don't forget to tie your discussion of values to a concrete business message.

∎ Do a "dress rehearsal" beforehand, getting feedback from one or two trusted colleagues. Also, make sure to get feedback from select members of the audience afterward, to help you continue to fine-tune your leadership values statement and your delivery.

CHAPTER 9

Self-Knowing and Authenticity

(Acting is) about using your own life and bringing what's appropriate and applicable and correct for the character. To find that, that's the trick. To find the fullest place, where you can bring the truth of your character and the truth of yourself so that there are no seams.

Joel Grey, Tony- and Oscar-winning star of *Cabaret*

REMEMBER JOHN KAVANAGH? HE WAS THE YOUNG ANGLO-IRISHMAN who developed real stage presence in standup comedy before going to work for the American oil company Phillips Petroleum in 1965. In Chapter 5 we told the story of John's speaking at Christmastime to Phillips employees in Belgium in their own language, Flemish—something no previous company leader had ever done.

After joining Phillips, John rose through the ranks and, ten years later in 1975, was sent to Bristol, in the United Kingdom, to run a manufacturing subsidiary there. It was comprised of two factories, one producing carbon black and the other producing housing bricks. The brick factory, called Severn Valley Bricks, was losing money hand over fist, and John's job was to turn the operation around.

The general manager who ran the brick company came from the well-educated upper classes. Aloof and unapproachable, he ran the company from a suite of attractive offices in a country village miles from the grubby industrial complex where the brick factory was located. He occasionally drove to the factory in his late model company Jaguar. His contact with employees mostly consisted of weekly walks through the factory when he ranted about laziness and inefficiency.

The first thing this fellow said when John arrived on the scene was, "Oh, you must be the chap the Yanks have sent to sack us." When John first met the union leaders who represented the working-class factory employees, they said, "Oh, you must be the bloke the Yanks have sent to sack us." Everyone feared Phillips was going to shut down the business.

John did close the comfortable offices in the distant village. He moved management and sales, including his own office, into a cramped space hastily constructed on the factory grounds. He took away fancy company cars and gave everyone, including himself, the same Ford sedan. Shortly after, when the general manager quit, John took on the job of running the brick company himself. He worked closely with the sales staff and put in place an aggressive sales compensation plan with lots of incentives.

John took to walking the factory floor and outdoor brick-storage yard daily. He talked casually to the workers, alternately telling jokes and asking their opinions about manufacturing issues and their work. Soon he identified a bright production foreman and promoted him to management with the mandate of improving production efficiency and product quality.

Changes began to appear. Productivity improved. Faults per thousand bricks dropped dramatically. Morale improved. Without being told, factory workers began wearing the green company overalls, with the company logo on the breast pocket. And the stacks of bricks previously strewn about the storage yard were now stacked in laser-straight rows. Sales and production volume rose too.

One hot Friday afternoon, at the end of a month in which the company shipped one million bricks out the gate for the first time ever, John called the entire company to the cafeteria.

As everyone waited, he backed his car up to the cafeteria door and opened the car trunk to reveal a keg of beer, from which he personally drew pints for all present. He toasted everyone and made a simple speech thanking and congratulating them for their achievements.

He then did something else no company executive had ever done. He drew a simple graph on a blackboard that showed their current revenue, the revenue they needed to break even, and the revenue needed to satisfy the parent company. He then translated this into number of quality bricks shipped per month. It was a challenging number but an achievable one. Now, finally, the employees knew what they needed to do and felt able and inspired to take some control over their own destiny.

John led this turnaround, not by dramatically changing the work conditions at Severn Valley Bricks, but by treating people differently, based on two values in particular: First, he believed people deserved dignity and respect regardless of background or breeding. The former general manager would just say, "Work harder and we'll do better." He revealed who he was and what he stood for, which was fairness—"We're all in the same boat"—and that made a difference. John didn't put the burden on the workers' backs.

Second, he believed people should succeed based on merit, and he believed merit could be found anywhere, even in the lowest-paid worker. He valued the knowledge and opinions of those doing the work. He promoted the best of them to positions responsible for improving performance. He believed reward should be earned rather than inherited. He was someone who'd risen up from poverty and was going to show them they had the same opportunity.

John, to our knowledge, never wrote down a formal statement of what he believed. But he was a brilliant storyteller and engaging conversationalist. In his many casual talks with workers at all levels he expressed what he believed in one way or another. If you could have followed him around as he connected with employees through his working day you would surely have heard clear statements of what he believed and valued.

Most important, his actions reflected his values and revealed who he was. There was a deep connection between his work and his values. He remained true to his own working-class origins, which we're told he never forgot through a long and successful career in which he rose to head all of Europe and Africa for Phillips Petroleum.

Authenticity, leadership, and acting

We like the story of John Kavanagh. It's the story of someone from working-class Liverpool who honed his presence as a standup comedian and went on to the top tier of a great international company. Values—his beliefs and principles—were an important part of his leadership, but they were part of something greater. John had a quality hard to define but easy to recognize. He was authentic.

Authenticity was the key to his success as a leader and the context that made his values so powerful. He came across as genuine. He was a "what you see is what you get" person. He would often talk about business around the dinner table with his wife and family, who would marvel at how he seemed to know, almost organically, what to do and say, no matter what the situation. In spite of his background and lack of college education, he was still able to mix with captains and kings as well as the workers on the factory floor. He would return from business trips and regale his family with stories of meeting heads of major corporations and several times the heads of state.

Often he took his wife, Joan, on these trips. She said, "It was hard for me. I'd get nervous before we would meet powerful people." He would always tell her, "Be yourself. Don't try to be something you're not. People can tell. Be yourself and you'll be fine." That was the message he always gave her.

From this core of authenticity, based on his values and his strong sense of who he was, John did more than motivate his workers. He inspired them to do what they'd not been able to do before.

We've often talked about Leadership Presence as the ability to connect *authentically* with the hearts and minds of others. We've talked about how to connect. Now we want to talk about how to connect authentically, because what we have found in our experience working with leaders is that merely connecting is not enough. What's important is that you create a connection in a coherent way between who you really are and the people who work for you.

People feel you're authentic when they know what you're about and they see that you act in ways congruent with what you say about yourself. People feel you're authentic when you're able to admit your mistakes in context. People feel you're authentic when you don't pretend to be someone you're not.

Too many business leaders try to behave in ways they think their role demands, rather than authentically being themselves based on their values. They come across as inauthentic and therefore not to be trusted.

As Rob Galford and Anne Siebold Drapeau say in their book, *The Trusted Leader*:

> *If you are to be trusted about matters of strategy, staffing, marketing, mentoring and so forth, you must first be able to understand what your natural tendencies are. . . . You must first be comfortable in your own skin. And you must also be able to share your understanding of yourself with others so that their expectations will be in line with your delivery.*
>
> *Above all else, trusted leadership means not faking it.*

Ironically, to play a fiction truthfully, actors must be real and authentic. According to Lindsay Crouse, who was nominated for an Oscar for *Places in the Heart*:

> *People think I practice telling lies all day, until I'm so good at it that you can't tell the difference. But that's exactly what acting is not. . . . (It's) the struggle to bring out the truth of your being, the fullest dimension of yourself. Acting is not pretending, but being, having the craft and the courage to let the truth of the moment filter through you.*

Great actors, the ones who convince us of the authenticity of the characters they play, are committed to the truth of a role and the reality of the play. To achieve that authenticity, they must bring their life experience to whatever role they're playing.

That's the parallel with leaders. Leaders need to bring their life experience and themselves as people to their roles as leaders. Just as an actor needs to connect with the character played, a leader needs to connect her work with her own life in ways that reach beyond sales and profits.

So leaders can learn from actors about revealing who they really are, including their "shadow" sides, those parts of themselves they're less comfortable with and prefer to keep hidden. Actors are often challenged to look at and accept their shadow sides, in order to play characters with those same characteristics authentically. That's a crucial element of authenticity, an ability to recognize and acknowledge shortcomings. The benefits of authenticity for a leader are trust and credibility.

Three rules for authenticity

We've found that some people are authentic naturally. They simply know themselves and act authentically. But most people we've worked with must do some work to understand themselves, as we described in the last chapter, so they can know what makes them tick, be clear about their values, and acknowledge candidly their own shortcomings. One of the hallmarks of authentic people is that they're willing to learn from difficult challenges. The leaders who get in trouble are often the ones in denial about their own limitations. As we've learned more about authenticity, we've distilled that understanding into three simple rules for authenticity, which we use with executives we coach. We believe the behavior in these rules is what distinguishes those leaders with genuine Leadership Presence. The rules are:

1. Accept yourself and be open to growth.

2. Live your values.

3. Connect authentically with your work.

Authenticity rule #1:
Accept yourself and be open to growth

We've noticed that self-knowing leaders, in spite of their acknowledged shortcomings, seem entirely comfortable with themselves. While they recognize their limitations and work to improve them, they also accept them, and work with and around them, as part of their natures. While they're always trying to grow, they're not trying to be someone or something they're fundamentally not.

Nigel Morris of Capital One said this about himself:

> *When I'm upset about something, it's pretty clear that I'm upset about it. I think it's okay to be upset so long as I make sure nobody walks out of a conversation with me feeling somehow I've personalized it, or subjected them to my own negative feelings. I have to make sure those feelings don't end up in anger or any kind of brusqueness. That's something I have really worked hard on in the last ten years. But I am an emotional guy. I actually don't want to change that. That's an important part of my makeup.*

In working with executives, we've found that leadership styles can provide a convenient way to think about your own preferences, approaches, and limitations. At this point, you have some sense of which leadership role you prefer to play in most situations: captain, conceiver, coach, or collaborator. You probably also know which role you find hardest to play, the one you seldom or never use.

Has that knowledge of yourself changed you? Knowing your limitations can help you develop the skills you need to overcome them. If you're a natural captain and find coaching difficult, but you recognize the importance of coaching, you can work to develop coaching skills. That's something we encourage, because the most effective leaders are those who can play a variety of leadership roles, as circumstances require, though they may prefer one role more than others.

But overcoming your limitations isn't the only response. For a leadership role that makes you uncomfortable, developing the appropriate skills may be difficult. In that case, your best response might be to accept your limitations and find someone else to play the role instead.

Actors are constantly made to face their own limitations, and to work through them. For example, every audition leads to failure for all but one of the actors who try out. The best actors accept who they are and work with that. Actor Christopher Reeve said:

> As an actor, you use as much of your personality as you can, and where it's not appropriate, you have to get rid of it. Certain things that you do, you just know are not right for the character. You're generally not going to be given something that is hideously wrong. Donny Osmond is not going to play Othello. He just knows it is not a smart thing to do. You've got to have a realistic sense of who you are and what you can do.

In his autobiography, *My American Journey,* Colin Powell, a career soldier and currently the U.S. secretary of state, doesn't claim every leader must play every role equally well. The leader only needs to know himself accurately and make sure the necessary roles are all present:

> In every successful military organization, and I suspect in all successful enterprises, different styles of leadership have to be present. If the man at the top does not exhibit all these qualities, then those around him have to supplement. If the top man has his vision and vision only, he requires a whip hand to enforce his ideas. If the organization has a visionary and a whip hand, it needs a "chaplain" to soften the relentless demands of the others.

In order to accept yourself and accept making mistakes it's helpful to view life as a never-ending journey of personal transformation.

This frame of mind opens you up to accept commentary about

yourself and your performance, including criticism. Instead of being defensive and frozen, you are freed by this point of view to make changes in yourself.

Christopher Walken has appeared onstage and in many movies, including *Catch Me If You Can*. On one occasion, after playing Macbeth and getting badly panned, he said:

> *I never regretted doing [Macbeth] for a minute, because I came away from the production with this tremendous insight about myself and about acting that I could not possibly have gotten anywhere else. It was taking on that monster and being trounced by it, but still learning something. . . . Failure teaches you that you never get anywhere being careful.*

The prospect of continuous learning is often so attractive that it's what motivates those who've already achieved success. Nigel Morris at Capital One said:

> *At this point in life, why do I do this? Why do I put my body through sixty-five to seventy hours a week under a lot of pressure? I think it's because I believe that I am growing and learning and that's what this is all about now. To be able to go on a journey with the people that you really care about and really respect, who are open-minded and share the same beliefs and goals. To be willing to challenge things that you believed in only a year ago. I think that's what gets me up in the morning now.*

When we saw in our workshops how much some leaders had learned from challenging times, and how inspiring it was to hear them talk about those times, we began encouraging *all* the executives we work with to focus on the difficult passages in their lives.

See difficult times not as failures but as opportunities for learning. Shift your thinking about an experience from "It was terrible" to "What did I learn from this?"

Making just that simple change in attitude can make an enormous difference in your ability to learn from experience.

We don't mean to make this kind of self-reflection sound easy or painless. It's often not. Listen to Madeleine Homan, the actress-turned-executive and coach we met whose acting background helped her remain calm and grounded when she was verbally attacked on live television. She commented on the moment in her career when she learned to take critical feedback.

> [It was] a moment in acting class with Larry Moss. The whole notion in acting class is that you come in, bare your soul, and then get critiqued. I would come in super-prepared and expect to be perfect, and I never was, of course, the whole point is to always get better, but it would kill me. Larry said to me, "You take criticism or feedback of any kind so personally that you become paralyzed. You need to deal with that." I was twenty-four and I had to learn how to psychically kill who I was and re-create someone who was more capable. It was incredibly painful and I'm glad that I did it when I was in my twenties because I see people [she coaches executives] who are trying to do it (later in their lives) and it's just like pulling teeth. They are trying to kill themselves as they know themselves today. It's like they need to be able to shed a skin because who they are needs to become bigger. Leaders who can't take critical feedback and use it are no good to anyone.

As you examine your experience, you are learning about yourself and that is different from other forms of learning. Gib Akin at the University of Virginia interviewed sixty managers about their learning experiences. He found their descriptions "surprisingly congruous," and he wrote,

> Learning is experienced as a personal transformation. A person does not gather learnings as possessions but rather becomes a new person. . . . To learn is not to have, it is to be.

Or, to say it another way, to learn about yourself is to *become* someone new. That's actually what developing Leadership Presence is all about. It can be painful, and most of all exciting, because it's a journey of growth and transformation and not merely the acquisition of new skills and techniques.

Authenticity rule #2:
Live your values

In our workshops when leaders are writing out their leadership values statements, we ask them to think over the major programs and problems sitting on their desks at work. Look for opportunities, we say, in that ongoing, daily work to apply your values. Begin a practice of regularly reviewing your work in this way. Think of the decisions you'll be making soon. Do your values offer any guidance? Think back over recent decisions. If you had already developed an explicit set of leadership values, would you have made different decisions, or implemented them differently?

You want to find actions that make your values visible. For instance, if you value open communication, if you value forthrightness, then you might create a quarterly meeting of your team where you ask people to speak their minds candidly. If you value creative thinking, you might institute very open brainstorming sessions at the start of every project. If you value teamwork, then you might review your compensation system and look for any disparity between rewards for individual performance and rewards for team performance. If you value work-life balance, are you offering flextime?

When he was CEO of the Boston Consulting Group, John Clarkeson was widely acknowledged by his people as a leader who valued and demonstrated integrity. Early in his tenure, he got a call from a fellow who was running a high-tech job fair. "Some of your consultants are here doing competitive research," this fellow told Clarkeson, "but they didn't say that's why they're here. I kicked them out, and I want you to know I think what they did was unethical."

After hearing the fellow out, Clarkeson apologized for the upset that was caused. He said he would get to the bottom of it.

The consultants were working on a project for a large metropolitan newspaper concerned that the number of high-tech job ads it ran was beginning to fall off. The newspaper wanted to understand what was happening in the job marketplace and hired BCG to find out.

As the BCG project team planned its research, it occurred to team members that going to a job fair and talking to representatives of all the firms there would be a brilliant way to gather information. The team members who went were new to the firm and some were summer interns, students between their first and second years of business school.

They went to the fair—which arguably competed with newspaper classified ads as a way for companies to find new employees—and were able to sign in as though they were job applicants without actually saying anything untruthful. Once inside the fair, the BCG people were completely forthright as they talked to representatives from several high-tech companies about the state of the job market. It was because of their forthrightness, in fact, that word of what they were doing soon got back to the fair organizers, who kicked them out and called John.

Clarkeson took the opportunity to make a point about integrity and honesty, two values important to him and BCG. He wanted to make certain things clear. Consultants were encouraged to be creative in everything they did for the client, but even that value could not supersede honesty and integrity. There was never a valid reason for a BCG representative to misrepresent herself.

Clarkeson chose to make this ethical misstep very public; he had a case written about what had happened without identifying the consultants individually and it was discussed throughout the company, especially in training and orientation sessions for new consultants.

The case, Clarkeson said,

> . . . *allowed me to do two things. Young people who do the case are going to get the lesson very quickly and say, "Wow, okay, that's a good lesson. I can make mistakes. Entrepreneurism is rewarded and encouraged, but we do have to be careful." Secondly, it's a reminder to the senior people that these are very talented*

but inexperienced people. It's your responsibility to provide the guardrail.

What gave the case extra punch was the odd circumstance that this particular client was Clarkeson's—he was the lead partner—and so, though he was not directly responsible for running the project itself, it was his responsibility.

"I think," said Clarkeson, "a lot of people really felt that, 'Gosh, he's exposing his own dirty linen.' " That had some impact too.

This incident occurred early in Clarkeson's tenure as CEO and it helped to communicate the high value he and the firm placed on integrity, a value that years later would still be recalled by his colleagues as a hallmark of his leadership.

Are your actions aligned with your values?

After a rehearsal, an actor typically receives not only director's notes but also checks in with other actors to clear up any problems and makes sure everyone is on the same page. This is similar to 360-degree feedback in the corporate world—and is analogous to the kind of rigor that can be brought to checking in with others to see if they feel your actions align with your values.

We suggest leaders take two related steps regularly, to make sure their actions are congruent with the values they espouse:

- Ask others in some formal, disciplined way if they perceive you as someone who lives your values. In fact, we often suggest leaders undertake a 360-degree review, conducted by a third party, that includes questions about consistency between the values they claim and the values reflected in their actions.

- Second, every time you talk about your values, ask people to tell you whenever your actions don't live up to what you've said. Ask for ongoing, real-time feedback. You may have to ask many times before anyone will tell you. People will need to trust that you don't shoot the messenger.

If you discover that people think there's a gap between your words and actions try to understand what's causing the gap and develop a simple but conscious action plan for closing it.

Bob Garland, national managing partner of assurance and advisory services, at the big accounting firm Deloitte & Touche, believes every leader must work hard to understand how people actually hear the message he is sending. For example, if people snicker when the leader says, "I believe in treating people fairly," that's a reaction the leader must try to understand.

One way to minimize the risk of making a big mistake is to create an environment where people understand that dissent is permitted and encouraged, and honest, critical feedback is sought. One technique Deloitte uses is to hire an outside company to get confidential feedback on how the firm is viewed by its people. It may take a couple of years of no repercussions for those brave souls who speak the truth, before people in general realize it's safe to be candid. Once you've earned people's trust, you'll get to hear what they really think.

In situations where some distrust already exists, Garland suggests gathering people in small groups and saying to them, "I heard this. What are you hearing that other people think?" Some people may be afraid to say what they think and choose to disguise it as what they hear from other people. You'll more likely get what's really on their minds. There must be some vehicle, Garland says, for honest feedback. "We all do stupid things and we all need pushback."

John Clarkeson at BCG had his own way of getting pushback. He believed it wasn't enough to ask people, and he didn't want to wait until after making a decision to find out that some people saw a disconnection between the decision and his or the firm's values. He tried to make sure, before making any important decision, that all viewpoints were heard. In fact, he became known for seeking out people who would articulate "every negative argument." He particularly valued a couple of BCG executives who argued "either on instinct or just because they liked to argue the dark side, the negative side."

He would let an argument go on, often longer than others liked, because, he said:

> It's when you get kind of frustrated, that's when somebody bursts out and says, "Yeah, but you know what I really hate? I really hate the way we do X!" How do you inject values into any discussion? It's creating conditions in which you can listen to other people's emotional instinctual reactions. People's values are partly logic and partly emotional. Making a checklist isn't going to do it.

It was only after going through this kind of arduous process that he felt confident of a decision and felt people would fully support it.

Problems when words and actions don't match

Imagine the results if John Kavanagh had talked instead of acted. What if he had come into Severn Valley Bricks and spoken— expressed explicitly in memos and presentations—the values he held, but without the action steps he took?

What if he kept the offices in the pleasant village far away, and the fancy company cars? Suppose he hadn't gotten to know the workers, or promoted some of them. Imagine he didn't show up and toast the workers for shipping a million bricks, or make clear what was needed and expected of them.

Of course, if he'd not done any of those things, the workers probably wouldn't have shipped the million bricks and John wouldn't have had occasion to make his toast. But that's the point. Actions always speak louder than words. Words unsupported by actions will likely get you nowhere. Indeed, they'll probably do you harm.

Remember President Richard Nixon, who took office in 1969 espousing "law and order?" It was impossible for anyone to take him seriously as the Watergate affair revealed the unlawful acts of his own administration.

The penalty for incongruence between espoused and lived values is more than mere disbelief. The leader is branded as dishonest and hypocritical—in a word, inauthentic. Once people perceive he is failing to live up to his own expressed values, he will lose the trust and credibility needed to lead effectively. Nixon had to resign for exactly that reason.

Authenticity rule #3:
Create an authentic connection to work

Leaders need to connect their values, their interior life, to the work they do, in order to be most authentic and inspiring to others in that work, just as an actor has to find an authentic connection to his character.

For example, here's how actor Simon Callow connected with his own interior life as he approached his role in *A Room with a View*:

> *I played the Reverend Beebe, who seemed to exude benevolence in the script. I asked myself what it might mean to be a priest. I have a Catholic background and earlier in my life wanted to become a priest myself, so I'm moved, as many people are, by the thought of a goodly priest. . . . I tried to dwell in Beebe's character, to submit to his ideas and his impression of the world. I asked myself what the sensation was of my own benevolence and endeavored to amplify it. I drive these inquiries to quite an extreme, so that I'm not just getting a glimpse of a character but a bucketful!*

Like actors, leaders must find an authentic connection to the work they do, so they can inspire others in that work. The culture at Boston Consulting Group stresses thorough evaluation within the organization. Through 360-degree feedback, all employees learn how they're thought of in the firm. Through this system of extensive and systematic feedback, partner Barbara Berke was recognized as a role model for her contribution to the firm and her commitment to BCG's values, particularly, learning and development.

What about her led to this distinction?

When Barbara managed consulting engagements in the seventies and eighties to help Midwestern automakers compete with the Japanese, it wasn't just about bottom-line profits for her. It was also about her personal passion for the creation of opportunity through individual enterprise and for the prosperity that this work created.

These are values revealed in her story of growing up in Cleveland:

> My father used to take us down to the flats, an industrial river valley full of bends and bridges. When the ore boats were coming down the river to unload at the steel mills, one by one the whistles would sound and the heavy iron bridges would be raised as the boats passed underneath. Farther up the river, we would watch them pour ingot in open-walled factories as the sun set. There's nothing like it. I love industrial businesses and I love the scene. I also saw what happened to the city as Ohio steel became uncompetitive and the work left. There is something deeply rooted in me about people who create value, who take raw materials and make something out of them. I have enormous respect for industry and enterprise and what they create for people.

For Barbara, then, her work was a way of pursuing something important to her personally. As it did for John Kavanagh's work, hers satisfied a deep belief. For John, it was helping people realize their potential regardless of their backgrounds. For Barbara, it was helping people and companies create value for themselves and their communities through hard work and enterprise.

Later in her career at BCG, Barbara reduced the time she spent traveling because of her need to care for young children and an aging parent at home. She became the BCG partner in charge of worldwide training and development. In this new role she was still able to find a connection between her work and an important personal value.

She told this story about her childhood in Cleveland:

> I used to take art lessons at the Cleveland Museum of Art. I was scared to go. I was an incredibly shy kid. I loved art, but I was really

afraid of going to those classes. My dad was invariably late pick-
ing me up and I would be left standing alone at the museum en-
trance wondering if anyone was ever going to come and get me.
Every Saturday morning, I would be doubled over with stomach
cramps until my mother gave me this advice, "There is always
somebody who needs more help than you. You'll always feel bet-
ter if you find someone else to look after." So, I did. I always
found that one other little kid weeping in the corner. To this day,
in tough situations, I overcome my fears and worries by thinking
first about what other people need.

The story reveals Barbara's deep belief in not only helping others but also in personal growth and transformation. This belief
came from winning her battle with shyness. It's a value she lives.
One coworker said of her, "She is . . . visibly committed to helping
people develop to their full potential," and another commented,
"Barbara's energy, warmth, and interest in *me* as a person really
made a big difference in my motivation and professional development." Her ability to articulate her values in a personal way
through words and actions gave her great credibility and authenticity. Barbara continues to be inspired by the values she grew up
with in her new role as the member of Governor Romney's cabi-
net responsible for business, technology, and economic development in Massachusetts.

When a leader has an authentic connection with work, then
work becomes more than a way to pay the rent or improve company profits. If the leader is inspired by her work and shares that
with others, it will inspire others to find their personal passion as
well.

Capital One and the 9/11 telethon

If people truly believe your talk about values and see you walk
your talk, what they hear and see will have a power all its own
that allows the organization to grow and do great things. Authen-

ticity and living values can result in astounding organizational performance.

Here's a story of how an organization inspired by leaders' authenticity and values rescued a very important and very visible event.

Most of us remember the telethon, *America—A Tribute to Heroes,* that raised millions of dollars for the victims of 9/11. It began as the idea of a few Hollywood producers and snowballed into a two-hour live production involving Tom Hanks, Julia Roberts, Tom Cruise, and dozens of other stars, broadcast over every television and radio network in the land.

What most people don't know is that four days before the telethon the company handling the call center operations backed out. The millions of anticipated calls were too big a job for it to handle.

The telethon organizers scrambled desperately to find another company able to take on this huge task. The only alternative was to scroll a donation mailing address across the TV screen, but they knew that would raise far less money than could be taken with credit card contributions over the phone.

No other company was willing even to try, except one.

The associates at Capital One, working around the clock for three and a half days, cobbled together a virtual twenty thousand-seat telephone call center capable of handling the unprecedented volume of calls. They recruited five major call center partners—AT&T, WorldCom, Verizon, Convergys, and Bank of America—and ran the program office for the entire event, managing and coordinating work among the television networks, the telecom carriers, the call centers, Internet service providers, and the United Way. In all, Capital One, with its partners, pulled together thirty-five thousand volunteers working from seventy-seven call centers.

On the Friday night of the telethon, the first calls began arriving half an hour before the live broadcast at 9 P.M. Eastern Time. By the end of the telethon on the West Coast five hours later, the call centers had received 1.5 million calls and collected $150 million for the United Way's 9/11 Relief Fund. Capital One people alone fielded 310,000 calls from around the United States, Canada, the United Kingdom, Mexico, and Puerto Rico.

Nigel Morris, Capital One president, said in a speech afterward:

> In the future, business historians may look back at Capital One and comment positively on our earnings, or on our charge-offs, or on our account growth. But in our hearts, those of us who were here during this time will remember this night and our role in this fund-raising effort.
>
> Faced with what appeared to be an impossible task during a most difficult period in our history, the associates of Capital One pulled together and poured all of their skills, abilities, and heart into making this telethon a reality.
>
> To borrow from Winston Churchill: "It was our finest hour."

Why did Capital One agree to do the telethon? Catherine West, the executive vice president of U.S. consumer operations and the executive who actually led Capital One's telethon operations, described what happened when the call for help first came in:

> I got a team together and we asked ourselves, "Can we even accomplish this?" Around the table, the team said, "Golly, we don't really think we can do it." But we said, "Let's say 'Yes' and see how far we can take this." I got Rich Fairbank (the CEO) and Nigel involved.

Nigel, Catherine's boss, was skeptical. He wasn't sure Capital One could or should take on such a huge and highly visible challenge. He worried that the company might take it on and then fail on nationwide television, with all the damage that could do to the Capital One name, to the morale of the people involved, and, ultimately, to the victims and their families themselves.

But Catherine believed it could work if the people of Capital One would get behind it, and so she and her team went on the company intranet and asked Capital One employees if they would be willing to volunteer. She said:

*Within one hour of asking, we had five thousand volunteers. We
ended up with seven thousand, but all we needed was five thousand. So we went back to Nigel and said, "Listen, people are willing to volunteer their time. We think operationally we can pull it
off."*

Morris gave the go-ahead, and Catherine's team began a thirty-
six hour race against time. They pulled together the logistics,
phones, headsets, desks, and food for seven thousand people—all
the time ensuring there would be no disruption to their core business and that Capital One customers wouldn't get busy signals
when they called in.

The night of the telethon Catherine and her team, along with
Nigel Morris and Rich Fairbank, visited the phone center sites,
serving drinks and pizzas and even manning the phones when
call volume peaked.

An inspired organization

We wanted to understand better what led the people of Capital
One to take on this unprecedented challenge and pull it off. So we
talked to many of the people involved. What we heard was that
they stepped up to the telethon because of values embedded deep
within the Capital One organization.

Catherine explained it this way:

*There's such a spirit of wanting to do the right thing because
that's the foundation of the company. Wanting to do right for the
company and wanting to do right for the community and wanting to do right by people. . . .*

We heard those same words, almost a mantra, from many others. For example, from another executive:

*When something like that happens, you just know what the right
thing to do is. You don't have to question, Should we do this*

telethon? Should we step up? You actually know the answer to that, because those values are just so embedded in every conversation and every interaction that you have. It's all about giving back.

It was the people of Capital One who rose up and pulled off this amazing feat. They believed, if they were doing the right thing, they could and should move heaven and earth.

That spirit was generated by the values expressed and lived authentically by company leadership, which over time had permeated the company.

Since its founding several years earlier, Capital One under Nigel Morris and Rich Fairbank had a history of active support for "doing the right thing" and "giving back." Those were values management had clearly expressed in frequent "Road Show" and "Town Hall" meetings held throughout the company. It was more than talk. The company sponsored a variety of volunteer programs in support of education, local communities, and children at risk, and encouraged employees to contribute their time. In fact, 67 percent of Capital One employees do contribute time to company-sponsored programs.

So it was no surprise, when the call for help came from the telethon organizers, that the people of Capital One said, "Yes!" Morris and Fairbank and other top leaders didn't push Capital One people to take on the telethon. On the contrary, their first response was cautious. It was the people themselves who said, "We should do this. We can do it." They were far ahead of their leaders.

The telethon was the work of an inspired organization, one into which life and spirit had been breathed by leaders authentically speaking and living their beliefs over a period of time.

In the end, it's about meaning

The ultimate purpose of theater and acting is to create meaning and context in our lives. Actors, with the playwright and the director, create meaning for the audience by revealing some broader and deeper context of life, by revealing the bonds that tie together all of life and humanity. We come away from a good play or movie feeling lifted up and better able to understand ourselves and one another. Think of *Schindler's List*, *The Deer Hunter*, *To Kill a Mockingbird*, *Gandhi*, and *Billy Elliot*.

Actor Simon Callow said:

> To me, nothing could be more important than people's fundamental sense of the meaning of their lives, because a life without meaning is not a human life at all, in my view. . . . And that's what the theatre is about: enabling you to identify the meaning of your life, if not the meaning of life itself.

In the same way, leaders create meaning for groups and organizations they lead, and they do that by authentically connecting what's important to them to their work as a leader. What makes this so powerful is that it allows the leader and the led to connect with something bigger than themselves and their own self-interest. That's been true of every leader whose story we've told in Chapters 8 and 9: John Perkins, Barbara Berke, John Kavanagh, John Clarkeson, the leaders at Capital One. In fact, it can be said of every leader we've discussed in the entire book.

All of us want to spend our days laboring in some endeavor that extends beyond our own personal needs and desires. We all want meaning. We all want to be connected with something valuable in human affairs.

Stage and film actor Frank Langella, best known for his portrayal of Dracula on Broadway and in film, expressed it this way:

> I think that, for the last ten or fifteen years, we have been living in an era of such mechanization, such nonhuman contact, and such a flattening and leveling out of the human spirit that, if an audience gets a chance to be in the same room with a man of heroic dimension like Cyrano or Dracula, and if they get to see him played at a heroic level, it unleashes in them all the passion and desire and want and excitement that they had in youth.
>
> When we're young, we all dream of being the best baseball

player or ballerina or doctor that could ever be. But as we get out into life we start getting pummeled, and more and more of our dream goes away. Then we look up one day and realize we've lost that heroic thing we set out to do. We find ourselves in a commonplace life.[10]

It is the job of the leader to recover that "heroic thing we set out to do"—to find and keep the authentic meaning of work in the hearts of those performing it. That's the ultimate and inspiring purpose of Leadership Presence.

Self-Knowing and Authenticity

Authen- ticity rule #1:	Accept yourself and be open to growth

Understand Your Limitations— Change or Accept Them

Purpose:	To break free of posturing, needing to be the perfect leader, or feeling stuck in a role
Exercise:	Self-knowing leaders, in spite of their shortcomings, seem entirely comfortable with themselves. While they recognize their limitations and work to improve them, they also accept them and work around them. While they're always trying to improve, they're not trying to be someone they're not. Take a few minutes to explore these questions in your journal:

- Overcome Limitations. From the exercises in Chapter 3, you have some sense of which leadership role you prefer to play in most situations—captain, conceiver, coach, or collaborator. You also know which role you find hardest to play, the one you seldom or never use, and the one that makes you most uncomfortable. How has that knowledge of yourself changed you? How has knowing your limitations helped you develop the skills you need to overcome them? Describe the leadership skills and behaviors you have developed that did *not* come naturally to you at first.

- Compensate for Limitations. For a leadership role that makes you uncomfortable, developing the appropriate skills may be difficult. Your best response might be to compensate rather than overcome—to accept your limitations and find some way around them. We cite the example of Colin Powell; he admires leaders who surround themselves with others whose qualities balance the leader's own skill set. How have you done this—or not—in assembling your own team? In what other ways have you compensated for your own limitations?

■ Commit to Change or Acceptance. Brainstorm a list of your weaknesses and faults as a leader. (It can help to refer to memories of challenging moments, failures, and defeats—consult your River of Life.) Then divide the list into two groups: those behaviors and qualities you are committed to changing in yourself, and those you wish to accept. Pick the three most important items from each group:

• The first is entitled: "My Commitment to Change." Write a statement listing the three most important items you wish to change, how you intend to go about changing them, and when. Make sure to tell others about your commitment, and get regular feedback on how you're doing.

• The second is entitled: "What I Accept About Myself." Write a statement listing the three most important items you intend to accept and, in your own words, thanking your inner critic for helping to teach you compassion for yourself and for others.

Authen-ticity rule #2:	Live your values

Find Actions That Make Your Values Visible: Walk the Talk

Purpose: To create trust among those you lead

Practice: ■ Top of the Agenda. Summarize the key points of your leadership values statement, in bullet form, and display them in a place that is visible to you when you work.

■ Daily Planning. With your leadership values statement in

mind, think over the major programs and problems sitting on your desk. What opportunities may exist on a daily, ongoing basis to apply your values and make them more visible?

- *Values-based Decision-making.* Begin a practice of reviewing your work in this way regularly. Think of the decisions you'll be making soon. Do your values offer any guidance in making those decisions?

- *Reflection.* Think back over recent decisions. If you had already developed an explicit set of leadership values, would you have made different decisions, or implemented them differently? (What's involved need not be of great import. Almost any problem or dilemma will offer an opportunity.)

Check That Your Actions Are Aligned with Your Values

Purpose: To overcome feelings of inauthenticity or distrust among peers and followers

Practice: In this post-Enron business environment, leaders need to be very honest with themselves about whether they are truly living their values. We suggest taking these related steps regularly:

- *Three-Hundred-and-Sixty-Degree Feedback.* Ask others if they perceive you as someone who lives your values. Undertake a 360-degree review, conducted by a third party, which includes questions about consistency between the values you claim and the values reflected in your actions.

- *Real-time Reality Check.* Every time you talk about your values, ask people to tell you when your actions don't live up to what you've said. Ask for ongoing, real-time feedback. You may have to ask many times before anyone will tell you—people will need to trust that you don't shoot the messenger!

- *Mind the Gap.* If you discover that people think there's a gap between your words and actions, try to understand what's causing the gap and develop a simple but conscious action plan for closing it.

| Authenticity rule #3: | Create an authentic connection to work |

Purpose: To discover your authentic connection to work

Exercise: Think about what makes you want to go to work in the morning. Write in your journal the answers to the following questions:

- Do you believe there is something particularly valuable about your product or service that excites or inspires you?
- Do you feel passionate about the process of your work or about your team?
- If the work itself does not excite you, can you find a connection to something larger, such as providing for the families of your team, generating prosperity for them or for your community?

Purpose: To help others find meaning in their work

Practice:
- Communicate regularly with your team about why you feel passionate or personally connected to your work. Help them feel authentically connected to their work by:
  - stressing the biggest mission—for example, safety, saving lives, or somehow making lives better.
  - helping each team member find their own personal connection (sharing yours will help, but each person's may be different).
  - giving them opportunities to see how and why their work is important or valuable—for example, making sure home office people know what's happening in the field, and are aware of satisfied customers and clients.

Epilogue

When you start discovering who and what you are, it's bigger than any-
thing you ever imagined yourself to be. And, by definition, it's generous.
It's a generous exploration. The more of you you find, the more of you
there is to give to those you love. Alan Arkin

WE HOPE THIS BOOK SURPRISED YOU, AT LEAST A LITTLE. WAS IT WHAT
you initially expected? Many who come to our workshops think
because we teach skills and techniques from acting and theater
that they will learn how to magnetically command the attention
of others. They think it will be about how they can be bigger,
more prominent, more the center of attention. They think it's
about them.

We understand why people make that assumption about what
we do. Perhaps you made it too when you first began reading this
book.

The problem arises from what we call the paradox of the theater. While the *business* of theater seems to attract people who are
full of themselves, who need to be the center of attention, the *art*
of theater requires actors to give themselves up to the characters
played, to the text spoken, to the music sung, to the other actors,
and to the audience. Acting is not about the actor.

When she was ten years old, Cherry Jones and her parents were
traveling through the Blue Ridge Mountains and they saw a stage
performance of *The Country Girl*.

I'll never forget, we were sitting in the front row, and this mar-
velous actress . . . came to the lip of the stage and delivered the fi-
nal lines of the play. I remember them being very poignant, and

*the lights slowly coming down, dimming on her, and as they
went out . . . there was a final burst of dim light. . . . I thought it
was her spirit surging one last time. That sort of did it. I knew I
wanted to do that.*[2]

It was only later that Jones learned what had happened. A
quirk of those old-fashioned spotlights caused them, as they
dimmed to darkness, to give out one last burst of light. It was
called "ghosting" and it made the actor seem to glow. That final
burst is what Jones thought was the actress's "spirit surging."

But the important point is what Jones *thought* she saw, because
that's what changed her life. That young girl saw an actress lit
from within, shining her light out on the audience. Though she
knows about those old lights now, the adult Cherry Jones still has
the same aspiration: to be the kind of actress whose inner light
shines outward for others. For us that captures the essence and the
paradox of acting. Each of us came to similar realizations, though
later in our careers and after perhaps longer journeys.

Kathy: One performance at the New Repertory Theatre stands
out for me. We did an adaptation of Charles Dickens's *Hard Times*,
a three and a half hour show in which six of us played all the characters in the novel.

On this particular night the stakes were especially high for one
of the actors. Besides acting, he taught drama at a local university
and he was being evaluated that night for tenure. He came on
with such energy that it literally jolted me and the rest of the cast
to another level of acting.

For the three hours of the play I felt like I was riding on this
great wave. I felt both tremendous energy and a sense of effort-
lessness. There was no experience of time, only this flowing energy between the actors, and the actors and audience. I was aware
that there was no little voice in my head, no self-critic, in fact, no
thinking at all!

It felt as if I was part of something much bigger than myself, and
I realized that at the heart of acting was something quite profound.

Before this experience, acting for me had involved a lot of self-
consciousness, concern about how I was doing, how the audience

was receiving me. That little voice in my head would ask over and over: "How's my performance? Do they like me? Am I good enough?" It was all about me. After that performance, it was about a deeper, bigger experience that I can only explain by saying it's about "not me."

Belle: I remember a concert that continues to be a touchstone. It was a time in my life when I was very consciously building a career, aware of getting the right reviews, and being seen by the right people.

Somehow I got a grant from the Italian government to do a concert tour in the small towns of Tuscany. I remember driving for hours in the hills and finally coming to a town square where the elders of the town were building a stage for me in front of the church. Someone explained to me that this was the first time someone was performing on a stage in this square for one thousand years! The last thing that had happened on a stage in front of this church was that someone was burned at the stake.

As it got near concert time, I could see what seemed like every member of the community sitting on green benches on the gray cobblestone square. I saw grandparents and children hanging out from windows framed by green shutters.

As I started to sing and to explain the songs as best as I could in Italian, I could feel the community longing to be entertained, to be touched. This wasn't about building my career. This was about giving these people an evening they would treasure. It was about bringing them together, touching their hearts and souls by finding and giving more of myself than I ever had before.

Finding that generosity in myself as a singer was a gift from that audience that I strive to bring with me in everything I do today.

For both of us acting and performing has been a means of personal growth and development. For Belle, it's been a journey from ambition to generosity. For Kathy, it's been from self-consciousness to letting go of self. For both of us, it has been from "about me" to "not about me."

No wonder we believe acting skills are more than superficial ways to attract attention. Now, after a decade of working with companies and leaders, we've come to realize that our personal journeys as performers were not so different from the journeys required of leaders.

We believe there is a paradox of leadership, like the paradox of theater. Leadership is better and more inspiring the less it's about "me" or ambition. Instead of being about personal power, it's about generosity and forgetting oneself and connecting with others in a truly authentic way.

All of Leadership Presence, the whole PRES model, is about Being Present and completely available to others. It's about Reaching Out, sending out your light, your values, and connecting with others. It's about Expressiveness, feeling your emotions and sending them out so people can be motivated and inspired.

As Zen Master Dogen said, "To know yourself is to forget yourself." For only by Self-knowing, becoming more confident and comfortable, having a stronger ego, will you be able to let go of yourself and be more open and generous for others. That's the lesson Cherry Jones learned—it's not about being in the spotlight, it's about shining your light on others. The more presence you have of the kind we're talking about, the less your leadership needs to be about you.

When the two of us decided to form a company ten years ago we chose the name, "The Ariel Group," after the character, Ariel, in *The Tempest*. It is Shakespeare's last great play and it embodies the leader's journey in the story of Prospero, the deposed leader of Milan. Guided by the spirit of Ariel, through the alchemy and magic of theater, Prospero undergoes a transformation and returns to Milan a more compassionate, Self-knowing leader.

We adopted the name because we hoped in The Ariel Group to serve the same role as Ariel played in *The Tempest*, and also because, in one of those small twists of fate, the role of Ariel was the only role that both of us in our careers had played in common. In the spirit of Ariel, we wrote down a decade ago the "Ariel Vision":

A world where people authentically engage with one another and unlock their most generous selves.

That's our wish for you, and for everyone we work with.

Rules and guidelines

Guidelines for Being Present in the moment

1. Focus on the physical.
2. Change your perspective.
3. Let thoughts go, let feelings be.

Rules for Being Present in action—flexibility

1. Be open to unexpected outcomes—"Yes, and . . ."
2. Adapt your role to the reality.
3. Be generous toward others.

Guidelines for Reaching Out and empathy

1. Know what makes your people tick.
2. Make the link to your own feelings.
3. You can empathize with anyone.

Rules for Reaching Out and making connections

1. Listen to build relationships.
2. Acknowledge the person.
3. Share yourself.

Guidelines for emotion and Expressiveness

1. Generate excitement by expressing emotion.
2. Express authentic emotion.
3. Invest passionate purpose into your words and actions.

Rules for Expressiveness using voice, body, and story

1. Conquer your fear of overexpression.

2. Use your voice and body congruently.

3. Tell stories to unleash your Expressiveness.

Guidelines for Self-knowing, self-reflection, and explicit values

1. Pursue some regular process of self-reflection.

2. Write down your personal leadership values.

3. Speak your leadership values.

Rules for Self-knowing and authenticity

1. Accept yourself and be open to growth.

2. Live your values.

3. Create an authentic connection to work.

Notes

Chapter One: Presence: What Actors Have That Leaders Have

1. (William Shakespeare) *As You Like It*. Act II. Scene VII. Lines 139–142.
2. (Peter Brook) Peter Brook, *The Shifting Point* (New York: Harper and Row, 1987), p. 232.
7. (F. Murray Abraham) David Black, *The Magic of Theater: Behind the Scenes with Today's Leading Actors* (New York: Macmillan, 1993), p. 228.

Introduction to Act I

18. (Bush Story) Bill Sammon, "Part III: Soothing the soul, rousing the spirit," *Washington Times,* October 9, 2002.

Chapter Two: Being Present in the Moment

21. (Lao-Tzu) Stephen Mitchell, *The Enlightened Heart: An Anthology of Sacred Poetry* (New York: Perennial, 1993), p. 14.
23–24. (Laurence Olivier) Laurence Olivier, *On Acting* (New York: Simon & Schuster, 1986), pp. 128–29.
28. (Laurence Olivier) Laurence Olivier, *On Acting* (New York: Simon & Schuster, 1986), pp. 180–81.
35. (William Hurt) David Black, *The Magic of Theater: Behind the Scenes with Today's Leading Actors* (New York: Macmillan, 1993), p. 66.
36. (Meredith Monk) Robert Coe, "The Quality of Mercy," *Tricycle: The Buddhist Review,* Winter 2002, p. 63.

Chapter Three: Being Present in Action—Flexibility

49. (William H. Macy) Mary Luckhurst and Chloe Veltman, eds., *On Acting: Interviews with Actors* (New York: Faber and Faber, 2002), pp. 65–66.

53. (Laurence Olivier) Laurence Olivier, *On Acting* (New York: Simon & Schuster, 1986), p. 86.

55. (Bill Murray) Timothy Crouse, "The *Rolling Stone* Interview: Bill Murray," *Rolling Stone,* August 16, 1984, p. 21.

62. (Christine Lahti) Carole Zucker, *Conversations with Actors on Film, Television, and Stage Performance* (New Hampshire: Heinemann, 2002), p. 50.

Introduction to Act II

79. (Max Reinhardt) Carole Zucker, Frontispiece of *In the Company of Actors: Reflections on the Craft of Acting* (New York: Routledge, 2001).

79. (Romney and Giuliani) Yvonne Abraham, "Giuliani, Romney Tour North End," *Boston Globe,* October 9, 2002.

83. (Robert De Niro) Mike Sager, "The Man Who Acts Like God," *Esquire,* December 1997, pp 74–77.

Chapter Four: Reaching Out and Empathy

85. (Meryl Streep) Brad Darrach, "Enchanting, colorless, glacial, sneaky, seductive, manipulative, magical Meryl," *Life,* December, 1987, v10, n13, pp. 72–77.

90. Daniel Goleman, Richard Boyatzis, and Annie McKee, *Primal Leadership: Realizing the Power of Emotional Intelligence* (Massachusetts: Harvard Business School Press, 2002), p. 50.

91. (Kenneth Branagh) Kenneth Branagh, *Beginning* (New York: St. Martin's Press, 1991), p. 143.

91. (James Earl Jones) Jackson R. Bryer and Richard A. Davison, eds., *The Actor's Art: Conversations with Contemporary American Stage Performers* (New Jersey: Rutgers University Press, 2001), p. 146.

98. (Ben Kingsley) Jamie Painter, "Show and Tell," *Back Stage West,* June 7, 2001, v8, i23, p. 6.

98. (Alan Arkin) David Black, *The Magic of Theater: Behind the Scenes with Today's Leading Actors* (New York: Macmillan, 1993), p. 295.

98–99. (Anthony Sher) Carole Zucker, *In the Company of Actors: Reflections on the Craft of Acting* (New York: Routledge, 2001), p. 177.

99. Daniel Goleman, "Leadership That Gets Results," *Harvard Business Review,* March–April 2000, pp. 78–90.

Chapter Five: Reaching Out and Making Connections

105. (David Pottruck) Fred Andrews, "Hard Lessons Learned At Schwab," *New York Times*, April 30, 2000, section 3, p. 7.

105. (Christopher Reeve) David Black, *The Magic of Theater: Behind the Scenes with Today's Leading Actors* (New York: Macmillan, 1993), p. 25.

108. Craig Taylor, "Focus on Talent," *Training and Development*, December 2002, p. 29.

109. (Cherry Jones) Jackson R. Bryer and Richard A. Davison, eds., *The Actor's Art: Conversations with Contemporary American Stage Performers* (New Jersey: Rutgers University Press, 2001), p. 130.

111. (*Death of a Salesman*) Arthur Miller, *Death of a Salesman* (New York: The Viking Press, 1949), p. 33

113. Concept of "Listen for values and strengths" originated by Thomas Leonard and developed by Madeleine Homan and The Ariel Group, Inc., 1998.

118. Jack Welch and John A. Byrne, *Jack: Straight from the Gut* (New York: Warner Books, 2001), p. 421.

120. (Anthony Sher) Carole Zucker, *In the Company of Actors: Reflections on the Craft of Acting* (New York: Routledge, 2001), p. 179.

123. (Christopher Reeve) David Black, *The Magic of Theater: Behind the Scenes with Today's Leading Actors* (New York: Macmillan, 1993), p. 25.

125-126. Practice, "Naming Emotions, Strengths, and Values," developed with Madeleine Homan, 1998.

Introduction to Act III

131. David Gergen and Gardiner Morse, "How Presidents Persuade," *Harvard Business Reivew,* January 1, 2003, 2p, p. 21.

134. Albert Mehrabian, *Silent Message* (New York: Wadsworth Publishing Company, 1971), p. 43.

134. (Danny Kaye) Dennis Brown, *Actors Talk: Profiles and Stories from the Acting Trade* (New York: Proscenium Publishers, Inc., 1999), p. 171.

135. Michael Cunningham, "My Novel, the Movie: My Baby Reborn; 'The Hours' Brought Elation, But Also Doubt," *New York Times*, January 19, 2003, Section 2, Page 1, Column 5.

Chapter Six: Emotion Drives Expressiveness

137. Daniel Goleman, Richard Boyatzis, and Annie McKee, *Primal Leadership: Realizing the Power of Emotional Intelligence* (Massachusetts: Harvard Business School Press, 2002), p. 3.

140. Daniel Goleman, Richard Boyatzis, and Annie McKee, "Primal Leadership: The Hidden Driver of Great Performance," *Harvard Business Review,* December 1, 2001 10p, p. 51.

140. John P. Kotter and Dan S. Cohen, *The Heart of Change: Real-Life Stories of How People Change Their Organizations* (Massachusetts: Harvard Business School Press, 2002), p. x.

141–42. (Maureen Stapleton) Jackson R. Bryer and Richard A. Davison, eds., *The Actor's Art: Conversations with Contemporary American Stage Performers* (New Jersey: Rutgers University Press, 2001), p. 236.

147. (Kenneth Branagh) Kenneth Branagh, *Beginning* (New York: St. Martin's Press, 1991), p. 168.

149–50. (Jack Nicholson) Brian Bates, *The Way of the Actor: A Path to Knowledge & Power* (Massachusetts: Shambhala Publications, 1987), p. 160.

Chapter Seven: Expressiveness Using Voice, Body, and Story

159. (Martha Graham) Agnes de Mille, *Dance to the Piper* (New York: Brown Books, 1952), p. 335.

167. (Kenneth Branagh) Kenneth Branagh, *Beginning* (New York: St. Martin's Press, 1991), p. 55.

167. (Katharine Hepburn) Katharine Hepburn, *Me* (New York: Ballantine Books, 1996), p. 82.

169. (James Earl Jones) James Earl Jones and Penelope Niven, *Voices and Silences* (New York: Macmillan, 2002), p. 374.

171. (Martin Luther King and Taylor Branch quoted in) Howard Gardner and Emma Laskin (contributor), *Leading Minds: An Anatomy of Leadership* (New York: Basic Books, 1996), pp. 205–06.

172. (Maureen Stapleton) Jackson R. Bryer and Richard A. Davison, eds., *The Actor's Art: Conversations with Contemporary American Stage Performers* (New Jersey: Rutgers University Press, 2001), p. 231.

173. (James Earl Jones) James Earl Jones and Penelope Niven, *Voices and Silences* (New York: Macmillan, 2002), p. 374.

173–74. Michael Cunningham, "My Novel, the Movie: My Baby Reborn; 'The Hours' Brought Elation, But Also Doubt," *New York Times,* January 19, 2003, Section 2, Page 1, Column 5.

178. (Storytelling Bullet Points) Inspired by Jean-Claude van Itallie, *The Playwright's Workbook* (New York: Applause Books, 1997), p. 54.

178. (Tips for Telling Stories) Cowritten with author Norm G. Gatreau.

Introduction to Act IV

193. (Polonius) *Hamlet.* Act II, Scene III, lines 78–80.

196. (Susan Sarandon) Roy Grundmann and Cynthia Lucia, "Acting, activism and Hollywood politics: an interview with Susan Sarandon," *Cineaste,* Winter 1993, v20, n1, p. 6.

196. (Laura Dern) Jamie Painter Young, "Defining Moments: through portraying women in search of their identities, Laura Dern has learned to be true to herself," *Back Stage West,* November 11, 2001, v8, i47, p6(2), p. 6.

197. Howard Gardner and Emma Laskin (contributor), *Leading Minds: An Anatomy of Leadership* (New York: Basic Books, 1996), p. 200.

Chapter Eight: Self-Knowing, Self-Reflection, and Explicit Values

201. Warren Bennis, *On Becoming a Leader* (Massachusetts: Perseus Publishing, 1994), p. 40.

205. (The Tylenol Story) "Tylenol's 'miracle' comeback: a year after the poisonings, public confidence is restored," *Time,* October 17, 1983, v 122, p67(1).

208. (Hume Cronyn) Jackson R. Bryer and Richard A. Davison, eds., *The Actor's Art: Conversations with Contemporary American Stage Performers* (New Jersey: Rutgers University Press, 2001), p. 25.

209. (Anthony Hopkins) Tom O'Neill, "Anthony Hopkins: The *US* Interview," *US Magazine,* February 1998, Number 241, pp. 53–57.

215–16. Noel Tichy and Tom Brown, "Companies Don't Develop Leaders, CEO's Do: An Interview with Noel Tichy," *Harvard Management Update,* October 1, 1997, 3p, p. 5.

219. (River of Life Exercise) Drawing the River inspired by Ira Progoff, *At a Journal Workshop* (New York: Dialogue House Library, 1975), pp. 104–5.

Chapter Nine: Self-Knowing and Authenticity

225. (Joel Grey) David Black, *The Magic of Theater: Behind the Scenes with Today's Leading Actors* (New York: Macmillan, 1993), p. 13.

229. Rob Galford and Anne Siebold Drapeau, *The Trusted Leader* (New York: The Free Press, 2002), p. 30

229. (Lindsay Crouse) Carole Zucker, *Conversations with Actors on Film, Television, and Stage Performance* (New Hampshire: Heinemann, 2002), p. xii.

232. (Christopher Reeve) David Black, *The Magic of Theater: Behind the Scenes with Today's Leading Actors* (New York: Macmillan, 1993), pp. 29–30.

232. (Colin Powell) Colin Powell and Joseph Persico, *My American Journey* (New York: Ballantine Books, 1995), p. 179.

233. (Christopher Walken) Dennis Brown, *Actors Talk: Profiles and Stories from the Acting Trade* (New York: Proscenium Publishers, Inc., 1999), p. 34.

234. (Gib Akin) Warren Bennis, *On Becoming a Leader* (Massachusetts: Perseus Publishing, 1994), p. 56.

240. (Simon Callow) Mary Luckhurst and Chloe Veltman, eds., *On Acting: Interviews with Actors* (New York: Faber and Faber, 2002), p. 10.

247. (Simon Callow) Carole Zucker, *In the Company of Actors: Reflections on the Craft of Acting* (New York: Routledge, 2001), p. 36.

247–48. (Frank Langella) Dennis Brown, *Actors Talk: Profiles and Stories from the Acting Trade* (New York: Proscenium Publishers, Inc., 1999), p. 227.

Epilogue

253. (Alan Arkin) David Black, *The Magic of Theater: Behind the Scenes with Today's Leading Actors* (New York: Macmillan, 1993), p. 290.

253–54. (Cherry Jones) Jackson R. Bryer and Richard A. Davison, eds., *The Actor's Art: Conversations with Contemporary American Stage Performers* (New Jersey: Rutgers University Press, 2001), p. 126.

Index

About the Authors

Belle Linda Halpern

Cofounder of The Ariel Group, Belle brings the skills of a professional consultant, speaker, educator, singer, and actress to her work. Belle has developed and delivered leadership programs for clients in the U.S., Europe, and Asia for the past ten years, including Boston Consulting Group, General Electric, the Federal Reserve, and Merrill Lynch. She has been featured in *Fast Company*, the *Boston Globe*, *Harvard Management Communication Letter*, and on CNBC. Belle has spoken at national conferences including the American Society for Training and Development, and the Women in Leadership Summit. She has designed and delivered workshops at the executive education programs of Columbia Business School and the Kellogg School of Management.

As a cabaret singer, Belle has performed in New York, Boston, San Francisco, Paris, Munich, and the hill towns of northern Italy for eighteen years. She cocreated several cabaret theater pieces that she regularly performs in theater festivals and performance series across the United States. Belle has designed an innovative methodology for teaching singing to nonsingers and has worked with students at Harvard University, Longy School of Music, and the Roy Hart Theatre in France. She currently teaches singing each summer at the Tuscany Project in Italy. Combining her singing talent with her work in leadership, she has delivered combination cabaret/lectures on leadership at the annual meetings for Instructional Services Association and for companies such as Ericsson and Capital One. She is a graduate of Harvard University.

Belle lives in Boston with her husband, Mitch, and her children, Aviva and Lev.

Kathy Lubar

President and cofounder of The Ariel Group, Kathy offers her clients the experiences of a consultant, teacher, leader, and actress. She has developed and delivered a range of programs for some of the top names in professional services and industry, such as Deloitte & Touche, Société Générale, Computer Sciences Corporation, and Capital One. As an educator, Kathy has worked with a wide variety of students, including business professionals, lawyers, teachers, actors, and women prisoners. She has taught workshops at the executive education programs of Columbia Business School and the Kellogg School of Management as well as the Leadership Institute at Harvard Business School.

Kathy has spoken at conferences in the United States and Europe, including the Performance Theater Leadership Conference in London, Linkage's Leadership Conference in San Francisco, and the United States Department of Labor's Senior Executive Service Forum Series. She has been featured in *Fast Company*, *Investor's Business Daily*, *Boston Magazine*, and *Harvard Management Communication Letter*, and on CNBC.

A graduate of Stanford University, Kathy acted professionally for fifteen years, performing in New York and Boston, and playing leading roles in a number of national tours. She cofounded Boston's New Repertory Theatre in 1984. Kathy lives in Massachusetts and Hawaii with her husband, George and her daughters, London and Rachel.

Keynotes, Workshops, and Coaching in Leadership Presence

The Ariel Group teaches the theories described in this book through an extensive range of experiential programs and executive coaching for individuals and organizations.

The authors and senior consultants from The Ariel Group also deliver lectures and keynote speeches to audiences around the world.

For further information on Ariel programs, individual coaching, or to book us for a speaking engagement, please visit our Web site at:

www.arielgroup.com